A PLUME BOOK

EVERYTHING YOU EVER WANTED

JILLIAN LAUREN is the author of the *New York Times* bestselling memoir *Some Girls: My Life in a Harem* and the novel *Pretty*. *Some Girls* has been translated into eighteen languages. Jillian has an MFA in creative writing from Antioch University. Her writing has appeared in the *New York Times*, *The Paris Review*, *Vanity Fair*, *Los Angeles Magazine*, *Salon*, *Elle*, and *The Moth Anthology*, among others. She is a regular storyteller with The Moth. Lauren blogs about motherhood and writing at www.jillianlauren.com. She lives in Los Angeles with her husband, Weezer bass player Scott Shriner, and their son.

Praise for *Everything You Ever Wanted*

"Lauren's writing is brave and honest, and she calls out hypocrisy wherever she sees it." —*Kirkus Reviews*

"Lauren proves she is a master storyteller." —Catherine Burns, artistic director of The Moth

"In this ferociously brave, funny, and heartwarming memoir, Jillian Lauren parses the challenges and rewards of motherhood with true grace and humility. No other parenting book has ever made me feel so validated about the big, messy, beautiful picture of what it means to care for another human being. I closed the c◌◌◌◌◌◌◌◌ e of both the author and of parenthood itself." —Claire Bidwell Sm◌◌◌ ◌ritance

"With humor and poignancy, Lauren interweaves her struggle to become a mother with her own story of being adopted as an infant. It's a love story—between Lauren and her rock star husband and also between a couple and their new son. Like all great love stories, the beauty is in the struggle."

—Kristen Howerton, founder of *Rage Against the Minivan*

"A transformative, unflinching account of the creation of an adoptive family. Jillian and Scott and their son, Tariku, show us—painful, frustrating, and joyful step-by-step—how to attach, heal, listen, trust, and then let go. A testament to the fierce and fallible journey of any mother. Reads like a novel, moves you like any great story of survival would, to tears of joy and triumph."   —Jamie Lee Curtis

Praise for *Some Girls*

"Riveting . . . [Lauren writes] with humor, candor, and a reporter's gimlet eye."

—Jennifer Egan, Pulitzer Prize–winning author of
A Visit from the Goon Squad

"[Lauren] is a deft storyteller and not afraid to provide candid descriptions of her life."   —*The Miami Herald*

"Lauren . . . imparts equal parts poignant reflection and wisdom into her enlightening book. A gritty, melancholy memoir leavened by the author's amiable, engrossing narrative tenor."

—*Kirkus Reviews*

"*Some Girls* is a heart-stoppingly thrilling story told by a punk rock Scheherazade. Lauren writes with such lyrical ease—the book is almost musical, an enduring melody of what it is to be a woman."

—Margaret Cho

Also by Jillian Lauren

Pretty

Some Girls: My Life in a Harem

everything
you ever
wanted

a memoir

~

Jillian Lauren

A PLUME BOOK

PLUME
An imprint of Penguin Random House LLC
375 Hudson Street
New York, New York 10014
penguin.com

Excerpt from "Somewhere That's Green" from *Little Shop of Horrors*, music by Alan Menken, lyrics by Howard Ashman. Copyright © 1982 by Universal - Geffen Music, Trunksong Music, Ltd., and Menken Music. All rights reserved. Used by permission. Reprinted by permission of Hal Leonard Corporation.

Excerpt from "Good Morning Starshine" (from *Hair*), music by Galt MacDermot, words by James Rado and Gerome Ragni. Copyright © 1966, 1967, 1968, 1970 (copyrights renewed) by James Rado, Gerome Ragni, Galt MacDermot, Nat Shapiro, and EMI U Catalog Inc. All rights administered by EMI U Catalog Inc. (Publishing) and Alfred Music (Print). All rights reserved.

LIBRARY OF CONGRESS CATALOGING-IN-PUBLICATION DATA
Lauren, Jillian.
    Everything you ever wanted : a memoir / Jillian Lauren.
      pages cm
    ISBN 978-0-14-218163-8 (paperback)
    1. Lauren, Jillian. 2. Women—California—Biography. 3. Identity (Psychology) 4. Women novelists, American—Biography. I. Title.
    PS3612.A9442275Z46 2015
    813'.6—dc23
    [B]

                                                                              2015005344

Printed in the United States of America
10   9   8   7   6   5   4   3   2   1

Set in Dante Regular

Penguin is committed to publishing works of quality and integrity. In that spirit, we are proud to offer this book to our readers; however, the story, the experiences, and the words are the author's alone.

While the author has made every effort to provide accurate telephone numbers, Internet addresses, and other contact information at the time of publication, neither the publisher nor the author assumes any responsibility for errors or for changes that occur after publication. Further, the publisher does not have any control over and does not assume any responsibility for author or third-party Web sites or their content.

Neither the publisher nor the author is engaged in rendering professional advice or services to the individual reader. The ideas, procedures, and suggestions contained in this book are not intended as a substitute for consulting with your physician. All matters regarding your health require medical supervision. Neither the author nor the publisher shall be liable or responsible for any loss or damage allegedly arising from any information or suggestion in this book.

For Tariku Moon

Author's Note

THIS is a work of creative nonfiction. My son, Tariku, disagrees. He insists that this book couldn't be nonfiction, because real nonfiction contains photographs of planets and lizards and stuff.

I have changed names and identifying characteristics at times, to protect the privacy of those involved. That said, to the best of my ability, planets and lizards aside, this book is the truth.

I'm his December bride.
He's Father, he knows best.
Our kids watch Howdy Doody
As the sun sets in the West.
A picture out of Better Homes and Gardens magazine,

Far from Skid Row
I dream we'll go
somewhere that's green.

—Alan Irwin Menken and Howard Ashman,
from *Little Shop of Horrors*

everything
you ever
wanted

～ Prologue

THERE are three kinds of daylight in Los Angeles.

There is the midday light—flat and relentless. Usually partnered with heat, it catches and suspends you, like a formaldehyde solution. It has weight, singes your lungs, would poison the rain if the rain ever fell. Makes you wish the bloody red sunset would hurry up and come already.

There is the light after a rare rainstorm—the cerulean blue sky that frames the Hollywood sign and breathes new life into a thousand impossible dreams. Shatters your heart into glistening David Hockney swimming-pool pieces. You feel rich. You want to be driving down Sunset Boulevard through Beverly Hills in a convertible. Forget that. You want to be driven down Sunset in a Bentley with tinted windows. Only tourists admit they want to be seen.

Finally there is the dawn—cool, pale, and still smudged with shadows from the night before. In Hollywood, for many people it still *is* the night before. But for those of us who wake with the dawn instinctively, it is forgiving. It is forgiveness. It is soft, from the humbler east, more understated than the garish twilight displays over the ocean. It yearns for something clean that never comes. No matter—it is the yearning that counts.

The dawn is my time. I always rise before everyone. More often than not, I dress quickly, have a few sips of tea, and walk out the door to exercise.

On the morning of my eighteen-month-old son Tariku's final adoption hearing at the Children's Court in Monterey Park, I wake at five. The hearing is a formality, but a significant one. After this, he will be irrevocably ours. My husband, Scott, and T are sleeping next to me. The pale predawn light seeps around the edges of the curtains. We don't have to be there until ten. I slip out of bed and lace up my sneakers.

In our neighborhood in northeast L.A., there is a hill on the southern border. A road cuts over it, but the back side is undeveloped, with trails I've yet to explore. The road is steep and winding. A good hike, I think, and doable in time. If I walk at a brisk clip, I don't even need the car.

I feel strong as I push toward the top. When I reach the crest, the trail looks clearly marked. I figure fifteen minutes to the bottom. Perfect. When I arrive home, Scott will have just woken up with T, the morning chores will be under way, and I will plunge in.

But now I'm headed down and something is wrong. I hike enough to be able to feel when a trail is going wrong—probably heading to a dead end. I go back to the last fork and take another trail, which also ends abruptly. Through the branches, I can see the back of what looks like a high school down below. I figure I can bushwhack my way through the brush, then walk through the campus and back out to the street. It won't be far. After that my home is just over the next familiar hill.

It's harder than I thought. Burrs invade my shoes; an errant twig scratches my face; another tears my favorite leggings. At the bottom, I remember that this isn't the era I grew up in, of smoking pot and getting felt up in the woods behind the library. This is the era of high-security schools. A tall chain-link fence blocks my passage.

My chest seizes and I recoil. When I was a kid, the jagged end of chain link ripped my hand open. I still remember the pale blue T-shirt I was wearing, the smell of damp earth after I hit the ground.

It always takes me a minute to remember . . . this injury never actually happened to me. It happened to my father.

When I was little, I used to ask my dad over and over again to tell me how he got the thin white scar that bisected his palm and ran down his forearm nearly to his elbow. I heard the story so many times it became almost as much a part of my own body as it was his. In my dreams, it's always me: stumbling, light-headed, nearly bleeding to death, trying to hold my torn skin together with my blood-soaked T-shirt.

I'm not delusional. If I think about it, I realize that of course that scar is my father's scar. Still, the memory comes to me with a momentary stab of fear.

I'm chilly in the shady grove, my sweaty shirt cooling in the morning breeze.

It's one of my greatest fears that my hurt will become Tariku's, in spite of my best efforts to give him a whole new world. Maybe the legacy of our parents' pain is unavoidable. Maybe these scars are not just psychological but somehow cellular. Maybe the darkest moments of my story are so deeply inscribed in my body, my voice, my very soul that I won't be able to help transmitting them.

I steel myself, wedge my toe into the diamond of chain link, and pull myself over the top.

Maybe so, I think. But I can also transmit this: Even shaking with fear, you can still scale the fence.

~ Chapter 1

WHEN I meet Scott in September 2003, I am midway between the before picture and the after picture. The before picture is
not one I'm eager to frame and put on the wall: addiction, depression, a past checkered with ill-advised intimacies and even-less-well-
advised sources of income, including a short-lived career as an
exotic dancer and an unlikely stint as a member of a harem in
Southeast Asia (yes, really). But the after picture—ah, the after picture. I'm like the endearingly trashy character Audrey in *Little Shop
of Horrors*: working in a flower shop, teetering around on too-high
heels and dreaming of that tract house of her very own (before she
gets noshed on by a carnivorous houseplant as comeuppance for
such hubris). I imagine a sun-drenched vintage kitchen with tiny
handprints smudged across the yellow cabinets, a vestibule scattered with pint-sized sneakers, a garden overflowing with heirloom . . . heirloom whatevers, just so long as they're heirloom. I'm
sure I'll get there, if I just work very, very hard at being very, very
good.

I first see Scott at a bowling party. He's wearing his light brown
hair slicked back, overdyed jeans cuffed at the ankle, worn but polished steel-toed boots. He is square at both the shoulder and the jaw
and holds himself ramrod straight, like the former U.S. Marine he

is. He is a force. I know from friends that he is a bass player for a popular band. I've heard he's a heartbreaker. I resolve to be aloof.

"What do you do with your days?" he asks.

Not my favorite question, but I suppose it's unavoidable. I should mention here that between the before picture and the after picture is a no-man's-land I've been dwelling in called cosmetology school.

"I go to beauty school."

"Beauty school is hot."

"Beauty school is not hot. Anyone who thinks beauty school is hot is a pervert." Scott is not deterred.

"Aw, come on," he says. "How about I pick you up at beauty school and take you to Norm's?"

Norm's is a 1950s throwback diner, but not in a shiny, hip kind of way. It's an L.A. institution, with cheap breakfast specials and grime worked into the linoleum floors. At Norm's of West Holly-wood, senior citizens share a counter with rock musicians looking for a nostalgic breakfast. The invitation to a date at Norm's is a clever nod to Frankie Avalon's version of beauty school.

Scott sees beauty school as some kind of holding pen for gum-cracking bad girls who wear lots of eyeliner and have dropped out of high school. The truth is less romantic. My story is, I'm a few months out of rehab and scrambling for some way to pay the bills.

Just a year before, I was hiding amid dust bunnies, syringe caps, and cigarette wrappers under a bed in a filthy flophouse in East L.A. while I hoped against hope that the men who had jimmied the lock and broken in looking for my dealer wouldn't find me instead. As I held my breath and focused on the laces of their track shoes, I re-discovered the long-lost (like, since my bat mitzvah) value of prayer in my life and made a little bargain with God that if I lived through it, I'd walk my stupid, stupid self right into rehab. I miraculously emerged unscathed, and that's exactly what I did. Every day, I'm still surprised to be alive and just as shocked that I'm nearly thirty years old. Chastened by the dangerous, Burroughsian roller coaster I have just exited, I stuff my artistic aspirations in the darkest corner of my furthest drawer and barely even take them out to look at them anymore. A job as a hairdresser seems fine. Not exciting, but haven't I had my fill of exciting? Since childhood, I have romanticized the life of the artist, and all of my poetic aspirations have gotten me nowhere but teetering on the edge of an early grave. What was it I once dreamed of? To write something? A book even, one day? What comic naïveté.

So, no, beauty school is not hot. Beauty school is humiliating. Beauty school is penance. I definitely don't want a cute guy popping by to see me doing roller sets on creepy doll heads in my white regulation smock. On the other hand, I'd be a fool to say no to the most interesting date offer I've had in a long while. A reputation as a heartbreaker should serve as a caution, but of course the exact opposite is true for me. I agree to go.

Our first date is on a balmy night in early fall. Scott arrives promptly at five and waits while I punch the time clock before he ushers me out the door and into his shiny green Ford Crown Victoria. I would once have avoided getting into that kind of a car, because I would have thought he was an undercover cop.

The start of the date is flawless. He opens every door for me, is inquisitive and polite. He is that rarest of things: a nice guy. Moreover, he's my kind of nice guy—a working-class musician with icy-blue eyes, full sleeves of tattoos, and a gold tooth that glints when he smiles.

And me? What am I? I'm not sure yet. So I wear a flattering dress that I hope will compensate for my lack of redeeming qualities and I pray that the past won't come up before he has the chance to get to know me a little bit.

~

We face each other across a two-top at Norm's. At the counter, World War II veterans eat pancake dinners elbow-to-elbow with aging musicians whose careers on the Sunset Strip haven't quite panned out. Years of wear have turned the rockers' audaciously big hairdos into slack, thinning ponytails. Their worn black leather jackets are shot through with tan cracks.

I have to give it to him: Norm's is a sweet choice for a first date. But we might as well be at Wendy's, for all I notice my surroundings. There's an immediate, brain-tilted, toes-buzzing chemistry between Scott and me. An electrical charge shoots between our nearly touching knees, like the static shock before your hand touches a doorknob. Here is a door. I am reaching for it. I am duly shocked.

He leans in and puts his elbows on the square of Formica between us. I am grateful for its presence. If not for the tabletop I might fall right into his gravitational pull and get lost entirely.

"I want to tell you that I'm looking to start a family," he says. "Soon. I'm not about fucking around. So if that's not something that you want, you should probably tell me now."

Here's something that almost never happens: I am struck dumb.

Talking about babies on a first date is not generally recommended, at least according to about a thousand self-help books featuring lists of the rules on ensnaring a husband. But I have never much been one for rules. Or ensnaring.

So what's the honest answer?

Do I? Yes, I do. I have always wanted kids, maybe even lots of them. At war with this desire are the sorority's worth of voices in my head telling me I'm not good enough to take care of someone. That girls like me don't deserve families. We might have our share of explosive romance, but we are ultimately slated only for loss and loneliness.

Across town, my closest friend, Jennifer, is sitting amid the debris of her drug addiction and shattered marriage, probably snorting OxyContin off her half of the wedding china. Every time I visit her, I fear I'm looking into a crystal ball. Girls like us are unworthy of happily-ever-afters. Like Audrey in *Little Shop*, girls like us may dream of somewhere green but always wind up getting sacrificed by the end of the show. If we're lucky, we get to deliver one final zinger. This is the time bomb I have long suspected I carry inside of me. Things may look pretty snazzy at present, what with this delightful date and all, but all you have to do is listen carefully and you will hear the bomb's unmistakable tick tock tick tock.

But I know better than to express these doubts to a man I'm trying to impress.

I say, "Yes. I want a family very much."

He follows with, "So, I heard you were a slave in China. Is that true?"

Surprisingly, this is more comfortable territory for me. I already have a custom-made set of invisible armor for questions like this. I can don it instantaneously, anywhere, anytime.

"Where did you hear that?" I smile.

"My friend Dan saw it on some *E! True Hollywood Story* called 'The Sultan and the Centerfold.' He said they blurred out your eyes in the pictures but it was definitely you."

His friend Dan is right. It is me in the pictures. Fifteen years ago, I spent a year and a half as the kept mistress of the titular Sultan's younger brother Prince Jefri Bolkiah of Brunei. The Sultan of Brunei was, at the time, the richest man in the world. His wilder brother Jefri was known in the press as "the Playboy Prince," due to his proclivity for jewel-draped, Chanel-clad international beauties, whom he mostly kept stashed away in one of his many palaces—his harem, after a fashion. It's a hell of a past to have to explain right away.

"Well, I wouldn't exactly use the word 'slave,'" I say. "And it wasn't China."

And so, within the opening moments of our very first date, it all comes spilling out around the half-full salt and pepper shakers and the smudged steel napkin dispenser—my teenage years as a stripper in New York; my failure at acting, at college, at writing; the years spent in the harem; my subsequent heroin addiction that came on the heels of that life; my endless attempts to change; the car crashes; the rehabs.

I wait for his reaction. My experience is that men generally think a past like mine grants them permission to objectify me. The moment I catalog my indiscretions, I drop down a few pegs in class, brains, and general worth. Many times, I've watched the relief in men's eyes as they realize that they aren't obligated to summon all the sensitivity training from their freshman year at Wesleyan in an attempt to respect me.

Scott is different. He listens and nods. His eyes don't drift—they definitely don't drift downward.

He says, "You know, when I said beauty school was hot, I was just playing with you. I know that place is a crappy, mind-numbing bitch. And I think it's great that you do it anyway. I think you've got guts for trying to change your life."

He drives me home, after a first kiss on a park bench, lit swimmy blue-white by a low, full moon.

For the next two weeks, we spend nearly every night together, until I graduate from beauty school and we celebrate with a road trip through the American West. Our only rule is that there are no plans, no itinerary. We drink black-and-white milk shakes for breakfast before we leave, pull out the classic yellow *Rand McNally Road Atlas*, and choose a direction.

We keep moving through that whole first day. Darkness falls and still we drive, as the road climbs the spines of mountains and curls back down again. We can't stop talking. I can't stop touching him. We finally pause at a seedy motel on the outskirts of Sedona.

When I wake, I leave Scott sleeping in one of the twin beds that we have pushed together. I pull on my jeans and walk, bleary, out to the road, my hand shielding my eyes.

Wind kicks my hair back and forth, blows sand into my eyes.

The sky is dead clear, the kind of blue that begs to frame a host of cherubim. It backs straight up to the deep pink orange earth and everything is set in high relief by the altitude and the shock of morning sunlight.

I have never seen the Southwestern desert. I have always wanted to. It is everything I hoped it would be. How corny. When does that ever happen?

I feel unnaturally still. I am going to marry this guy.

A year later Scott, with an enormous candy bar in his hand, walks into the hair salon where I work and says, "I thought you might be hungry. Also, how about you quit this job you hate, marry me, and go to graduate school?"

Straight out of the final scene of *An Officer and a Gentleman*.

I say yes. Duh. Of course I say yes. I go to graduate school to get my MFA in creative writing, like I always dreamed. And we live happily ever after.

~ Chapter 2

IN November 2006, I borrow a friend's dress, and Scott and I skip town and get married alone, barefoot, on a deserted beach in Kauai, during a half-cloudy but still glorious sunset. I wear a floor-length veil—also borrowed—that tears on a jagged rock when the wind catches it. A jovial old Hawaiian guy and his smiling-eyed wife bear witness. Only the bouquet and the husband and the moment are truly mine. Waves of joy, ambivalence, hope, cynicism, anxiety, and calm crest and break in me, over and over. Part of me feels like I'm living a borrowed fantasy, something purer and more innocent than that to which I'm entitled. I smile for the pictures and hope that I'll look at the photos later and see someone who fits perfectly. It is a beautiful wedding and true to where we are—not at a happy ending, but at a quiet and hopeful beginning.

As soon as that borrowed white dress is on the hanger, ready for dry cleaning, Scott and I are on a mission. An added dimension of intentionality infuses our lovemaking during each starry, guava-scented Kauai night. From that point on, each sexual encounter between us figures in my head into some future narrative. I construct the story as I live it, the awareness of the moment heightened by the tale I plan to tell our children. A portion of my consciousness is always reserved for documenting. It's a blessing and a curse. I'm never fully present, but I have a purpose—a reason for weathering even the most grievous of life's injustices. Material, I say to myself when things get shitty. Material. As if everything can be justified by art. As if everything is somehow redeemable.

When the honeymoon is over, we return home. My friends are getting pregnant in droves. This being Los Angeles, at every luncheon or shower or birthday party, phone numbers are traded for doulas, acupuncturists, custom baby slings, prenatal Kundalini yoga classes. Far from judging the privileged culture of bourgeois-hip maternity wear and celebrity midwives as I normally would, I want *in*. I want in on their invite-only message boards, their secret language, their knowing smiles. After my nights with Scott in the teak bed in Hawaii, I'm sure it will be mere weeks before I'm gently complaining about nausea. I think weight gain will be my biggest problem. Or maybe it'll be whether we can fit one of those inflatable birthing tubs into our living room.

This is my second chance, my redemption story. My own childhood began as an unwanted pregnancy, my unwed birth mother stranded alone in a snow-blanketed Chicago, feeling terrified and foolish. Across the country, my soon-to-be mother cried herself to sleep in her West Orange, New Jersey, apartment every night, longing for a child. A deal was struck, a baby passed from one set of hands to another. I was adopted just barely before the passage of Roe v. Wade in 1973.

To be so unwanted and so wanted at the same time can carve a fault line in you. I expect motherhood to finally unite this duality. It will settle the question of whether or not I'm needed. Motherhood (which is ultimately going to be my true calling, I am sure of it) is going to be the story that justifies my life, riddled with mistakes and missteps though it may have been.

I can't tell you how many times I am absolutely certain that I'm pregnant, am sure that I hear the whisper of an angel telling me as much.

I am wrong every time.

With Project Baby inexplicably stalled and my MFA program letting me work independently, I join Scott's band on tour. It seems like just the thing to take my mind off my growing sense of unease.

When we're not touring, Scott and I live in a ratty, weird apartment with mirrored closet doors, curling linoleum, industrial gray carpeting, and Cottage White walls. We moved into it blinded by new love, with the thought that he'd mostly be on tour and we'd save money to buy a house. Every time Scott and I head out for another leg of the tour, we leave the crappy apartment full to bursting with the beginnings of a married life. Or rather the beginnings of the accumulation of stuff that I sometimes think signifies a married life. Each appliance testifies to my health and growth. I have a Cuisinart food processor. I am here. I am whole. I have monogrammed tea towels, therefore I am.

I also sometimes think, What the fuck is a tea towel anyway?

We're both relieved every time we drag our bags out the door. As depicted in a thousand movies, the touring life is grueling and hard—the travel, the exhaustion, the repetition. Touring notoriously wreaks havoc on musicians and their families. But for Scott and me, life on the road is a kind of rolling meditation. We love living out of suitcases. We both feel less secure when we're settled down than when we're on the move. I am never more myself than when waking up, ordering room service, and poring over the map of a new city. I'm even happier if breakfast contains one or two things I can't name. Scott and I both feel like we should have been born into a circus family.

And in a way, that's what being in a band is—a dysfunctional, nomadic family, united by a common purpose and facing common obstacles, buoyed always by the electrical force of the music. There are perpetually shifting alliances. You become an old married couple, content to read next to each other at a café, not enmeshed but never exactly alone. Except you're not a couple, you're a group of ten. It's easy to get lonely on tour, but you are never without a witness. Scott belongs on that stage and I belong with a notebook in my lap, perched on a flight case in the wings, and we both feel plugged in to this planetary organism in our exact right place at the right time.

I tour with him all summer and into the fall, curling up in the back lounges of the tour buses. I watch columns of light shoot up into the purple sky over the California desert, while the crowd boils and churns and clamors for guitar picks. I gossip for hours with the other wives and girlfriends. I watch Scott play grungy Dutch clubs and cavernous American hockey rinks, and, how bizarre, the site of the Nuremberg Rallies. I wake dazed in St. Louis, Toronto, London. Liam Gallagher offers me cocaine in a bathroom in Paris, which I don't accept, but still. I step over passed-out, topless Scandinavians. I wander the 8th arrondissement, the red-light district of Hamburg, downtown Detroit, Walt Disney World. And even though it's not my first time to this particular rodeo—I've been with my rock musician for years now—I still fall in love with Scott anew every time I watch him step onto a stage, into the persona he wore in his childhood dreams. It's as if I can see my husband imagining himself into existence right there in front of me.

The jet lag clouds my vision. Gauzy threads connect everything, strings floating lazily in the air, though I can't see exactly what they're attached to. I am convinced I could grab the end of one and follow it back to a street my ancestors once lived on in Poland. Me, the book with too many themes, with no satisfactory conclusions. An American girl, probably Irish and Scottish by blood, adopted by Eastern European Jews, married to a blue-eyed German musician from Toledo, Ohio. In every city, I walk streets that are, for a heartbeat, somewhere I might belong. If you don't quite fit in anywhere, you belong on a rock tour, where all frayed threads are hastily stapled into a makeshift hem in time to run for your next plane.

~

Traveling with the band, I'm a "Wife." I sit in the other room with the Wives. Ride to the show with the Wives. Why don't you see if the other Wives want to go shopping with you? Wives Allowed. No Wives Allowed.

I'm of two minds about the "wife" label. I like being a part of something—a couple, an institution. But I don't like being merely an appendage of the artist, even though all I have to show for a career of my own is a stack of rejection letters for the earnest essays I've been unsuccessfully submitting to magazines and a pile of student loans for the graduate program that's teaching me to write said earnest essays.

When you're the wife of a musician, you can start to feel like Wife may be the best you're going to do. Still, I pull out my journal, sit cross-legged in the corner of the first-class lounge, and scribble furiously. Because even if you're a failure, even if you're a fool, you still have to do what you do.

Nowhere is the drifting feeling of being on tour more profound and satisfying than in Japan. It's not like traveling in Europe, where I'm pulled into a vague undertow of anxiety as I search for the right word buried somewhere deep in my high school French file, just out of reach. I stutter and stumble, as people's eyes glaze over with impatience. In Japan, I harbor no illusion that I'll ever say anything more complicated than "hello," "excuse me," "how much?" "thank you very much," and "do you have that in a bigger size?" (I memorized that one.) Even the letters of the alphabet are nothing more than a set of hieroglyphs to me. The tour takes us on bullet trains from Osaka to Fukuoka to Nagoya to Tokyo. In each city, neat packs of schoolgirls in blue and white uniforms wait outside our hotel in the snow to ask for autographs. It is like meandering through an exquisite foreign film, but I am just an extra, free to observe as I please, not required to learn any lines or jump in on the action.

When we get to Tokyo, I go to the rock shows, write, and occasionally make deranged fashion choices, inspired by my shopping trips to Harejuku. The city of Tokyo is a pinball machine, a sci-fi movie set, a wonder. I spend my days drifting dazed under its massive television screens, its neon signs slashing through space in every direction. I wander the rolling streets of Shibuya, a neighborhood packed with love hotels and sex shops—some bizarre, some barren, some lit up like a rowdy bar and grill. I try to peek into doorways.

Red-light districts fascinate me. I look at the photographs of the rooms advertised in the love hotels and picture the lives inside them, as if one may offer a parallel life of my own. I'm time traveling and dropping in on a self I once was. These thoughts are like a bruise that I keep pressing on, just to see if it still hurts.

In Shibuya, unlike in the red-light district of Hamburg or Paris or Amsterdam, the working girls are invisible. When do the Japanese girls walk to work? Where are they? In the United States, you'll sometimes see a random girl strolling in the door of a club, wearing sweats and Ugg boots, baseball cap over blond extensions, dance bag over her shoulder. Never in Japan. They live hidden, somehow. Hidden from me, anyway. Maybe if I knew what to look for I would be able to see them.

There were once hotel rooms that hid me away, too. Mine were in the Four Seasons New York, the Ritz, the St. Regis, the Hilton Kuala Lumpur, the Westin Stamford Singapore. I danced in clubs not unlike the ones behind the pink neon of Shibuya, and there I met businessmen from Japan. Lots of them—with their clean skin smelling of soap, their square shoulders, their pressed suits. When I worked in strip clubs, all the customers were foreign, not just the ones from other counties. They existed in a different dimension, as if they were people and we girls were ghosts. Their goal was to become pure flesh for a moment; our goal was to become as distinct from our bodies as possible.

When I think of that girl, it's hard to grasp that she was me.

Meet me for lunch and I'll tell you stories about her, but they will be stories about someone else—a shadowy figure zipped into a shiny girl suit.

This shiny, shadowy, fake girl, who spent nights with Japanese businessmen in the Four Seasons, with foreign royalty at the Hilton Kuala Lumpur—she's still here, floating next to me, her hazy borders moving in and out of the me that is now firmly grounded in this corporeal world, winding through the back alleys of Tokyo in a pair of purple clogs, looking for a great bowl of soba. Whenever I find myself in a red-light district, I unconsciously seek out faces of girls with whom to make eye contact. I want to tell them that I understand, that I was once like they are. But the girls in Shibuya have become ghosts so effectively that I can't see them at all. Even if I could, they wouldn't believe me. There's a password, but I have long since forgotten it.

~

I'm driven back to the hotel early one night by the first twinges of menstrual cramps. I know the intensity will pick up momentum quickly and I want to be in a hot bath before I'm leveled. My cycle has always been true to its popular moniker: the Curse. Sometimes on the first day I can barely walk. Sometimes I vomit into trash cans and it feels like an unseen hand is digging a set of claws into my uterus.

The initial twinges came earlier in the day but I convinced myself they were something else. For months now, we have been diligently trying to get pregnant and this means that we've been unsuccessful—yet again. Scott, I know, will be his usual optimistic and unperturbed self about it. I, on the other hand, am besieged by despair.

As I lie in a fetal position on the hotel bed, my palms clammy and my upper lip beading with sweat from the waves of pain rolling through me, I watch out the window as snow falls over Tokyo. I think about the invisible girls down below. Can a ghost cross back to the land of the living? Maybe I left my body behind and now there's no getting it back. Aside from the metaphysical, there have always been physical problems for me—cysts and surgeries and bleeding and pain.

I shake off the doubt worming its way into my brain. I don't believe in being broken beyond repair. I believe in second chances. I believe in an infinite number of chances, in fact. I believe in re-birth. I believe in the redemptive power of love.

Don't I?

Tick tock tick tock.

~

Scott and I stay in Japan after the tour is over and call it our second honeymoon. After the rest of the band is on a plane to L.A., we take the bullet train to Kyoto. We stay at a lovely traditional inn, with tatami mats and sliding doors. Outside our window is a court-yard with a rock garden and a bonsai frosted with snow. There is a wooden tub sunken into the floor with a hot bath already drawn when we arrive. Kimonos hang in the closet. Everything is delicate and quiet and I feel brash, my clogs something that belong on Gul-liver, my jeans too low-slung in the back for all this kneeling. I plan to cover my thong with the kimono.

That first night in Kyoto we eat dinner in our room and it's an elaborate affair, with course after course of mystery custards and fish that might still be alive. I soft-focus my eyes as I bring the food to my lips.

"I think this is the worst and the best food I've ever eaten," says Scott.

Afterward, we watch Korean horror films on Scott's computer late into the night. We make out like teenagers, in no kind of rush, and eat mochi candies, thinking they're the most delicious things we've ever tasted. We stock up on boxes of them for home, though

I suspect that when we bust them open in our L.A. living room, they will taste flavorless and pasty. Everything is colored by love, by adventure. We collapse in laughter together. We feel lucky.

We spend a day sightseeing with my friend Yoshi. Yoshi is a music enthusiast and political activist I met in L.A. when I volunteered with Food Not Bombs. We have kept in touch over the years. Repaying us for Weezer tickets in Osaka, he promises us a temple tour, a fantastic dinner, and some authentic Japanese karaoke, which he assures us will surprise us with its volume and rowdiness. He asks us what we want to see. Kyoto is famous for its temples and its geishas. I'd like to see both, which turns out to be easy. Hidden around every turn is a gold shrine that catches the light as you round the corner, a bright flash of lipstick on a pale face as it ducks into a doorway. Scott intertwines his fingers with mine and we wind through the streets.

At the Heian Jingu shrine—a massive, soaring temple surrounded by winter gardens and crowned by stacks of curling red pagodas—Yoshi teaches us how to pray properly. First you bow before you enter the torii gate with its two upright columns and two crossbars, slashes of crimson like brushstrokes in the sky. I've always been interested in devotional rituals. I spoke to God all the time as a child, and even though I lapsed into silence for a while, when I picked it up again under my drug dealer's bed, I fell easily back into the habit.

My family has belonged to a big Reform synagogue in northern New Jersey for four generations. I was raised in the heart of the temple, its roof laced with stained glass that lit up the sanctuary like it was on fire in the late afternoon. The upstairs lobby on a weekday afternoon was hushed but still humming with the promise of activity from the Hebrew school below. I would take the world's longest bathroom breaks from class and wander the back hallways, lined with black-and-white photos of the old temple in Newark. I'm not sure that what I experienced there was the presence of God, exactly, but I did inhabit a spacious silence that seemed to act as both a bolster and a helium infusion, making me stronger and less tethered to gravity at the same time. I loved it there.

"The shrines are just pathways, like telephone lines, for the *kami*, for the gods," Yoshi says. "Like the essence of a thing. Like, have you seen *Spirited Away?*"

He thinks the only gods we Americans will understand will be in the form of cartoons.

He points to the gate.

"This is what makes different ground that is common from ground that is sacred," he explains.

Yoshi demonstrates how to use the hand-washing basin, left then right, before washing your mouth out. Then you ring the bell that hangs on the temple, to announce your presence. You bow twice. You clap twice. With the second clap you keep your hands pressed together in prayer in front of your heart and you pray.

We arrive at the Fushimi Inari shrine as the sun is setting to find that there are not one but *five thousand* torii gates under which you have to pass to get to the shrine. I suppose sometimes you need lots of chances to cross over. We wind up the hill through the gates, the small cemeteries and shrines along the path strewn with alternating ribbons of light and shadow.

"Inari is the goddess of rice and fertility and good fortune. And foxes. This is where businessmen pray for success," says Yoshi.

I'd never pray for such a thing, I think. I'd feel too greedy. I'm not someone who has ever prayed for money, even in my crappiest night in my crappiest apartment, facing my crappiest day job. I've always believed that you're not supposed to pray to get things, as if God is Santa Claus and you're sending your personal Christmas list.

And yet, when we reach the top of the hill at the Fushimi Inari shrine, I break all my own rules. I surprise even myself when I turn from Scott and Yoshi and toward the gods. I wash my hands in the right order. I'm careful to wash them well. I invest almost as much hope in the washing as I do in the prayer. I ring the bell and imagine that I am calling to this goddess. Of rice, of prosperity, of foxes. Of fertility.

I roll out the Christmas list. There is only one thing I really want. An undertow of urgency pulls beneath my prayer.

I look out from the corner of my eye and see, indeed, businessmen praying. But I also see women praying. My inner feminist scolds me—how could I be so regressive? Maybe these are businesswomen praying for success. Perhaps they are. But there may also be others like me—women with their eyes closed and their palms pressed together hard, who have turned from their friends and unlocked a private door in their heart. Others who are, right at the same moment I am, putting aside doubt and living for a minute in a desperate sort of faith.

What I have—marriage, life on the road, writing—might be almost all I've ever dreamed of, but there is one thing without which I will never be home. I'm sure it's this last thing that will make me finally whole.

Please, I pray. Please. Make me a mother.

~ Chapter 3

THE following spring, our Realtor calls. Our bid has been accepted on a house in Eagle Rock, a trendy, family-oriented neighborhood peppered with grassy parks, cute cafés, and strollers. The restaurants and boutiques have Swedish-looking play areas, populated by toddlers and their tired young mothers, who are sucking down amphetamine-grade lattes. Of the many houses we've looked at, it's the one we love the most, by far—an adorable Craftsman built in 1921, on a block lined with camphor and jacaranda and palm trees. There's a music studio in the backyard and a second-floor office surrounded by windows, perfect for writing. I can't believe I'm going to have a home this beautiful. This is the moment that the tide turns and everything starts looking up, I'm sure of it. This portends a change in our astrological circumstances—Venus moves out of the sixth house at 4:28 P.M. on March 3 and *bam*. Magic.

It's the outskirts of Los Angeles, so our street has been used in countless movies and television shows. It's "the charming street," a harmonious mix of architectural styles common to California in the 1920s. In a city that generally knocks everything down and starts over every decade or so, this neighborhood has been oddly forgotten by time. It's a popular street for shooting both pharmaceutical commercials and horror movies. It's meant to signal normalcy. Sweet. Perfect. In the case of the pharmaceutical commercials, there's no irony. The horror movies, though, recognize that something dark always lurks beneath a polished veneer.

We pack the Crown Vic with paper bags full of condiments and open cereal boxes, along with pillows, guitars, laptops, a bin of half-full shampoos and body products. The odd-sized things, the last things to go from the crappy apartment. As we pull away, I feel a pang, a little internal lurch of reservation. What if this next house isn't all I'm hoping for? What if we aren't happy there after all?

We got the house, which had multiple bids at the top of the housing bubble, on the virtue of a letter I wrote to the owners, explaining that we wanted to start a family there. When we pull in, the husband is parked in the driveway, moving the last of his things. All four car doors are flung open, spilling over with bedding and plants and children's toys.

"Oh, hey, hey. Sorry about this. You have no idea. This move has been a nightmare," he says. "I long for the days when it was just the two of us moving from an apartment like you're doing. Just wait until you have kids. And you will. This is a fertile house, I'm telling you."

He fidgets and tries to wedge a houseplant into a crate. Would it be rude to just walk into the house as he's still clearing it out? A distinctive voice sails into the yard from the street.

"Jesus. And men are supposed to have all the talent for engineering?"

An attractive dishwater blonde who looks like she's from Connecticut drags a towheaded toddler up the driveway and stands, hands on designer-cargo-pant-clad hips, surveying the scene. She squints into the sun and the skin around her eyes crinkles in an appealing way, like in an ad for night cream. I think I recognize her. A TV commercial, maybe? A sitcom I saw once? She introduces herself as Suzanne and tells me she lives in the stately green house across the street. The toddler regards me with suspicion.

"And this is Hank," she says of the child.

She hands him a yellow toy car, with googly eyes on the front, which he rolls roughly back and forth along the pavement. She pushes the keyboard player out of the way, systematically unpacks his car, and lays all the crap out on the sidewalk, then lickety-split stacks it all in again in a much more efficient and logical way.

"There. Jesus."

Hank begins to crawl toward the street. Suzanne's face transforms with sudden panic as she wheels around abruptly, then scoops him up and places him back within her immediate reach.

"My first child was killed. He was run over. It was an accident with a neighbor. So I'm always nervous with this one near the street."

Her words knock the wind out of me. It leaves the world changed, tilted slightly. I am suddenly aware of the position of the sun behind the trees, the breeze on my bare arms, the bass vibrations from a car stereo blocks away.

"I'm sorry," I say.

I sense that the abrupt conveyance of this information is some kind of test. I don't know if I pass. I could have done better, I guess, but then again I could have done worse. I could have said one of those horrid phrases people sometimes use when unsettled by another's tragedy, like, "There's a reason for everything."

I hope I do pass, because, jarring as the encounter is, there's something about this woman's straightforward energy to which I instinctively respond. Maybe she could even become a friend—my friend across the street. How Ozzie and Harriet would that be?

That night Scott and I sleep on a mattress on the floor in an upstairs bedroom. We have almost nothing. We abandoned our IKEA bed at the old apartment. We didn't have any furniture worth salvaging. I like the house like this. It feels light and spare and promising.

In times of duress or transition, I often have night terrors, so

Scott is braced for some late-night unconscious histrionics. Our first night in the old apartment, I pulled the curtains down on top of us. Scott told me it looked like I was trying to climb them.

I dream of Suzanne's dead child. I dream that there is a faceless baby in my arms. He looks swimmy and white, almost like an ultrasound. He is hungry and I try to breast-feed him, but I can't. I put him down and leave and other stuff happens involving staircases and Malcolm Gladwell. Somewhere in the midst of it, I realize that I've left the baby behind. I go back for him and he is sick, starving, nearly dead. As I watch him die, I know that I have killed this child through my neglect.

I wake with my heart slamming against my chest, unable to get a good breath, feeling disoriented—low to the ground on the mattress, far from the ceiling. As Scott breathes evenly beside me the space around us swims with jagged lines of shadow and light, strange electrical charges. It takes me a few minutes of conscious breathing and logically talking myself down before I shake off my fear enough to cross the room and go to the bathroom, where I turn on the light. I hold my head in my hands. It's just anxiety, I tell myself. It's not a premonition. It's not a sign.

Morning breaks at last. I throw on my robe and wander through the labyrinth of boxes in the living room, the blissfully bare dining room. There are only a few brief moments when a room will ever be this peaceful and empty: a place where no mistakes have yet been made, where all the decisions are still in front of you.

I grind the coffee beans Scott likes and fill the French press. While the water boils, I gaze out the front picture window, with its eighty-year-old glass. Hot pink camellias and fat white roses and birds of paradise encroach on every porch on the block. A flock of wild parrots, the stuff of local legend, screech from their perch in the jacaranda tree outside.

I wish I could pause this and rewind just a little. Our fresh start has already begun and the clock is now running.

Scott lopes down the stairs, whistling. My husband is happy most of the time. He loves his stereo speakers, his coffee grinder, the power tools he never uses. He's an inherently Zen kind of guy. I am the opposite. I seize on shifting spiritual agendas and enlist him. A brief sampling of some of our endeavors have included: Transcendental Meditation, the master cleanse (twice—horrible), Eckhart Tolle, Shlomo Carlebach, Bible study, Burning Man, and Peruvian psychedelic ceremonies (Scott backed out of that one). Scott is a good sport. Left to his own devices, he is more apt to quote the guy from *Harold and Kumar Go to White Castle*: "The universe tends to unfold as it should." This is exactly the kind of thing that drives me crazy.

"The baby's got a house now," he says, drawing me into his arms. "That's all she was waiting for."

~

The months pass. He is wrong.

Everyone has unsolicited advice.

Just relax.

When you stop trying you'll get pregnant.

Go get stoned.

Have sex in the car.

Stop thinking about it.

I have a friend (everyone seems to have this same anecdotal friend) *who tried every which way for years and then just when they started the adoption process they finally got pregnant.*

I share a birthday with Madonna—the day of the relentless. I am a pit bull with a locked jaw when I set my sights on something, and I have set my sights on a baby. Pregnancy seems more elusive with each passing month and in inverse proportions, it grows in size and volume in my consciousness. At the suggestion of one of the fertility books, every day I "chart" my basal body temperature along with any fluctuation in every possible bodily function. I have blood workups and aura readings alike. I am not panicked yet. Things have never come easily to me, but if I am tenacious they usually come, in one form or another.

Reading the pregnancy books, I first see the word "infertility." I read sentences like, *Infertility is assumed if pregnancy has not occurred within a year*, and my stomach drops. But I tell myself we haven't been trying, exactly; it was more like a process of being less and less careful until we weren't careful at all. So that doesn't count, right?

I'm a task-oriented individual. I like lists and goals and any project with bullet points I can tick off, so charting naturally appeals to me.

. . . Many women find that using the chart to predict their fertility window becomes a fun challenge!

The fun doesn't end there! There are other contributing factors to note on the chart: exercise, travel, illness, stress, PMS, symptoms, ovulatory pain . . .

The good news is that all of this gives me the impression that I can control this fertility thing. I love control! Control is my favorite!

The bad news is the flip side of that sentiment: it's my fault.

I can almost feel my ovaries. The insides of me, which have previously been just energy and motion and weight, now become a color-coded, labeled illustration, like the one in the book. I'm hyperaware of all the delicate pink bits, the ones you can see and the ones you can't. The ones that always seem so fragile but prove time and again to be more durable than they appear or they would have been torn to pieces long ago.

Through it all, I feel a cold hand on the back of my neck. I keep brushing it off, but it returns when I read things like, *Ovarian surgeries can seriously compromise your fertility*. I've had three major occurrences of ovarian cysts, two of them requiring surgery. My first cysts occurred when I was just thirteen and had barely started menstruating. I remember the doctor with the unfortunate bedside manner in San Francisco—the one who brusquely dismissed my concerns that the surgery would one day affect my ability to get pregnant. I always knew that guy was a jerk; I just hadn't considered the fact that he might also be wrong.

Based on the information in the chart, I can be pretty sure about my ovulation window. But I decide to pad it to be safe and I start us on a regimen of lots and lots of sex. I get no arguments from Scott. He is always cheery about it and ready to go, any hour of the day or night. Sometimes the sex is nuts-and-bolts pragmatic: not-a-lot-of-time, kind-of-tired, get-it-done sex. Sometimes it is tantric sex magic and afterward I end up lying on my back, hips on a pillow (in recommended get-pregnant fashion), feeling like I'm hardly a body at all—more a shimmering fingerprint of light on the planet's face.

On the fertility websites I've begun to peruse (reluctantly, as if my browser history will seal some metaphysical deal), there are suggestions for keeping your sex life from becoming a goal-obsessed misery. *Get a pedicure together! Set aside time for self-care. Remember—sex should be fun!* But this effort to get pregnant has not yet devolved into that for us and I'm convinced it never will. Because the extra effort still has, in spite of my mounting anxiety, an undercurrent of joy. We're trying to start a family. We're this close.

We lie in bed and imagine how amazing it's going to be to have a baby there with us—how soft, how sweet, how good it will smell. In our talk, in our thoughts, the baby becomes an entity, almost there between us already. We come up with a name for her: Bluebell. Who's dropping off Bluebell at preschool this morning? Oh, no! Bluebell lost one of the mittens you knitted for her.

Every time I look down and see the first pale red stain on the toilet paper, I feel like a failure. I read the blood as a sign, maybe a message from God. I am broken. I have come this far just so he can laugh harder at the expression on my face when it all falls apart. This is my deep suspicion when I lie awake late into the night. But there's always the relentless optimist warring with the naysayer within. And so I continue to fill out the chart.

Chapter 4

MY initial impression of Suzanne is right. She is smart and saucy and we become fast friends, often taking walks together with her son in the early evening. On one such night, I unload my anxieties about pregnancy, detail my litany of efforts. As we stroll up the hill, Hank tries to leap over the long shadows cast by the palm trees next to the sidewalk. Suzanne stands on tippy-toes and reaches for a ripe plum hanging over a neighbor's fence. When she turns around, plum in hand, she tells me that she's going through the same thing. She loves her specialist, says that he's one of the best in the city. Stop fucking around with psychics and shamans and magic books, she tells me. Go see a doctor already.

A week later, Scott and I sit in the Pasadena Reproductive Clinic, all soft, Southwestern colors, smiling young nurses, and a flat-screen the size of the Asian continent playing footage of tropical fish. On the reception desk is a little calligraphy sign that says: *The presence of children can be painful for some of our patients. We love children, but we thank you for leaving yours at home.*

I used to think fertility treatments were for fortysomethings in power suits, or fringe weirdos with septuplets and their own reality show. Not for boho graduate students in their thirties.

But by the time I walk out of there, my shoulders are thrown back and there's a bounce to my step. I clasp my own personalized three-ring binder to my chest, as if the Secrets of the Universe are contained within. The strapping doctor and his smart, sexy staff have infused me with fresh optimism. How could you not get pregnant under the care of such caring, such . . . *attractive* people? They treated Scott and me like we were intelligent, worthy. They were hopeful. Even if the whole thing did seem a little bit bizarre, as if we were in a scene from the movie *Species* and the warm fuzzy vibe was just a cover-up for diabolical experiments. Once the patient is under, the doctors remove their handsome masks and alien tentacles unfurl, dripping in ectoplasm.

"How much?" says Scott once we're in the car.

I look for the numbers in the binder. My mood crashes. The treatments are prohibitively expensive. Of course they are.

No matter. I gather my resolve. We will find a way to pay. And pay and pay, if that's what it takes.

~

I always blanch at blood tests. I had lousy veins even before I ever sat in a moldy San Francisco basement, letting a girl with an orange Mohawk tie a bandanna around my biceps and feel for a vein in the crook of my arm. The end stage of my heroin addiction was pretty much spent in a bathroom twenty-four hours a day, face slick with tears, trickles of blood running down my arms, legs, neck, like something out of a horror movie, trying desperately to mine some last uncollapsed blood vessel deep under the surface of my skin. My veins have never recovered and, as a result, blood draws are often long, frustrating, and shameful. Not that the phlebotomists (who often hover around my arm in packs, consulting with each other) know the cause of my being such a "tough stick," but I know. It's enough to bring tears to my eyes, not because it hurts, but from the knowledge that I did such brutal and permanent damage to my body.

I think of my friend Jennifer, who is now in the grips of a full-tilt heroin relapse and is probably in some shady motel room working on her own damage. Sometimes she calls twice a day, forgetting that she's already spoken to me. Sometimes she doesn't call for weeks. When she does, she either cries or lies. I can hear the telltale fading in and out of her voice as the sense memory of the drug burns inside my chest. Though it seems like a lifetime ago, I can still remember that heroin felt, for a brief moment, like that first view of the Sedona desert: love, connection, relief. Heroin is like an abusive lover, who seduces you with promises of a floaty eternity hanging around being skinny, listening to Velvet Underground records, and forgetting about your past, your pain. It's only when he finally reveals his true self and socks you in the kisser that you realize he has closed and locked the door behind you.

I don't tell Jennifer about the fertility tests. I've stopped telling her much about my life. These days, more often than not, I press Decline when she calls. I try to tell myself that I don't want to enable her, but maybe that's not exactly accurate. Maybe I also don't want to be reminded of where I came from.

Except for the needles, the first round of tests is relatively simple and painless. The second round of tests is neither. As I start the first of the fertility drugs, I'm equally convinced of both outcomes. I'm sure it is going to work and that all of this suffering will recede until it seems just a bad dream, and I am sure it is never going to work and that the bad dream will stretch on into a childless eternity.

One room in our house remains empty, or rather has become a repository for every object we can't find a home for—a de facto storage room. We keep the curtains drawn. We keep the door closed. We do not call it a nursery.

The advice keeps coming. Every time I leave the house, I return with a new phone number for someone's miracle healer. How come everyone has their miracle already except me? Still, I'm desperate and I call them. Every one. It becomes a full-time job.

Along with every conceivable medical intervention, here are some things I try: acupuncture, acupressure, chiropractic, Reiki, quitting wheat, quitting dairy, quitting sugar, quitting meat, unquitting meat, eating lots of ice cream (because fat supposedly helps?), expensive supplements, charting ovulation, Chinese herbs, yoga, breathing, meditation, hypnosis, Ayurveda, muscle testing, homeopathy, Kabbalah classes, church, colonics, wraps, fasts . . .

I take out my piercings because an acupuncturist suggests they are "obstructing the flow of my qi." At the behest of a buxom tarot reader in my neighborhood, I burn a candle shaped like a penis on the first night of a full moon. I order special magnets online and place them under the bed.

Every first half of the month is a new leaf, a resolutely cheery fresh start. And every second half I start sneaking into the back of a Pentecostal church in East L.A. on Sundays, where nice Latina moms lay healing hands on my belly and pray with me and no one cares if I cry. Every time it doesn't work it's like my chest is caving in and I think that maybe I won't ever be able to sit up straight again. I live with the flutter of failure trapped like a bird under my rib cage all the time.

I feel wronged by God. I'm deeply ashamed of this feeling. I'm not being raped and murdered in Sudan. I'm not an underage factory worker in Bangladesh. I'm not Suzanne, grieving a dead child. I'm a spoiled brat, who should be nothing but grateful for my life, my "first-world problems."

But I want this like I will die without it. Every month, I crumble and I hate myself for it. Then I stand back up and call the next number on the miracle list.

Rinse. Repeat.

~

When we start in vitro, Scott is recording a new album with his band out in Santa Monica. To spare him the daily commute they house us in an apartment on the ocean, overlooking the pier. It should be my best time, I realize. I'm approaching graduation and I, who could never stick to anything, will have a master's degree in creative writing. I'm married to a great guy. It's *Baywatch* outside my window.

And yet, I have rarely been so unhappy. I keep dreaming that I've left a baby behind to die. My mother once told me she had the same recurring nightmare. It's true in life as well as in dreams—I'm living the same hell my mother lived through before she adopted me. Sometimes I think about calling her to talk about it. My mother is a great listener. I remember her often pacing the kitchen late at night, winding the spiral cord of the phone around and around her finger as some friend or another poured her heart out to her. But who wants to admit to our mothers that we are turning out just like them? Or to ourselves. She and I chat nearly every day, but still I avoid the subject and she doesn't press me.

My marriage now walks with a limp. Scott spends hours in the studio, even more hours at the gym. He has never been so buff; I've never been so doughy. Every night as we lie there with an ocean of guilt and blame and fear between us in the bed, I remember how things were not so long ago, when we were so wildly in love.

The book *The Secret* comes out, and we receive about twelve copies as gifts. The premise is about "the law of attraction," which means that whatever you think about will manifest in your life. Apparently, the reason we didn't hear about "the law of attraction" until now is that it was a *secret*! A secret that the successful have been keeping from the rest of us schmucks for centuries.

I read it front to back and find it odious. I have no problem with thinking happy thoughts, but take *The Secret* to its logical conclusion and everyone who is sick is sick because they're not thinking right. Everyone who is starving is starving because they just haven't envisioned a BLT with enough conviction. Everyone with a giant house in Malibu is just more righteous than you, with a purer soul.

I can't help wondering, if you could think the world into existence, would a house in Malibu be the best you could do? While
babies starve in Africa?

But this is L.A. and hordes of people are full-on into this law of
attraction idea. A pregnant friend actually offers to shop for maternity clothes with me, because she thinks that's exactly the kind of
positive thinking that will help manifest the reality of a pregnancy.
I suppose in some circles shopping for maternity clothes when
you're not pregnant is called positive thinking and in others it's
called psycho. I personally cannot imagine the humiliation of it—
the envy, the emptiness. I do not go.

Even as I deride *The Secret*, early each morning, when I pinch a
thick fold of skin on my bruise-mottled thigh and inject the precious yellow serum, I try to think myself healed, fixed, fertile. I
think to reverse all the brokenness and toxicity of my old life. I think
with all my might. The rest of the time, I walk around with a raw
throat and a ringing in my ears and Xanax in an Advil bottle. And
every minute of every day, it feels like someone has caught my
heart with a fishhook and is yanking from behind.

~

They fertilize my eggs in a laboratory, where they grow for five
days. At the end of the five days, we hope that the embryos will
grow to between six and eight cells, at which point they're called
blastocytes. They call them "blasts," which I think sounds really
zippy and cute. Blasts! Zing! Except we have no blasts. None of
the embryos have made it that far. We have a couple with five cells,
and they implant them in my uterus. I return to our Santa Monica
apartment for the recommended three days of bed rest.

It's my birthday. Scott buys me a small diamond moon pen-
dant. My beloved Patti Smith plays out on the pier under our window and we can hear her clearly when the wind blows the right
way. Scott and I sit quietly together as the sky turns from apricot to

bruise purple to gray black. For the first time in a long time, I relax. I have done all I can do. I look across at my intrepid husband, who has endured all of it with grace—every appointment, every humiliation. As strained as things have become, I know he loves me. It's enough, for just this moment, to be loved.

I swear off the IVF forums and blogs for the next two weeks, while we wait to see if it has worked. I vow not to Google every real or imagined next symptom to see if it is a possible indicator of pregnancy. My resolve lasts about thirty-six hours, until I finally give up and surrender to trolling the Internet, looking for hope, for answers.

I wait. I walk our dogs along the beach. I try to do my schoolwork. I try not to imagine signs from God in the clouds, in my tea leaves, spelled out in the lacy foam on the waves.

After ten days I go for the blood test and it goes smoothly. They get it on the first stick. I return home to wait for the answer. The physician's assistant calls a couple of hours later.

That answer is no.

I am not pregnant. The eggs haven't implanted.

"I'm so sorry, sweetie," says the physician's assistant. "We're not giving up yet! I still think we're going to get you pregnant."

I sink to the floor.

The joyful screams coming from the roller coaster on the pier sail in through the open window. I remember kneeling, lonely, in my childhood bedroom, my ear pressed to the closed door, straining to hear the laughter and music of my parents' parties—listening to the muffled sounds of an elusive happiness so close I could almost touch it.

Chapter 5

I run into an old friend one morning on Sunset Boulevard. She, too, has been trying to get pregnant for a while and has had difficulty. I've long been jealous of her slender figure, fashionable clothes, and chic circle. She always seems to be coming from Soul-Cycle with Cameron or a book club at Beyoncé's. I call her name. When she turns around, I see that I now get to add a baby bump to the list of her things of which I'm jealous.

With a beatific smile, she tells me that she got pregnant with the help of Maori tribal healers from New Zealand, who happen to be in town again right now.

"I heard about them from [insert movie star]. Have you seen her baby [insert name of fruit, Hindu god, obscure blues/country singer, or day of week]? Adorable! Ridiculous! The baby was breech and she almost had to have him in the hospital, which she obviously did *not* want to do, but the Maori healers laid hands on her belly and turned that baby around and three days later it shot right out of her before [insert rock star husband] even had time to fill the birthing tub."

When I get home, I Google these healers before my coat is off. Indeed, they are in Santa Monica right now, being hosted at the home of a Vedic astrologer, whatever that is. I get an appointment for the next day. I am elated.

I show up at a charming 1950s beach house, painted powdery pink. Two dachshunds dressed in lederhosen—little Peter Pan collar shirts, embroidered suspenders, the whole thing—greet me at the door. You can read that sentence again if you need to. They are followed by a plain-looking woman in the kind of shapeless dress you buy at the Hare Krishna store on Venice Boulevard. She rubs her pregnant belly. Of course she does. Everyoneeveryoneeveryone in the world is pregnant.

"Wow. The dogs are so cute," I say, because it would be strange to not remark on this canine cast of *The Sound of Music*. "Are you doing a photo shoot or something?"

"No, no. They just like to dress up. I sew all their clothes. I would never make them be models or anything. I don't think the rejection is healthy."

She gives me that same pregnant smile my fashionable friend gave me. The one I uncharitably imagine to be smug, but maybe it's something I just don't understand.

"I'm sure you'll make lots of great baby clothes," I say awkwardly, still haunting her doorway.

"I've already got a closet full of gender-neutral clothes for three different ages. After all the dog outfits, it was really challenging to figure out the right place to put the baby arms and legs, but I've got the hang of it now." She gives a snorty little laugh. "Would you like to come inside?"

I'm thinking this dog clothes thing is strange and maybe sad. And then I check myself. That's not exactly getting off to a non-judgmental start. Maybe if the astrologer were a drag queen, I'd think the dogs in suspenders were eccentric or charming. Because how these things read is really all about context. It's all about tribe. I suppose you never know where you may find one. Maybe mine is right through the door in the next room. There's no way I'll know, if I go in there with a closed mind.

The astrologer and her Teutonic wiener dogs lead me into a

room with two massage tables set up in the center, and about eight people sitting on couches around the edges. Some of them look like what I imagine Maoris to look like—thickset and wide featured, with caramel skin and almond-shaped eyes. Some of them look more like the dog costumer's friends, tanned and be-flip-flopped and stylishly tousled. I steal glances at the skin that peeks out above the Maoris' collars and below their sleeves, hoping to catch a glimpse of the famous and fierce Maori tribal tattoos, but I don't see any.

No one looks up or stops their conversation. I stand there, hovering somewhere between the doorway and the couches, for a few long moments before I start to panic. I'm such a schmuck, I think. I've handed two hundred dollars over to yet another charlatan. I remember the angel healer I saw the week before, who had a visitation from the archangel Michael, telling her that all I needed was a ritual cord-cutting, where she would sever the invisible cords tying me to my past. She could have done it right there and then, for another three hundred dollars. Or the storefront psychic who told me that there was a curse upon me, which could only be lifted if she traveled to the village in which she was born and at the foot of the mountain there buried a jar of nails that I had peed on. All she would need from me was my urine and two *thousand* dollars.

One of the men starts asking the rest of the people in the room what they want for lunch. He hands around a Chinese menu. He turns to me.

"You want some moo shu or something?"

"No, thanks. I'm just here for . . ." What do you call it anyway? "For this."

Without getting up, another one of the men offhandedly indicates that I'm meant to lie on the table. I haven't even told them why I'm here yet. No one appears to be leaving or stopping their conversations. Are we really going to do this here in front of the dog lady and everybody? Do I have to admit in front of all these men that I can't get pregnant?

I lie down. I've paid. Even if they are just carnival hucksters, how bad can it be?

Another of the men, slight and muscular, approaches the table while his friend orders Chinese food over the phone.

"Why are you here?" he asks me.

I'm grateful when he leans in close so I don't have to speak loudly. When I am through, he walks over to an ample woman of impossible-to-determine age, who has been sitting the whole time on the couch with her eyes closed and her hands on her knees, like a statue. He whispers in her ear. I don't even know what language they're speaking. I don't know anything about these people and I'm completely at their mercy. Is this what smart people do?

This is what happens when you want something so intensely. You lose all your power. You wind up with a shelf lined with snake oil and still you invest your faith in the next carnie with a good pitch, because what else should you do? Nothing?

Maybe a Buddhist would say I'm suffering because I believe that happiness resides outside of myself. I am suffering because of desire. I tried Buddhism once and I sucked at it. My entire soul has been sculpted by desire; longing is my best talent. Nonattachment has never seemed an appealing goal. What would I do with my nights? Miracles, on the other hand . . .

Just think of [movie star mom], I tell myself. The breech baby who turned around. The miracle she got. The miracle she deserved.

Upon hearing what the man whispers in her ear, the woman on the couch opens her eyes like an angry, awakened spirit. Or maybe I'm imagining that. Maybe she's just annoyed that her nap was disturbed. She stands and removes her gray hoodie, then strides toward me with an impassive face but a caged energy in her body, something in her about to spring. The Chinese-food-ordering man and the question-asking man flank her as she approaches the table. The other people in the room make no attempt to leave or to halt their conversations, but they do talk a bit softer.

One man stands at my feet and pins my ankles down and the other stands behind me and puts his hands on my shoulders. The woman gingerly lifts my shirt and folds it back. The girth of the arms stretching the sleeves of her red T-shirt is impressive. She says nothing, just shapes her fingers into what look very much like talons and then, with all her mass behind them, brings them down onto my stomach and begins to dig. She feels for the outlines of my organs and then I believe she actually tries to move my uterus around in my body, to draw my pelvic bones apart, to reposition my ovaries. At least I think that's what she's doing. I can't say for sure because pain explodes in the center of me and radiates toward my extremities. I instinctively leap up and the two men pin me back down so that I'm immobilized. I scream for her to stop. When she doesn't, my screams turn into sobs.

She's hurting me for being a fool. For being an asshole from L.A. who believes that movie star moms have the answer. For thinking I can just insert myself into the middle of her tribe and hand her two hundred American dollars and be healed.

She's punishing me for believing that I'm entitled to a miracle.

Everything in me contracts around the pain. My feet hurt and my ears ring and my hands feel like ice.

A wizened old Maori man with a shock of white hair stands up from the couch and shambles over. He shakes a rattle behind my head and begins to chant.

The guy holding down my arms and shoulders leans down and explains in my ear, "He's calling the spirit of your child." He gazes into the space above me, as if looking at something. "Your child is here. We see him. He just can't find you."

The chant is beautiful. It soothes me. Something bright and calm breaks over me. The healer lets up with her claws and as the pain recedes, I begin to laugh. The Maoris laugh along with me, though we never check in with each other about our own particular punch lines. It ends soon after, with little fanfare. I thank them and walk out, feeling exhausted and famished and spent.

Little waves of laughter surprise me the whole ride home. Because, after all, it is *funny*—all the bizarre things I've done in pursuit of motherhood. It is human—to be miserable at achieving nonattachment. And it is worthy of compassion—to try so hard and to fail.

I finally feel a shred of this compassion for myself, as opposed to just wild fluctuations of self-hatred and self-pity. If motherhood ever does find me somehow, this may prove a useful thing.

Later that afternoon, I go for a walk on the beach.

I remember the physician's assistant's words: We're not giving up yet!

The sand stretches out in front of me. Life stretches out in front of me: the blank check to the fertility clinic, the drugs, the waiting, the sleepless nights in online forums. The miracle healers and their strange dogs. And everybody telling us that if we'd just relax already, we'd get pregnant.

It is as clear to me as anything I have ever known. The doctor might not be giving up, but I am. I'm giving up.

Chapter 6

I tell Scott that night. I fear this will be the end of us. Not immediately, maybe, but eventually. My husband wants children more than anything, and here I am quitting the race before the finish line. But I'm pretty sure that continuing on the same path will mean the end of us, too. We're sitting around on the rented furniture of our rented beach pad and eating takeout from the hippie joint around the corner. He puts his head in his hands. He's the best thing I've ever had and he is going to leave me, I think. Here it comes.

Instead, he says, "Thank God, baby. Thank God."

I walk around for the next few days blanketed by a luminous calm. I have no idea what comes next, but I know in my bones that I did the right thing. I do a lot of walking—suspended in the cool, sun-kissed days, drifting in a kind of limbo. I'm aware that it's temporary, that I will soon again be longing desperately for a child. But for now, releasing the endless cycle of hope and despair has left me with an odd sensation of freedom, my first in years.

One day, I wander into a coffee shop and a yellow poster on the wall catches my eye. On it is a smiling family, arms around each other, a jumble of ages and races. It advertises a seminar called "Adoption Options," at something called the Center for Children and Families. I haven't seriously considered adoption to this point.

I've always thought that maybe I'd foster or adopt somewhere down the line, but it seemed so vitally important to me to carry a child in my body first. Being adopted myself, I've never been able to look at the world and see a reflection of myself. I never had a parent or a sibling who looked like me, never experienced any sort of visual evidence that I wasn't dropped from an alien spacecraft. A pregnancy was meant to fix this problem. I'd finally feel connected to the world in a physical, primal way. I look at the flyer and in an instant reconsider this whole perspective. What do I really want, a Mini-Me or a family?

Scott sounds as enthused as if I've asked him to go to a quilting bee.

"No, I don't think I'm ready to go to that," he says. "Why don't you go and then tell me about it?"

Considering the circumstances, I can't imagine why he wouldn't jump at this chance to learn more about adoption.

"Why?"

"I have reservations," he says.

I'm still confused.

"Reservations about what?"

He pauses.

"About adoption."

This completely blindsides me. In spite of my own messy search for a sense of belonging, I have always loved adoption. It's not perfect, certainly. In my own life it has proved confusing at times. But it has also inspired me to search, to reach. It has provided me with a crazy tapestry of a family tree that I have grown to treasure.

As a child, I grew up thinking that adoption was a badge of honor. When I was sad as a child, I asked my parents to tell me the story of how I came to them, because I found the tale comforting. While it was true that I was different in this way from most of my friends, my parents told me that I was special, also true. Adoption is complicated, but also rich with narratives of strength. As a kid, I kept a running list of famous adopted people—all of them colorful and unique and sometimes even triumphant. Babe Ruth, Debbie Harry, Steve Jobs, Melissa Gilbert. Marilyn Monroe. Superman.

I liked belonging to this club. This may seem naive, but it had honestly never occurred to me that some people might not think adoption was so awesome.

"I mean, you just don't know what you're going to get," he says.

It rolls over me like a ten-ton truck. Does his easy faith, usually outshining mine exponentially, stop short of adoption? This is the only time I have ever hated him. If he can't love an adopted baby, he can't love me.

I lie awake that night shot through with pure, sharp anger. I should leave. Leave now. Stop this domestic charade and be who I really am—a firecracker, burning every bridge behind me. Go to India, Israel, Argentina.

If I don't, I think, he will. It's just a matter of time. He's probably sorry he married me right now. Just look at me. I'm a wreck. Maybe the problem isn't that he doesn't see me, but that he sees me too clearly.

I get up and go into the other room, unable to live with the voices in my head any longer. I'm usually a morning writer, but this night proves the exception. I sit down at my computer and write in a white-hot fury for three hours. I write and write, not about adoption and Maoris and babies and shadows, but about a time long ago, when I was younger and bolder and this whole search for meaning, for a home, first started. I write the beginning of a story about a wild child with dreams of stardom, who gets mixed up with some unsavory characters and winds up in a harem in Southeast Asia.

I should write a book about this, I think.

No way, I think next. No one will believe it.

But it's too late for reservations. The moment of conception has happened.

~

It takes Scott one day to change his mind. I have not talked him into it. I've been so angry I've been unable to talk.

"Let's go check out that seminar," he says, thawing the chill that has descended upon our house. "No promises, okay?"

This concession is not enough but it is. I sigh into his body, inclining my head into the exact-right-height indentation in his broad chest that has always seemed made for me. I will have to believe for two right now. I wonder if it's possible. The fertility disaster has left me hollowed out. But there in the recesses, I can feel the faith in me, small yet glowing.

~

The Adoption Options seminar is held at the St. Margaret's Home for at-risk pregnant or parenting young women, a building that looks like a cross between a hospital and an office complex. The Center for Children and Families offices are located there. Toys are scattered about on the sidewalk—a little pink shopping cart, a grimy yellow stove.

We show up at eight A.M., braced for a long day. Fifteen other couples file in, huddling in their own little teams of two, venturing funny little remarks about the meager breakfast buffet of stale bagels, crumbly cookies, orange juice, and coffee. The couples are an eclectic mix—straight and gay, all colors and shapes. I remember the Pasadena Reproductive Clinic, feeling like I was in a movie of someone else's life. I have the exact opposite sensation now. We fit right in here. This just seems like a roomful of people we should be with.

For several hours, we sit in a semicircle of folding chairs and listen to lawyers and social workers. I'm engrossed, but Scott has to pinch himself to stay awake. We have a different idea of interesting, he and I. But he's game; he's trying.

After the lunch break, adoptive parents tell their stories. This is truly riveting. A dad with kind eyes and a horseshoe of kinky salt-and-pepper hair talks about bringing home his five-year-old boy from foster care.

"When I first showed my son the house," he says, "I took him into my room and opened the closet door. The look on his face was . . . He ran and hid under the bed when he saw the belts. He had been beaten so badly. He wouldn't come out no matter what I did. Finally I just lay down on the floor next to the bed and talked to him. My wife came in and she lay down, too, and sang to him. We promised him he was safe. It took two hours before he finally came out. I mean, the first three years with him were basically a version of the same thing. I'm not going to lie to you: it wasn't easy. Most of the time, the best we could do was just wait with him until he was ready to trust us. He's nine now and doing wonderfully. Just wonderfully." The man tears up. He hands around a picture of the two of them at a Little League game. "He's my hero."

Will this capture Scott's heart or affirm his worst fears? I turn to him and see that he's no longer fidgety. He dabs at his eyes with a thin paper napkin off the buffet table.

The adoptive parents who speak are an eclectic mix: two Brooks Brothers–clad gay dads, a blond pixie of a woman who looks like a kindergarten teacher, an older African American couple with orthopedic shoes but young eyes. As they tell their stories, my thoughts turn to my parents. What must they have gone through to adopt my brother and me? There were no such seminars for them. Adoption was shrouded in secrecy then, rife with sealed files and buried histories. If you had to do it, you usually just moved on and pretended it had never happened. They must have felt much more alone than I do now.

A long-buried memory bubbles to the surface. I almost had a sister.

When I was four years old, my parents were adopting a baby

girl. We had just moved from a one-bedroom apartment across from a huge hospital complex into a three-bedroom split-level with a broad green lawn on a desirable street, deep in the Jersey suburbs. It even had a creek running through the backyard. My parents let me pick out the wallpaper for my bedroom, an explosion of green and white ferns, with a green carpet to match, bright like a forest floor after a spring rain. Next to my room was the nursery, decorated in creamy shades of pink and white, diapers in the linen closet, baby bottles neatly arranged in the kitchen cupboard.

The morning my parents left to go to the hospital, I waited at home with my grandmother for their return. I was ecstatic—a sister! I stood sentinel by the picture window.

Later that day, my parents returned, empty-handed, looking stricken. I do not remember this part. I only remember as far as the waiting. They would have climbed the stairs from the garage. My mother would have gone to the kitchen to cook, soothing herself with measuring, stirring, tasting. My father would have found a way to explain to me, somehow, that there would be no sister. The birth mother had discovered we were Jewish and had changed her mind at the last minute, preferring to place the baby through a Christian organization.

I remember my reaction: a protracted fury. I, who by all accounts had been a dream child until then, suddenly started acting out: talking back, fighting, carelessly hurting myself all the time— testing them, blaming them. Perhaps I was going to be sent back, too, like the absent sister whose imagined softness I could still almost feel in my empty arms. One evening when my mother was getting dressed to go out, I was sitting on the edge of the tub and watching her, as I often did. As she tells it, I crossed over to her, reached my arm over the curling iron, and calmly pressed the tender skin of my wrist to the red-hot barrel.

The next day, my mother asked me to do something and I refused, on grounds that she wasn't my real mother anyway. This I remember, like I remember few other things from that time. I was wearing my Kermit the frog jumpsuit, sitting on the piano bench, not looking her in the eye. She went to her room and wept while I sat there, stone-faced.

"Why would you say that to your mother?" my father said. "Why?"

We later learned that the baby had a heart murmur and had died shortly before she reached a year old. My mother now considers it a blessing of sorts that we lost her. All her life, my mother has said a prayer for that little girl on her birthday. The daughter, the sister, we almost had.

"Are you okay?" asks Scott.

"I just remembered something," I say.

Tears run down my face and a sob gathers at the base of my throat as the blond pixie woman begins to speak. She hands around the kind of photo album you create in iPhoto, complete with narrative captions and decorative borders that look like travel stamps. It documents in great detail her trip to Ethiopia to adopt her eight-year-old daughter. I flip through the artfully constructed book, read the blurbs of text. In one striking photograph, standing in front of a row of brightly painted bunk beds, are the nannies who cared for the girl while she was in the orphanage. Each of them holds a little hand-lettered sign.

You are always laughing and dancing. Love, Fantu
We will miss you. Love, Abenet
God bless you always. Love, Mehiret

It blows my mind.

When I was adopted, parents generally didn't do things like make photo albums that lovingly chronicled their child's preadoption life. The oversight wasn't meant to be cruel. It's just that, on the whole, adoptive parents in the seventies didn't think knowledge of one's origins might be helpful in piecing together a satisfying sense of identity. When I tracked down my own birth parents in my early twenties, I felt like I was betraying my parents. I worried that I'd hurt them. That they'd feel displaced. Today's panel shows me a whole new world, a whole new model. There's talk of ethics, of rights, of identity and belonging. Listening to the parents speaking in front of me, I feel it growing in me like an embryo. There are so many ways it could look, this adoption thing. I look over at Scott. We could do this. Maybe we're meant to do this.

I sit for a while, holding the Ethiopia album in my lap, rightness settling into my limbs. I also have a twinge of fear. I'm standing before a door that I know will never close again if I should decide to open it.

I pass Scott the album and surprise even myself when I say, "That's where our baby is."

I fear he'll protest but instead he takes the book and begins to turn the pages.

On the way home in the car, the world seems tilted, unreal, the low-slung buildings that line the freeway whizzing by like scenery on wheels. Scott interrupts a comfortable silence by saying, "I think we should adopt a baby."

I have never loved him the way I love him in that moment.

~ Chapter 7

THE social worker who shows up to do our initial interview is named Kumiko, a hip young woman in jeans, a chunky necklace, trendy glasses, and no makeup. I cover my tattoos. I smile. I offer her tea and snacks. I'm good at this part. I learned it from my mother, a natural entertainer, with something freshly baked always around to nosh on, should someone happen to ring the bell. I don't often trot it all out, but it's buried in there somewhere.

Our plan is to tell the truth in response to the easy questions and get creative, if necessary, when things get hairy. At first, Scott is unwilling to tell even the smallest of untruths. He is nothing if not an honest guy. But I, both more determined and more dissembling than he is by nature, entreat him. The only way to tell the truth about who we really are now is to let a few things slide. I mean, the *truth* truth, with all its debauched sluttery, lascivious foreign royalty, and high-quality narcotics? No young social worker with her brand-spanking-new degree, scrubbed cheeks, and Mephisto sandals is going to hand a baby to that truth. On paper, I do not appear to be mother material at all. But the paper doesn't represent what's in our hearts or our lives. In the end I convince him to present a cleaned-up interpretation of our pasts. This may be our last chance.

How old are you?
How tall are you?
How much do you weigh?
How do you deal with happiness?
How do you deal with stress?
How do you deal with anger?
How did your parents discipline you?
How do you expect to discipline your child?
How long have you been married?
Have you been married before?
How do you get along with your parents?
Why are you seeking to adopt?
What is the cause of your infertility?
Have you sought treatment for it?
Have you sought counseling?
Do you have any health problems?
Do you have any sexually transmitted diseases?
Have you ever sought psychiatric treatment?
Do you smoke?
Do you drink?
How much?
What kind of medications do you take?
Have you ever committed a crime?
Have you ever done illegal drugs?
And on,
and on . . .

The visit is three hours long. I do most of the talking. Outside our picture window I can see Suzanne walking up and down the street, following Hank on his tricycle. Somewhere is the sound of a leaf blower. Somewhere else a dog is barking.

I can see why the invasive vetting process is necessary, but it feels like shit. I always imagined that a big pregnant belly makes you feel successful and blessed and loved. You feel the exact opposite when required to throw yourself on the mercy of doctors and lawyers and the State of California and the U.S. government. We make it through that interview, and the next, only whitewashing a few tricky corners. Really, how many people give an honest answer to, *Have you ever tried marijuana?* We put locks on all the cabinets and a regulation grate over the fireplace and everything, everything in its place (according to a ten-page checklist) for the home inspection. We jump through the hoops and we actually make it through. After all is said and done, we hold in our hands a piece of paper that certifies us as eligible to adopt a baby from zero to four years old, so says the State of California.

After much research, we decide to go with my initial instinct and pursue an international adoption from Ethiopia. Maddening paperwork follows—endless lines at the United States Citizen and Immigration Services, papers notarized and authorized and stamped and filed and lost and filled out again. Every step of the process comes with contradictory instructions. We show up at appointments carrying a checklist of documents only to find the rules have changed—there's a new checklist. We buy a rolling briefcase and stuff it with every possible piece of documentation, just in case.

During this time, I get a call from my agent. She has sold not one but two books of mine, the novel I wrote in graduate school and the memoir that I began that strange and hyperreal night after I decided to stop fertility treatments. I developed that initial seed into a proposal for a coming-of-age memoir that recounts my whirlwind shift from nice Jersey girl to harem girl. And back again, if not to Jersey, then at least to nice, or sort-of-nice . . . nice adjacent. And wonder of wonders, someone buys the thing. My first thought is, Holy shit, I'm going to have a book published! My next thought is, Holy shit, I'm going to have a book published about being in a harem.

What will my sweet ninety-year-old neighbor think of me? Will

Prince Jefri have a massive freak-out? Will my mother assume a permanent back-of-hand-to-forehead posture on her fainting couch? Will my husband and our future children be ridiculed? What happens when schoolyard taunts of "Your momma is a ho!" are actually factually confirmed by said momma in her ho-ish memoir?

My biggest fear of all: once it really knows me, will the world judge me unfit to mother after all?

I follow the advice of my sage writing mentors: write as if no one will see it. Just to be safe, I hedge my bets by squirreling away my advance and vowing not to touch it. I figure if I chicken out at the last minute, I can hand it back.

My contract says I have a year. My days begin to take on some sort of shape. I finally have a mission. Two missions, actually: book and baby. I write all morning and do adoption stuff in the afternoon. I would not say that I am happy exactly, because I am stressed and harried and scared that this adoption will fall through and that I'll lose the courage to write this tremendously exposing book that I so brazenly proposed. But there are moments, stepping-stones in the stream, islands of solidity and purpose and calm. I know who I am. I am a writer. I am becoming a mother. The finish line is far, true, but it's there. It's there.

The other thing that helps is my friendship with Suzanne, now three months pregnant with twins. We spend many afternoons together, something deeply lazy and serene washing over us. A happy suburban cliché, we drink lemonade on her porch while Hank plays in the yard. We talk like we have all the time in the world—like stoned college students up late at night and first falling in love with the world. We talk about Camus (changed us both) and the movie *Cabaret* (best movie ever made) and *Lost* (didn't get it) and all the things we wanted once upon a time and how we maybe got them and maybe didn't.

The fertility treatments worked for her. They worked for me in a way, too, by steering me in what I trust is finally the right direction. As the seasons shift in the subtle Los Angeles way—the slight chill in the air, the smell of the wet trees from the first fall rain, the morning slate gray sky—our eyes slowly adjust to the new light around us. We will both have babies. Soon.

One afternoon, as we watch Hank make precocious chalk drawings on the sidewalk, my phone rings. Jennifer. I almost ignore it, but instead sigh and pick it up.

"I'm afraid to close my eyes," she says. "I've done too much this time. Will you come over?"

I mouth Jennifer's name to Suzanne, who knows the whole saga. I don't always go when Jennifer calls, but today I hear something different in her voice, cracked and small. It's been months since I've seen her. I pry myself from my spot on the porch.

I drive across town, steel myself, and knock on the door of her once-lovely apartment. It takes her a long time to answer and when she does, she looks at me like she doesn't remember she invited me. Her eyes are lifeless blue marbles. She wears jean shorts and a stained off-white T-shirt from Fred Segal that probably cost a hundred dollars new. In better times, Jen was always a fashion plate, a true original, sure to show up at a formal affair in knee-highs, plaid hot pants, a vintage blazer, and Ann Demeulemeester motorcycle boots.

"Hey! Come on in," she says in an affectedly normal way, like a robot trying to sound human. "I was just cleaning up. You want some tea or something? I don't have much right now."

Before this drug relapse, her apartment was trendy and tidy. Now it looks like something from a postapocalyptic novel. There are mysterious holes in the walls, an overflowing litter box, clumps of cat fur in the corners of the room and under the empty bookshelves. Where did all the books go? There is a weight, a smell, to the sadness of it. The shades are drawn in the middle of the day and a man sleeps facedown on the couch.

"I want you to meet my new boyfriend," she says. "Mark. Mark."

Mark doesn't stir.

Those Demeulemeester boots of hers sit by the door. She wore them to her wedding, a hundred years ago. I was in the ceremony. The couple included a Buddhist hand-washing ritual, and I poured the water from a cut-crystal pitcher.

At the time of the wedding, I had yet to meet Scott. I was in a long-distance relationship with a blue-haired writer, who was reputedly also in a relationship with half of San Francisco. I spent the weekends that I wasn't in beauty school shampooing hair at a Beverly Hills salon. I barely had money enough to keep me off the pole at Cheetahs strip bar. I planned every night before bed to wake at five and write, but I only sometimes managed to do it and as a result spent the day disappointed with my life and disgusted with myself. I was exhausted and chubby. My apartment looked like something out of *Hoarders*. Jennifer, then a well-paid paralegal at a high-powered law firm, walked me through it all. I hoped that if I kept putting one foot in front of the other my life might look like hers one day.

Before the ceremony, the bridal party got dressed in her soon-to-be-husband's sister's old room. It still had the butter yellow carpet and white eyelet bedspread that the sister had picked out as a teenager. Blue ribbons and tennis trophies decorated a shelf over the desk. Jennifer sat in a kimono on a white wicker chair at a vanity while I did her makeup. I can still remember what the planes of her face felt like underneath my fingertips as her other girlfriends fluttered around us like breathless birds. The wedding was a triumph, a beautiful expression of who she was. She wore a full-length, black silk dress, with those boots peeking out from the bottom, a declaration that she'd never completely surrender to bourgeois respectability.

"Do you want to go to rehab? Do you want to at least go to a meeting?" I ask her. "I'll go with you."

"Yeah," she says. "I know. That's what I should do. I have some stuff I need to take care of first, though. Maybe, like, next week I'll look into it."

How many times had she held my hand while I cried in cafés?

It's been a while since I haunted the rooms of a twelve-step program. Though I loved it in my way, I drifted away from it, and don't regret my path. I still deeply respect these programs and I miss the fellowship sometimes. It's the best lifeline I know for a crisis.

There's a protocol for dealing with people in the throes of addiction. You're not meant to offer too much help, unless it's help getting their ass to a treatment center. You're never to give money. You're not supposed to enable them. You're not supposed to make it easier for them to slowly kill themselves.

It stinks like cat shit in here. I want to leave and I hate myself for it. I stand awkwardly with my hands at my sides and make small talk. I tell her about our adoption-in-progress and it is as if Jen, the real Jen, drops into this alien body in front of me. She looks alive for a moment and her eyes well up with tears.

"You're going to be a great mom," she says. "I always thought that."

I remember living in a room like this. I remember being addicted to drugs and walking around the world trapped inside a bubble, looking out at "normal" people and thinking: How do they live? How do they do it? Now Jen is in the bubble and I feel guilty for being the one on the outside. At the same time, I'm acutely aware of how much I treasure my world now, the solidity I feel standing in my own skin.

"I'm afraid," she says.

I can't think of anything else to do, so I ask, "Do you want to pray with me?"

Jews do not generally kneel to pray, and I almost always pray alone, but this is as good a time as any to make an exception. Jennifer and I kneel together in the middle of her filthy floor and say the serenity prayer. It comes like a muscle memory from my days spent in semicircles of folding chairs, nursing a coffee and listening to people tell their stories.

"What else?" she asks.

"I guess, 'Help,'" I say. "'Help' is a good prayer."

"Help me," she says.

I kneel there and put my arms around her as she clings to me and sobs.

To accept help, she'll have to change. Change is hard for anyone but for a drug addict it's nearly impossible. I wonder about the limits of healing. I usually like to say that you get as many do-overs as you need, but that's not true. You don't really get any, do you? Not strictly. You can build a new city, but you're always contending with the ruins of the old one. They don't just go away.

I sit there and hold her and think—am I crazy? Am I crazy to want a child so badly? When this is what can happen to the best and brightest and kindest and most talented among us? What if I have to watch my child live in this kind of hell? Will infertility and all its attendant tortures suddenly seem like a trip to Paris in June?

I take her hand and kiss her palm before I go.

"I love you," I tell her.

On the car ride home, I pray she stays protected. I pray that she gets through this and gets well again. It seems paltry, but once, long ago, someone prayed for me and here I am.

With a shudder, I remember bringing what I like to call the Decade of Despair to a close, drenched in sweat, lying on the bathroom floor of a lockdown detox unit and vomiting up my guts. In the still-dark early morning hours, a nurse came in to sit with me. In between heaves, I laid my head in her lap. She placed a small, cool hand on my forehead.

"Would you like me to pray for you?" she asked me.

Right then, I invented my still-in-place prayer policy. I'll take a prayer from anybody, to anybody, at any time. If you want to pray for me, please, by all means.

The nurse prayed to Jesus for mercy, for strength.

I rocked and heaved to the rhythm of her words until the sky outside the barred bathroom window brightened to cobalt blue and I fell mercifully asleep. I made it through that night and the next and the next. Eventually the most remarkable thing happened: I began to change, learning how to accept life just enough that I didn't have to dart for the nearest escape hatch every time things got uncomfortable.

It's so easy to slide into the hungry darkness; so hard to fight your way back. I still feel the shadows that shift underneath my skin. The voices that tell me I am not worthy of this human experience, this ordinary life with all its joy and suffering. I even sometimes still believe the voices; I just don't do anything about it anymore. I've gotten sick of living with the scars, so I try my best not to create too many new ones if I can help it.

I'm spent by the time I get home, but one more errand awaits. A lone envelope sits on the dining room table—the very last of our adoption paperwork. Though the shadows of a migraine threaten at the edges of my eyes, I take the envelope in hand, heft the weight of it, paper upon paper, this maddening maze I have somehow managed to navigate. With legs a thousand pounds each, I walk a half mile to the post office and send it certified mail to our adoption agency. There will never be a perfect, painless moment. Today, it is the action of sending the envelope that keeps the voices at bay.

We are now finally fingerprinted, authorized, and filed. We start our wait.

Chapter 8

Writing my memoir is harder than almost anything I have ever done. I am sunk in the story, having fallen down a trapdoor to the past, visiting a girl I would rather forget, when the present calls. I normally turn off my phone when I write, but the referral call from our adoption agency could come at any minute. On October 6, 2008, it does.

"This is Kathy at Children's Services. We have a beautiful boy for you."

When I hang up, I open my e-mail and find two slightly fuzzy photographs of a baby boy with a wide forehead and electric chocolate eyes. His skinny legs are framed by mismatched sheets and he sucks on two chubby fingers with what seems like great concentration. His face is confused and scared and sweet and gorgeous.

Kathy tells me that his name is Tariku. In Amharic it means "his story" or "you are my story." I look at the piles of notes sitting in front of me on the desk. The story I am attempting to write—my story. For me, the significance of his name, as seen through this lens, goes beyond fortuitous and into mystical. Kathy tells me we have a week to accept or refuse the referral. But I know that I have already said yes.

I sit for a moment alone with the baby before I call Scott, who is on tour in Seattle. The thought of Tariku slowly takes form in front of me, moving like wind through the house. For this last moment, it is just Tariku and me.

I forward the e-mail with the pictures of Tariku. I picture Scott in his nice hotel, with crisp linens and movies on demand and bath products that smell like lemongrass. I imagine his face as he pulls his computer into his lap and opens it, as I pick up the phone and call.

"My son," he says, his voice catching. "There he is. My son. He's perfect."

~

The pictures come with a social report, replete with cryptic and sometimes contradictory information, some of it worrisome, none of it sating my hunger for information about our son. Most of it is translated oddly. At the time the report is put together Tariku is nine months old.

> Tariku is a bright, curious and funny!
> Tariku cannot sit up without assistance and appears to have
>   some atrophy in his legs.
> Tariku has been give two courses of antibiotics for pneumonia.
> Tariku is a happy boy who loves to dance when his nannies clap
>   their hands!

They advise us to have the file reviewed by a physician before officially accepting the referral. The next morning I walk into our pediatrician's office with the paperwork in my hands, as proud and excited as if I am holding the baby himself. We found the doctor months before, through the recommendation of friends.

I perch across the office from him on a child-sized bench, my knees nearly touching my chin. There is a solar system painted along one wall, toys and books scattered around the room. Between us sits not a child but a stack of papers.

"There are a few concerns," says the doctor. "He's been ill, it says here. He's had pneumonia twice before he was eight months old. He's severely underweight, but that's normal, considering. He's a fighter at least. I don't know."

He doesn't know? I'm confused.

"All I need to know is if there are any major concerns we need to understand. Any *major* concerns. We're already in the process of this adoption. This is already almost our child."

He pauses.

"I just think that parenting is hard enough," he says. "This child is already almost a year old. I don't see why you'd want to take this kind of a gamble."

Something cold slides into place behind my eyes, where only a minute before there was a sweet, expectant enthusiasm. I thought everyone would be as joyous as me upon viewing these remarkable pictures. I look dead into the pediatrician's watery hazel eyes.

"I don't need counseling," I say. "We're adopting Tariku from a developing country and he's obviously not going to have all the perfectly controlled variables in place. That's not my question. I just need to know if there are any major health concerns."

"No," he says. "Not major."

"Well, then you should congratulate me, because I have a son."

I do not wait for his response. I stand and leave, shaken but feeling strong.

I call Scott. "Well, we lost a pediatrician, but we got ourselves a baby."

I shrink the pictures and wear them in a locket. I make wallet-sized copies to give to our relatives and friends. I blow them up and frame them and put them in nearly every room of the house.

We have about three months to wait before Tariku's case makes it through court in Ethiopia and we can go over there to bring him home. Scott is working his ass off, often out of town. Alone and impatient, I fill the months with preparations. There is plenty to keep me busy, lists upon lists. I never imagined I could summon such zeal for curtains and crib linens. I hire a friend to paint Tariku's walls with a mural of a fairy-tale forest, the ceiling a starry night sky. A toile-covered rocker sits next to a crib with bedding that cost more than our entire bed, including the mattress. The bookshelves and closets are already full to bursting with the gifts of well-wishers. There are open suitcases on the floor of the room for weeks before our departure. On the changing table sits a checklist for our trip that seems to only grow with each item I tick off: medication for every possible ailment, clothing in two different sizes for any weather condition, bagged jars of baby food, bottles, cans of formula, hats, blankets, hiking boots, "modest" clothes for us, water purification tablets, a first aid kit.

I sit on the bright green carpet, like the one I had as a child, under the painted sky above me, and pack and plot and plan, late into the night.

It is Tariku's room.

Terry's room.

T-Bone's room.

T's room.

I try out the nicknames on the room as if on Tariku himself. And through it all, his face is what keeps me tethered to the world. I look at the photos and it is the only time that I can calmly sit, the churning in my belly stilled, my eyes clear, my thoughts trained on the knowledge that lives somewhere deeper than all my grasping and all my fear, that it will all be fine somehow. That he will come home to us after all. The world is about to shatter into something entirely new.

Chapter 9

NEARLY a year to the day after I sent that final envelope by certified mail, Scott and I wedge into the cramped seats of an Ethiopian Airlines 747. It has been almost four years since our wedding. We are no strangers to long journeys by now, but it's the first time going to Africa for both of us. We travel there a week early, to get to know the land from which we are about to pull up the roots of our eleven-month-old son in order to replant them halfway across the globe.

I've filled suitcase after suitcase with donations for the orphanage, most of it hand-me-downs that friends have piled on our front porch in grocery bags. We had to hire a van to take us to the airport. By the time we are sitting on the plane, we have twelve (*twelve*) full-sized suitcases in the cargo hold. The rather enormous impracticality of this doesn't hit us until we have traveled for a full forty hours and arrive after midnight at the airport in Addis Ababa to find that not only has our guide forgotten to pick us up, but we have also sailed right by the money exchange and out through a door labeled *No Reentry*. It is hours before we are finally able to enlist the help of a friendly van driver and find a different hotel than planned. It takes us another hour to load in our baggage.

Scott and I spend that first week traveling around the country.

We see the savanna with its wide expanses of golden grass, low acacia trees, and herds of antelope and baboons. We meet the fierce Afar tribesmen, who herd camels and like to joke around with the AK-47s they carry everywhere. We visit the famous monolithic churches of Lalibela, carved down into the volcanic rock, a magical underground city. We see the building in which the original Ark of the Covenant is supposedly housed, but we can't get close because only one guardian ever gets to lay eyes on it and he is chosen by the angels. We see the robes of Haile Selassie. Highland villagers kill a goat in our honor and then sit fascinated by our iPhones for hours. We share a meal with nuns living in a cave. I stand in line with hundreds of white-swathed pilgrims in order to kiss an ancient relic.

On the outskirts of every town are miles upon miles of shacks with corrugated tin roofs. The buildings look like they're made of a few brightly colored pieces of wood, leaning precariously together, like a house of cards. All along the roads are people walking, many carrying bundles of sticks or yellow plastic jugs of water on their backs. There is the occasional horse-drawn cart or mule, herds of sheep and goats. In some of the towns we visit, it is like we have traveled back in time a thousand years. I am hyperconscious of our big cameras, our sun hats, our giant suitcases (we have stowed ten of them but are still dragging around two) that contain practically an entire aisle's worth of Trader Joe's trail mix. I feel like the princess in the Mel Brooks movie *Spaceballs*. Her spaceship crashes in the desert and she still insists on dragging around a trunk with a hair dryer the size of a Volkswagen.

The week is wondrous and transformative, but also hard, because of the heartbreaking poverty and (selfishly, embarrassingly) lack of creature comforts, and because I am worried the whole time, as much as I try to shelve my concerns and think positively. We recently had a friend go to Russia to adopt a child and come home empty-handed. I have been obsessing about this unthinkable possibility for weeks, checking and rechecking every single seal and signature on every single piece of paperwork. By the end of that first week in Africa, my nerves are so frayed that I sit doubled over on the small plane carrying us on the final leg of our journey, holding my head in my hands, willing the coming headache away. Underneath my enthusiastic adventuring is the fear that after everything, the rug is going to be pulled out from under us and we will not be going home with this child after all.

I am also entertaining some less significant worries about the fact that we'll be spending the next week in close quarters with eight other families. Our adoption agency sends people to Ethiopia in "travel groups," with whom you walk through the final steps in the adoption process. Before we left California, a woman I know, who had recently returned from a similar overseas adoption trip, called to warn me, "Just be prepared: the other families in your travel group are probably going to be super-conservative Christians." I'm not sure what "super" means exactly in this context, but I imagine that it's probably code for bad haircuts and not believing in evolution and not liking Ozzy Osbourne. Or Jewish people. Or something like that. This is what runs through my mind as we sit in the tiny plane on our in-country flight from Lalibela to Addis Ababa, where we will be meeting these Ozzy haters, along with a representative from the adoption agency. From there we will drive to the guesthouse where we'll be staying. The nine families have all been posting on a forum set up by the adoption agency and I have gleaned nothing alarming. They do seem blindingly polite and enthusiastic and organized. They are also extremely helpful with vaccine schedules and packing lists. And they use lots of emoticons.

I just got my yellow fever vaccine today. Ouch :(But the good news is that's the last of it!! :D

I'm afraid of being judged by these people and I have planned my wardrobe and demeanor accordingly. I'm not about to walk into what will probably be the most important week of my life and feel like I did on the playground in junior high: like the weirdo, the other. Instead, I am going to summon up all my college theater training and play the character of someone respectable. I vow to keep my tattoos covered, not swear like Courtney Love, and be relentlessly upbeat, like I imagine churchy people to be. For a week, I am going to be an übernormal expectant mother. By the time we disembark and meet up with the other eight families in the airport in Addis Ababa, my quest to seem squeaky clean has left me in a cold sweat and completely self-conscious. Scott expresses skepticism about this awesome plan.

"Do you think you're being a teensy bit narcissistic? Don't pull a muscle trying to be someone you're not. These people aren't going to care one way or the other about your tattoos. They just want to get their babies, like us."

The Addis airport smells of woodsmoke, coffee, frankincense, and bodies and hums with loosely managed chaos. We home in on the cluster of exhausted-looking white people surrounding an enormous pile of suitcases. In short order, I discover that I was totally off base in my assumptions about the other families. It's a diverse group, including artists from a self-sustaining farm in Virginia, outdoorsy liberals from Portland, a female rabbinical student from Philly, and a handful of friendly, shiny-cheeked couples from frozen Midwestern burgs, some of whom never left Wisconsin before they got on a plane to Africa. The courage that must have taken strikes me immediately, before I remember not to let my guard down.

Don't be fooled by all of this seeming-coolness, I tell myself. If they really knew where I came from, they'd probably tie me to a stake and break out the s'mores.

Strangely, I can find no evidence of this impending witch-burning. The other couples remain delightful, if tired, as we huddle there together for about two hours waiting for our driver. Finally, a smiling, unapologetic man shows up and herds us into a van that carries us wide-eyed through the city.

The wife in the outdoorsy Portland couple is named Karin.

She's a petite woman in cargo pants and hiking shoes, with a curly blond bob and a thoughtful, pretty face. She stands up while the van is moving, clasping her camera to her side and backing up down the aisle, which isn't a big deal because cars in Addis move at a crawl in order to accommodate the endless stream of pedestrians and occasional herd of goats.

Karin points her video camera at the group.

"Where are we going?" she asks, like a camp counselor.

As if rehearsed, every voice answers her, "We're going to get our babies!"

Something in me shifts, tectonic, palpable. We're not in junior high anymore; we're grown-ups; we're parents. We're going to get our babies. Our common goal is so incandescent that it outshines any imagined differences.

We're going to get our babies. Finally.

~

The nine families are divided between two stucco guesthouses with yellow bars on the windows, behind identical tall gates crowned with razor wire. We're right down the street from the orphanage, but they don't tell us where it is.

The guesthouse is a masterwork of asymmetry. There isn't a matched linen or a fully painted wall or a right angle in the house. All I can see are power cords and sharp table edges everywhere. Not what I'd call babyproofed. I think of our house at home, every outlet obsessively covered, a gate at every staircase, an ugly marshmallow blob of foam stuck to the corners of every table. An illusion of safety, but a comforting one.

We share the smaller of the two guesthouses with the southern artists and the rabbinical student traveling with her boyfriend and mom. Everyone else is in the other. Scott and I unload some of our trail mix stash on the others and we all drink mystery tea we find in the kitchen cabinets. We cannot stop talking to each other. We have all done so much reading about adoption, having gone through hours of classes that address issues of race and culture and attachment. Everyone is excited, brimming over with stories and plans.

We come up with a shower schedule, should we happen to have hot water. We ooh and aah at all the pictures of our children.

For the next couple of days, the families stumble from house to house, fill out some final forms, take obligatory tours of hospitals and schools, pace the living room jet-lagged late into the night, and share our meals. It is a kind of torture—to think our babies are sleeping somewhere right nearby. So close now. Every day is a new surrender.

~

One morning, I reach for the pancakes and my sleeve accidentally works its way up to my elbow, exposing my tattoos.

The Wisconsin mom with the thick blond ponytail says, *"Oh."*

Here we go, I think.

"Oh, that is so pretty!"

And that is that. No one mentions it again. I spent all those hours worrying about what they were going to think of me. Was I really prejudiced against them, based on my assumptions about their politics or religious beliefs? I'm ashamed of myself.

"It was never really about the tattoos," I tell Scott later that night, as we're lying on the fuzzy synthetic velour blanket that covers our lumpy bed. "I just thought, like, here's a chance to be someone else. This is the new me. The appropriate mom me. Who doesn't have a scandalous past and talk too loud and make jokes no one gets and try too hard."

"This is you trying not to talk too loud?" he says.

"Not working?"

Scott shrugs. He refolds his shirts military style, sharply creased, then falls back beside me on the bed. I nestle my head into his shoulder.

"Aw, c'mon, hon," he says. "People love you . . . *and* they think you sometimes talk too loud."

Every time I forget how to breathe, he reminds me.

As there are only three inches of space between the bed and the wall on any given side, I wedge myself out the door, onto the tiny patio outside our room. A full moon hangs low over Addis, casting eerie blue light on the city's ubiquitous construction projects, which make the whole place look either half-built or half–falling down. I hear dogs barking, club music, people either celebrating or fighting in the street. In the end, it's just too hard to try to be anyone else. Somehow I got us here, to this incredible turning point. So am I maybe not such a fuckup after all? I vacillate between the polarities of fear and hope, doubt and faith. As I stand and stare out into the night, my every aspiration for this fledgling family of ours rises to impossible heights and collapses into rubble again and again.

We're going to get our baby.

Chapter 10

WE board the van together and drive a few blocks down the road, to a three-story, pink stucco, eighties-style house. Balconies line the top two floors, their iron railings draped with onesies and blankets and tiny T-shirts hung out to dry. Compared to most buildings in the neighborhood, the orphanage is pretty nice. The yard is strewn with plastic toys and an empty inflatable baby pool sits on a patch of grass in front of some low, makeshift buildings out back, painted a muted shade of mint.

No one is chatty today. All the talk is practical, perfunctory. We walk stiffly, in the way of people being herded around. For the past couple of days we have found ourselves in cars, in buildings, in schools and hospitals, even in the bazaar, without ever really being sure how long we were going to be there or what was coming next. Today we know.

We take our shoes off at the door and put on oversize foam rubber slippers, then shuffle together through a marble foyer and into a living room with a high ceiling. Everything is decorated in shades of burnt yellow and rust red and rose. The colors remind me of the rugs sold by roadside vendors in Tijuana. The decorations are still up from Christmas. The place is clean and cheerful and we can hear the sounds of children playing in the hallways of the floors above us, echoing down the marble stairway.

We find spots in the living room, some perched on the edges of the furniture, as there are not quite enough seats. Some of us shift awkwardly; a few knees bounce up and down. Everyone is silent, save for a sniffle or two. I don't meet anyone's eye, just hold Scott's hand in a clammy death grip and sit absolutely still, staring at the big yellow rose in the middle of the rug. I am worried that if I let even one tear fall, I might collapse on the floor and never get up.

I glance around the circle, looking everyone straight in the slippers. This has been a long, long wait for all of us. A yoga teacher once told me: if you truly knew all that people had been through, you would get down on your knees and kiss the feet of every person you came across.

The social workers managing our cases appear. With no fanfare, they call the first couple by the name of their child.

"Will Maese's family please follow me?"

The artists stand. The wife wears a peasant skirt and a silver necklace bought in the bazaar. Her wide, soulful brown eyes brim with tears. The husband wears a neat plaid button-down, his hair long and tied back in a ponytail. He looks solid, like a guy who built their house with his own hands (which he did). He looks like a guy you'd want to be your dad.

They walk up the marble staircase. The rest of us look around at each other. What happens now? Fifteen minutes pass and it feels like three hours. When they come back down the stairs, a little gasp of relief and joy passes through the room, because there are now three of them. In the husband's arms is a frail, surprised-looking baby girl in a white dress, with an enormous matching white bow pinned to her scant hair.

"Will Mihret's family please follow me?"

One by one, each couple ascends the stairs, then comes back down with a child. The parents hold them like they're made of glass.

Here we are, watching these families be born.

It's breathtaking.

Finally, when everyone else is playing in the adjoining room with their children and only Scott and I are left staring out the wide windows, wondering if maybe our worst fears have come true and we have been denied or forgotten, our social worker, slight and polite, if a bit inscrutable, appears.

"Will Tariku's family please follow me?"

We stand and follow her up two long flights of stairs. I am unsure how exactly my legs are moving, because I'm barely anchored to my body. At the landing, a man greets us with an old video camera the size of a toaster. He follows us, the lens a few feet from our faces. There are no outside cameras allowed inside the care center, but they record everything and then edit it later into a "Video Life-book." It is nice not to have to think about taking pictures, but it does have the disconcerting effect of making me feel like I'm in the reality TV version of my life.

We walk into a room lined with multicolored wooden cribs. The middle of the floor is strewn with a patchwork of blankets, on which a puppy pile of adorable babies roll around and play with toys. Smiling nannies in blue shirts and matching kerchiefs sit along the edges of the blankets playing with the children. In a blue plastic baby chair, the still point of the turning world, sits our son, Tariku. I recognize him immediately from the pictures, with his wide forehead and sparkling eyes.

One of the nannies plucks Tariku from the chair, his little legs dangling, his face not yet registering anything uncommon about his day. What would be unthinkable for most babies has become totally usual for him. People come and go. They answer your cries or they don't. There is food or there is not food. One minute you have a mother and the next you don't. And then, one day, you do again.

He wears an orange cotton jumper a size too big. His tiny rubber-soled sneakers knock around at the ends of his skinny legs, as if on a doll.

The nanny hands Tariku to me and says, "Mama."

This meltdown I have felt on the verge of every minute of every day for the previous month dissolves into a kind of primeval calm. Tariku looks back to her and then looks at me skeptically. Like, What do you want, weird white lady? And then he looks at Scott, and something like understanding registers. I swear, I can see him think, Oh, *this* is who I was waiting for. Tears stream down Scott's face. Tariku reaches his perfect hand up and wipes a tear off his cheek. I am not even making this up.

"I am so proud of you," I say, surprising myself. I have no idea why that's what comes out of my mouth, or what I'm proud of, exactly. I suppose I'm proud of us all for coming this far.

"We got the best one," I whisper to Scott when we are out of earshot of the camera and on our way downstairs.

"Definitely."

"Oh, shit, he's wet."

Tariku has wet through his diaper. We, veteran parents of seven minutes, head straight back to his nannies, where we discover that the reason he has wet through his diaper is because he doesn't have one on. There are no more left. They are waiting for another batch of donations. They hand us a square of what looks like pleather and a square of what looks like a muslin rag and shoo us away.

We carry our wet baby down the stairs and into the room with the rest of the families. At least he isn't crying, yet. He regards us incredulously. We lay him down and unwrap him, then look helplessly at the origami project in front of us.

"Are we supposed to make some kind of a waterproof loincloth out of this?" says Scott.

Thankfully, the experienced parents come to our aid, and together we figure something out. In a long, low room with dropped ceilings and liver-colored carpeting, all nine families begin, shyly, sweetly, to get to know our children. Some are confident parents already, with tone of voice already memorized, actions sure and smooth. It is these families that I watch out of the corner of my eye. I shape my arms like those of the Wisconsin mom. I try to settle my face into a serene smile, like the beauty queen mom. Karin gives me a book out of her seemingly bottomless bag of tricks. It's called *Baby Faces* and it is exactly that. It delights my son; he is hysterical.

At the end of two hours, we are asked to return our babies to their cribs and leave. This is my reaction: panic. Panic is not a logical response; I knew we would be expected to leave our babies here for the night. There is a strict protocol for transitioning the children out of the orphanage and it is slower than any of us would like, but we understand the reasoning. I'm sure it's best for Tariku. After all, we're taking him away from everything he's ever known. But I also can't stand it. I simply cannot leave Tariku here. Not for one more second. My eyes dart around the room. I can just take him and run. I still have a deep vein of fear that this miracle is being dangled in front of me as a cruel joke by God and that at any minute it is going to be taken away.

Ultimately, I surrender to the inevitable, climb the stairs with labored steps, and place Tariku into his crib. I touch his soft belly one last time for the day. The laminated eight-by-ten-inch photo of us we sent at Christmas is taped to the inside of the bars. The rest of the stuff we sent in the package is nowhere to be found.

As we exit the gates, my whole body shakes, unreasonably chilled. The Wisconsin mom says to me, "I swear, I almost took my baby and ran."

I link my arm through hers and we get back on the bus.

When we return home, I calculate that it is about five in the morning on the East Coast. I call my mother anyway.

"They made me leave him," I sob.

"Oh, honey," she says. "He's yours. He's your baby. Just hang in there. You'll be home with him soon enough."

~ Chapter 11

THE next morning, the alarm is set for five, but I wake at four thirty with swollen glands and a raw throat. We make coffee and cross the rocky side streets to the other guesthouse. It's still dark and clouds obscure the last of the stars. The morning call to prayer echoes through the streets. Scott says it reminds him of boot camp: the insistent loudspeaker, the early morning, the unfamiliar place.

At the other guesthouse, we slap together some stale PB&Js and board the bus for the drive south to the city of Hosana, in the Kembata Tembaro zone, a rural part of the country that has been besieged by drought and famine for many years. Most of the five million orphans in Ethiopia come from the south.

It is the day of our entrustment ceremony, which has been organized by the adoption agency as a chance for the adoptive families to meet any living family members of our children or, for some, the "finders"—the people who found them abandoned and brought them to the steps of the orphanage. Finders are often deeply concerned for the futures of the babies. All the children in our group have people showing up to represent them at the ceremony. Tariku's birth mother will be there. I'm both excited and trepidatious. I want her to like us. I want to like her. I want to do this in the most respectful and conscious way possible. I want to remember it all, so I can tell him one day. I trust that, in this case, my being adopted gives me an advantage. I still remember my own childhood hunger for details about my story. I know what it was like to meet my own birth mother as a young woman, the way I studied her face for clues about myself.

As we drive, the rising sun spills liquid gold over the fields of maize and turns the acacia trees into black silhouettes against the sky. Entering the southern region of Ethiopia, the landscape shifts markedly and we begin to see tukuls—traditional mud huts with conical thatch roofs—surrounded by enset trees, with their wide, waxy leaves. Decorative paintings adorn the doorways of the houses. I listen to my "Hosana" playlist, a mix of music I chose before we came (during my maniacal to-do list period) to be both soothing and important enough for the occasion—John Lennon's "Imagine," Eva Cassidy's "Over the Rainbow," Jeff Buckley's "Hallelujah." A plaintive hour in, I am wondering why I didn't at least throw in a Clash song or two.

The mood of the group is both settled and expectant. In spite of the emotionally laden day we face, we have met our children. We have held our children. Now there is Tariku, the indisputable reality of him, soft and smelling like powder, with his fuzzy little nest of hair. This fact alone is remarkable ballast. I still feel fatigued, but also newly propped up from the inside, in a way that makes me realize how much sheer willpower it has taken to propel myself forward for the past few months.

Four hours later, we arrive at a low, nearly abandoned-looking building with a desolate courtyard. One of the social workers shepherds us into a room with a dot-matrix-printed sign along one wall that says *Entrustment Ceremony* in English and in Amharic.

Again we wait quietly, sitting on mismatched chairs and couches along the edges of the yellow room. Some of us write in journals; the artist couple draw in sketch pads. A TV in the corner plays a program about traditional Ethiopian music and dance. The energy in the room is hyperaware, everyone vibrating with adrenaline, wearing their nervous systems on the outside of their skin. Every time a shadow passes by the doorway my throat seizes. Finally, a rangy man with a wandering eye comes in and calls Scott and me by Tariku's name. He leads us down a pathway.

I first see Tariku's birth mother, Tsehai, through the window of the small room in which our meeting is going to take place. She cranes her neck to get a glimpse of us. She stands when we walk in the room and warmly hugs and kisses me, then Scott. It is like hugging a child, tiny and beautiful, with delicate bird bones. They told us she's nineteen, but I immediately realize that there's no way. She is fourteen or fifteen. My heart contracts.

My own mother never met my birth mother. It would have been radical at that time if she had. My birth mother actually wrote my parents a letter, but my mother threw it out unopened. My mother later told me that she hadn't wanted to know if the letter had contained bad spelling. An unfortunate choice, but I have always understood why she did it. She was just frightened of losing me. It was a mistake. What mistakes will I make?

I'm overwhelmed by the heaviness of the task, the slipperiness of time, the mystery of memory. Remember everything, I tell myself over and over. Remember.

Tsehai wears her hair braided under a red kerchief, a white button-up shirt over an athletic team T-shirt, and a long, brown flowered skirt, with sweats peeking out from underneath, as is the fashion among most of the rural girls I see walking by the roadside. She has a shy smile and looks off to the side a lot. There is something gentle about her, something luminous. She looks just like him. She smells like cloves.

I have an instant, overwhelming tenderness for Tsehai. How could I not love her face—the roundness of her cheeks, the shape of her lips, the bright eyes, so reminiscent of his?

There are three chairs and a desk crammed into the tiny room. We face each other in the chairs and the tall man perches on the edge of the desk. Tsehai mostly talks directly to him in response to our questions and the man translates haltingly. I wonder what's getting lost in the divide between what she's able to express in her own language and the words the translator is able to come up with in English.

The strict regulations governing the birth-family meetings state that we can give her exactly two things: a map showing her where we live in the world and a family photograph. We give Tsehai a double-sided frame with a picture of our wedding on one side and a picture of Tariku on the other. We also give her a framed map of the world with a red thread connecting Ethiopia to California, which I sewed before we left. I explain to her that it symbolizes the fact that our hearts will always be connected. Tears fill her eyes and a few spill over. She wipes them and composes herself, then clutches the frames in her lap for the rest of our interview, her fingers curled tightly around their edges.

We tell her about our careers, our house, Los Angeles, our dogs. She acts interested and smiles a lot.

I ask questions suggested by an adoption website, because I didn't trust my ability to think clearly in the moment. I'm glad I prepared, because I can barely see. My eyes leak uncontrollably and I wipe my nose on the back of my sleeve. The loss in the room—everyone's—flattens me. Thankfully, something in the center of me remains intact and I'm still able to talk, to breathe, to look her in the eye and try to inscribe her in my memory.

She tells us that she has no special recollections of her childhood. She comes from a farming village where they mostly grow corn and enset, and she has always worked very hard. She was raised picking cotton and fetching water. She lived with her parents, who were very poor, and there often wasn't enough food.

What do you do for fun? is one of the suggested questions.

It strikes me as inapplicable, under the circumstances. I change it to, "What makes you happy?"

"My joy is singing in church and praising God," she says.

Her answers are short and quiet, but she lights up a few times when she talks about Tariku as a baby.

"He was happy and smiled always," she says. "Except when he was hungry."

She laughs quietly and gazes into the middle distance, remembering.

This is the first adjective everyone uses to describe Tariku: happy. He is a naturally joyful kid. This is evident even in the scant few hours we've spent with him so far.

"Why did you name him Tariku?" I ask.

"When he was a baby, we had to leave the village because people wanted to kill him. We traveled all around to different relatives, different villages, trying to find somewhere to live. But I could not work and also take care of him and there was no food. *Tariku* means 'his story.' I named him that because he already has so much history for such a little boy," she says.

Kill him? Did that just get translated correctly? I ask her to clarify.

"Yes," she says matter-of-factly. "The father's parents wanted to kill him so their son could return to the village after being banished."

I catch a glimpse of something fiery in her as she describes this. Her eyes flash and she tilts her chin up. I see in an instant how hard she fought for him.

Our twenty minutes end and I feel like someone hollowed me out with an ice cream scoop. I stand up and a tremor starts in my stomach, radiating out into my arms, my legs, my jaw. Scott puts his arm around my shoulder and stands beside me with what I can only describe as great dignity. He is a mile wide, so solid. For once in my life, I chose wisely.

He says, "We love Tariku. We will give him every opportunity we can. I promise you we will raise him to be proud of who he is and where he came from."

After we exit the room, I make a beeline for my journal and write furiously. I plan to compose a letter to Tariku later, detailing every moment of our trip, so that I will have it for him when he starts asking questions about where he came from. As the other families finish their interviews, they file into the big yellow room, red eyed and looking emotionally pummeled. I don't know if there is another experience in the world that encompasses both such a well of sadness and such heights of joy at the same time. You learn to be fluid enough that the waves of each can move through you without knocking you over.

When everyone is done, we gather for the entrustment ceremony. A pastor officiates, wearing a simple brown suit and tie that look like they're probably from another decade. We hold hands and pray together. The social workers hand around sheets of paper, one in Amharic for the birth and finding families and one in English for the adoptive families. We form two lines and face each other. They then hand around candles and plastic Bic lighters. The birth families read from their prayer.

I try to catch Tsehai's eye, but she looks down. She lights her candle and hands it to us, then we say our prayer:

Through God's divine plan, our journeys have crossed and your children have created a sacred bond between us. We would like to express our gratitude, which is beyond words, for the willingness to share the joy of your children with us. Thank you (Amaseganalou) for the humbling privilege to open our homes to raise your beautiful children from this point on . . .

I feel like I'm engaged in an ancient and sacred contract that women have been making with each other forever. When need be, we take care of each other's children. I experience acutely our inter-connectedness, the way the past and the present intersect, the permeability of the membranes between our lives.

When it's over, we hug Tsehai one last time, and she ducks out the door. I hope it helped her to know he's okay. To see our faces.

I'm slammed to the seat of the bus on the way home, speechless. It is one thing to consider separation of a child from a mother. It is one thing, even, to have lived through it myself. It was another thing entirely to look at Tariku's birth mother's face. I drift off and, half-asleep, for a moment I am Tsehai. I am my mother, Helene. I am my birth mother, Sherri. I am something that started long before I was born and I am something new. I am me, here, now, not enough of a grown-up to be a mother, not enough of a child to be so unwise all the time. I know everything I need to know and I know nothing at all.

~ Chapter 12

THE next morning, we go get our babies, for real. Later in the afternoon, we'll bring them back to the orphanage for a short ceremony, but we will not leave them there. Never again will we have to leave them. This is the day of the final paperwork at the American Embassy—the last hurdle. I won't truly relax until the plane leaves the ground for America. My spirit of adventure and curiosity is wearing thin and I want to get him home already.

We go through the now-familiar routine: leave our shoes at the door, don our slippers, shuffle up the stairs to our children's rooms. I bundle T into his Ergobaby carrier, a gift from a mom friend of mine at home, and we tote the babies outside and file onto the bus for the embassy.

T starts to fuss, and it occurs to me—holy shit, I have no idea how to take care of a baby. I wasn't one of those kids with big families or lots of babysitting gigs. I have cooed over friends' infants and done a few rounds of "The Itsy-Bitsy Spider," before promptly handing them back. I may have changed a couple of diapers, but can't remember when. Why did I not think of this before?

I surreptitiously check out the other families. There seems to be bouncing involved. Bouncing, walking up and down, soft talking, singing. T falls asleep on my chest after a while and relief washes over me. I look around to make sure no one has noticed what an impostor I am.

When we arrive, there's more shuffling, more metal detectors. Taking off baby carriers, putting baby carriers back on, dumping out and repacking diaper bags. There sure is a lot of schlepping involved. Some of the kids are clearly a bit sick, uncomfortable all the time, half whining, half crying. It's likely that they're suffering from giardia, a common intestinal parasite. Some of the kids are smiley and quiet. Tariku falls somewhere in between. He looks like he's considering having a fit, but is too dazed and confused to do anything about it. We get inside and settle into a waiting room with plastic bucket chairs and a linoleum floor. A few people are scattered about, but no other adoption groups. We wait around and barricade off a little pen in the corner, where the kids crawl around together. Eventually, the social workers begin to call names. We go into the main room in groups, where we wait in yet more snaking lines.

The main room at the embassy looks kind of like a bank, with marble everywhere, columns, a vaulted ceiling, individual tellers, and bulletproof glass. Scott and I stand in line, me holding a half-sleeping, squirming Tariku in the carrier on my chest. When we finally get to the window, a man with an unreadable expression and bloodshot eyes looks at our paperwork for a long while. I smile. I shift from foot to foot. I rub Tariku's back. The man looks up at us.

"You're not eligible to adopt this child," he says. "You're only certified to adopt a child up to four months old. It says it right here."

He holds the paper flat to the thick glass and it takes me a minute to see where the mistake has been made. It's a typo. My body is a block of ice.

"Oh, no, no. That's a mistake. It's a typo. It was meant to be four *years*. A child up to four *years* old." I say.

The man has no discernible reaction. He speaks with a neutral, almost robotic tone of voice.

"Nope. Sorry."

He rises and leaves. I am stunned silent. I look to Scott. Usually so fast acting and unfazed, he appears to be caught in an invisible freeze ray. I look wildly around for help, I'm not sure from whom. I remind myself to suck in a breath.

It's going to be okay. He is going to come back any second laughing. Sorry about that! Our mistake!

But he doesn't. Five minutes pass, then fifteen.

Scott stands dumbstruck, while I begin to wander around the cavernous room like someone in shock, asking everyone, anyone who will listen, tugging on the sleeves of security guards, cutting in front of lines for I have no idea what.

I barge right in front of the people at other windows, stick my face to the hole in the glass, and say, with mounting hysteria, "What happened to the guy who was over there? Do you know where that guy went?"

Eventually, Scott collects me and we return to the waiting room. The rest of our group is packed up and ready to go. Their expectant smiles fall away when they see our faces. I tell the social worker what has happened, then *she* leaves, with no explanation of where she's going or when she'll be back.

I begin to babble. The tears erupt and then the sobs. I clasp Tariku. "I'll get an apartment here," I say. "I'll move here. I'm not going home without him. I'm not. I'm not."

Scott holds out his arms. "Honey, give me the baby. You're going to make him upset."

He gently extracts Tariku from my grip and brings him over to where the other babies are playing. The women in the group close ranks around me and speak to me in voices not unlike the ones they used to soothe their babies. They wait with us there for the next three hours. No one complains. I have long ceased crying and am lying with my head in Karin's lap when the social worker returns, with an offhand smile and our approved paperwork. As if it's no big deal, practically an afterthought.

"Here you go," she says. "I'm not sure why you were so worried."

We all get up together and take our cranky babies back to the bus, the adrenaline still pumping through my limbs.

On the bus, I look around at the people I initially made so many assumptions about, who I feared would judge me—I have more in common with each one of them than with most of our friends back home combined.

~

"How hard can it be?" Scott says as we pile out of the bus and head to the guesthouses with our babies.

Our baby. Staying with us. Like, forever.

"We just have to feed him, love him, change him, and put him to sleep. Right?"

Two hours later I look across the living room at Karin, who is limply draped across the couch with a knowing smile playing about her lips. I keep trying to interest the kids in boring things like toys and books while they instead insist on crawling straight toward the apparently much more engaging pointy edges, sharp objects, and steep drop-offs.

"Oh, my God," I say to Karin, who has two older sons at home. "What the hell do you do all day with an eleven-month-old?"

"I'm trying to remember . . . I think I went to the mall a lot?" she says.

For the rest of the day, there are awkward feeding attempts; there is unutterable sweetness; there are volcanic poop disasters (the stories of which I will spare you); there is exhaustion; there is boredom; there is beauty. And at the end of the day, mercifully, there is sleep.

Tariku drifts off snuggled in between Scott and me, his small head pressed into my neck. Every minute of the past—the messed-up day, the messed-up year, my messed-up life—falls away, dissolving into the sound of his breath. Here is my child sleeping beside me. Finally.

This particular day is an important one not for just us; it is also a historic occasion. At home, thousands of people are gathering on the National Mall for Barack Obama's inauguration. I hear the TV downstairs. I dare to pick Tariku up and bring him down with me to the couch, where I put my feet up and rest him on my chest. He doesn't wake. The other members of our guesthouse slowly file in to watch.

I watch Aretha sing in the morning. What a change, I think. What an opportunity. All of it. Our little lives and the big fabric of history and this child here breathing evenly as across the world, in his soon-to-be home, the dawn breaks on a new era.

~

Before we leave, we return to the orphanage to participate in a ceremony that allows the staff and other children to say good-bye. The nannies and the children are dressed in traditional garb. Tariku wears a pink pantsuit, with fringe at the hems and an embroidered Ethiopian cross on the shirt. The families form a big circle around the living room, while the nannies hold the children in the middle and say a few words about each of them.

Tariku's favorite nanny, Fantu, cradles the back of his head with her palm, tears streaming down her cheeks.

A translator interprets. She says, "He is such a happy boy. He loves to dance when we sing to him. Every day he makes me laugh. You are very lucky."

She hands Tariku to me. So many good-byes for this child.

We hold hands and pray.

Each child puts his or her hand in a tray of blue paint and leaves a handprint in a book, its binder swollen with these pages. I wonder if Tariku will want to come back and visit his print someday. Will he be the kind of kid who will care about such things, or will he shoulder his surfboard and beg to go to Hawaii instead of Africa for Christmas?

The ceremony is moving and sad and wonderful. A cluster of the older children perform a rousing version of "Old MacDonald" for us. I have often heard that adoption is not a solution for the orphan crisis, and while I logically understand that, I don't fully get it in my heart until I look in the eyes of the older children who will not be walking out the door today. These kids will watch the babies leave with their forever families and then will return to their row of cots, their schoolroom, their group meal. And for each of these children, there are thousands more with no cot, no schoolroom, no meal at all. I vow to myself that once we are on the other side of this, I won't forget them. Adoption isn't the solution, but I will find out what is and I will do my part to work toward bringing it about.

I don't quite believe that Tariku is truly ours until the next day when the plane leaves the ground and I feed him his bottle as we rise above the city of Addis Ababa. When the babies are finally asleep in our arms, the Wisconsin mom and I look at each other across the row, each of us illuminated by a circle of light from the reading lamp above. She takes in a big gulp of air, an enormous sigh. I follow suit and it is delicious, almost decadent. It feels like my first real breath since I saw his picture three months before.

I look around the plane, at all the members our group holding their babies. I remember how out of place I felt in the waiting room of the fertility clinic. I wanted to be pregnant so badly because I thought I needed it to connect me to the world in a deeper, primal way. I was wrong. Look around me. I have found my tribe. This tribe that assembles our families from the left-behind is exactly where I belong.

Chapter 13

T sleeps through much of the flight. T. The nickname starts to tumble off our tongues involuntarily. Can you hand me T's bottle? Where is T's hat?

The entire flight we can't stop staring at him. We can't stop saying to each other, over and over again, unoriginal things like:

Just look at him.

Just look.

We change planes, move through hours of customs, change planes again. Forty hours later we arrive at LAX. The travel is a breeze. I'm not being sarcastic here. We are finally moving through the world as a family and everything else fades into irrelevance. I float three inches above the ground; there will never again be an insurmountable obstacle in this lifetime.

My closest friend, Jo (now "Auntie Jo"), and her partner, Anne, pick us up at the airport. Jo and I have known each other for nearly twenty years. When we met, I had crayon red hair and wore vintage nightgowns and platform boots everywhere I went, a cross between Stevie Nicks and a Japanese manga character. She dressed like Elvis circa *Blue Hawaii* and liked to hang out with a bunch of performance artists who took psychedelic mushrooms and roller-skated on Wednesday afternoons. Somehow we have managed to stick together through many incarnations. Now she waits with Anne at baggage claim, carrying a poster board sign that reads *Welcome, Tariku*. Anne holds masses of balloons and a hand-knit mint green sweater and hat set, made with love during the weeks we've been gone. We gave them specific instructions: no shouting, no singing, no mobbing us. We told them to keep the energy low-key. What I actually said was, "The transition alone is going to be traumatizing enough without a couple of white lesbian ladies screaming and crying all over him, so can you try to keep it *mellow*?"

Instead they're a couple of white lesbian ladies who keep their voices low but still cry all over him. T looks at everything—the balloons, the aunties, the airport—with a supercilious, reserved skepticism. I can't believe our luck—Scott and I think we must have just been blessed with the world's most well-behaved child.

"I guess we got lucky," I say to Jo. "He's so easy."

The moment that we strap him into the car seat, T has finally endured enough. He has suffered the strange people, the plane, the hours of travel, the crowds. This indignity is the final straw. He lets loose with an alarming wail and doesn't stop.

"Should we pull over?" I ask, helplessly, on the way.

"And do what?" says Scott, genuinely asking.

"Um."

By the time we reach home forty-five minutes later, T is winding down and we are rattled. The relief of coming home, however, overrides any lingering dread derived from the car soundtrack of nonstop screaming.

I have done a great deal of research on adoption and attachment theory and we don't start blind. We've constructed a detailed plan for the next few months, meant to promote attachment and trust. We aim to turn back the clock and help to heal the many months of his young life that have been spent without a secure connection to a primary caregiver. We need to help our child feel safe, even after he has been taken away from everything he's ever known, not once, but multiple times.

One of the recommended practices we plan to implement is called "cocooning." It's not a hard-and-fast science and doesn't make sense in every case but it makes sense to us. The goal is to limit Tariku's contact with anyone other than us, keep close to home, keep stimulation and distraction minimal, and stay present in the moment.

Before we left for Ethiopia, whenever I discussed the cocooning plan, people tended to be dismissive. I finally just stopped talking about it. I realized that it was like a lot of things about parenting: best shared only with people who have common interests or experience. Even my mother thinks we're being silly. Of course, she has a vested interest in my loosening up on the cocooning rules because she'd like to be able to come visit sooner rather than later.

"That's ridiculous," she says. "Just take that kid home and love him up and you'll be fine. And remember to let him know who's boss. You've got to have boundaries. That was our problem with you; we just didn't have enough boundaries."

That wasn't their problem with me, by the way. Their problem with me was that my authoritarian father and my rebellious self locked horns constantly, resulting in an emotional *Attica* every day. We're both a lot better now, but I'm still not about to run out and buy his parenting manual.

I tell my mother she'll have to wait a couple of months to see Tariku.

Beyond cocooning, I'm not exactly sure what we're going to do. There are numerous camps into which my friends have divided themselves, and each is equally critical of the others. The culture of frantic self-improvement in Los Angeles reaches a fever pitch when it comes to parenting. Every mom I meet offers an endless list of things that can apparently make the difference between your child winning the national chess championship and winning the domino tournament in a maximum security prison. Cosleeping, sleep training, food plans, attachment parenting, RIE, Waldorf, invites to the "right" playgroup, co-op preschools, fancy preschools, yet fancier preschools, charter schools, wait lists, baby sign language, day care, nannies, TV or no TV, to vaccinate or not to vaccinate, to make them share or not to make them share, Music Together, yoga, Gymboree, Mommy and me . . .

The parenting books contradict each other, too. I know, because I've spent the past year of my life up late every night, poring over them. And I must, *must* do this right. This is the only proving ground that counts. Never mind all my previous failures and mistakes; this is my chance to absolve them all, my opportunity for redemption.

No pressure.

First things first: cocooning.

T's birthday is six weeks from the time we bring him home. I manage to stave off any family visits until then. For those six weeks, the plan is that no one will hold him, feed him, or nurture him in any way other than Scott or me. Ideally, he'll never be more than a few feet from my body at any given time. We will sleep with him, bathe with him, feed him, hold him skin-to-skin whenever possible, spend every waking moment playing games that involve eye contact and connection. After the first six weeks, we'll introduce other friends and family members to his life slowly, with the focus still being on attachment-promoting activities with us.

For the implementation of this plan, the bunker/cocoon is well stocked. I have a mill to make organic baby food. The cabinets are lined with bottles and organic formula. His room is a dream, with darling green gingham curtains on the windows and neat, labeled bins of toys in the closet. An absurdly tall stack of books about baby food and baby sign language and "respectful baby changing" and mindful parenting threatens to topple off my nightstand at any moment.

When we walk in the door of our house for the first time in weeks, I see my mistake in a flash. For all my obsessive preparations, I am completely unprepared. The knowledge drops into my belly like a penny into a can and rattles around there for a moment before I dismiss it and charge forward, always forward, into this new life.

~

The first week passes in strange fits and starts, as I engage in an elaborate juggling act of rocking, feeding, bathing, sleeping, repeat, repeat, repeat. Tariku is suddenly restless, in constant motion, and grows alarmingly more so with every passing hour. He rocks his head from side to side. He responds to diaper changes as if I'm prodding him with a hot poker. His relentless howling appears to have no rhyme or reason. What happened to the well-behaved baby who slept straight through the twenty-hour leg of the trip home? He eats almost no solid food, just craves bottle after bottle of formula, gulped down like a man dying of thirst in the desert.

Scott has to work with the band almost immediately, so he begins sleeping with earplugs and I take the night shift. Tariku sleeps once in a while, for a couple of hours at a time; I just can't seem to find a pattern to it. After a few days, the world feels alternately tiny and huge, heavy and light. Half-asleep, I see shadows pass and I startle awake, but when I look, there's nothing there. One afternoon, as Tariku naps for a moment in his crib, I bury my fingers in our terrier Peanut's fur and lie down next to her on the floor.

"You would never do this to me," I say to her.

She presses her head against mine as if to say, You're right. And also, Told you so.

I remember the cocooning directive: be present with your child in the moment. I have an article about this bookmarked on my computer and I go back and check it, in case there are any further instructions as to how exactly one is supposed to achieve such a thing. And even if you did accomplish such mindfulness, how could you possibly know, when all you can think is: *Holy shit, I'm so tired. How can I possibly be this tired? Tiredtiredtiredtiredtired. I can't believe I ever thought I was tired before.*

We use the crib in his room only for naps. At night, he's in our bed, between me and the bed rail, the two of us nestled like spoons in a drawer. When he sleeps it's bliss. At first, I'm concerned about my nightmares, but from the first night my sleeping consciousness shifts. I'm never so deeply asleep that I'm unaware of him. In a matter of days, motherhood has altered me, even at an unconscious level.

In spite of being sunk in this constant fatigue, we discover pockets of deliciousness. A few times a day, for as long as he will allow it—sometimes for hours and sometimes not at all—I remove my shirt and lay Tariku over my chest in only his diaper, his spindly little legs squirming around. He tries to crawl up and over my head, until he eventually calms and lies there breathing, breathing. He is severely underweight, an eleven-month-old the size of a skinny six-month-old, all belly and eyes and forehead. He has two teeth and a head full of fuzz that smells like some combination of powder and cookies and fairy dust and his skin is buttery soft and warm. We rock and sing like this, anything I can think of—lullabies and musical theater and James Taylor and Patsy Cline. These are the tiny fugue states in which I understand what I'm doing and why. And maybe even, just a little bit, who I am.

~

Two weeks after we get home, Scott begins going into the studio all day every day to record the next record with his band. I am suddenly alone with T all day long. After breakfast every morning I clear the coffee table from the living room floor, lay out a patchwork quilt, and bring out books and carefully selected toys that he mostly couldn't care less about. He does like the *Baby Faces* book, which Karin ended up giving us in Ethiopia. It contains baby faces, with words corresponding to their expressions.

Happy!
Stinky!
*Uh-oh!**

We read it again and again as he laughs and laughs.

I stumble around unable to remember what we did that morning, whether he has eaten or not, until our sleeping habits settle into some kind of a routine. My days coalesce again, as if I'm emerging from a heavy fog. He still wakes five or six times a night, sometimes screaming until he throws up on me, sometimes just crying and crawling for the edge of the bed, but at least there is a delineation between day and night.

Jennifer calls multiple times one day, until I finally pick up the phone.

"Why didn't you tell me you were home?" she asks, sobbing. "Why did I have to hear about it from Jo?"

"Jen, it's just a different world. I don't know. We're cocooning."

"You're what?"

"Cocooning."

"What language are you speaking? You hurt my feelings," she says. "You're my best friend." My stomach lurches with guilt. I have wanted to call her, but it's been a vague urge, dismissed shortly after I remember that the friend I want to call is no longer the friend on the other end of the line.

"I'm sorry. Oh, he's awake," I lie. "I have to go."

This baby gives me such a sanctimonious excuse to dismiss everything else in the world, but it's not an entirely true excuse. I could have made a quick call and told her about our trip. I could have just asked how she was.

Cocooning week two: I sit across the living room from Tariku

*Margaret Miller, *Baby Faces* (New York: Little Simon, 1998).

at eleven A.M., feeling like it's six P.M., wondering what the hell you're supposed to do in a cocoon with an eleven-month-old baby. You read "happy" and "stinky" and "uh-oh" four hundred times and there are still 23.5 hours left in the day. I communicate with almost no one—just Scott, Jo, my mother, and Suzanne. My every second revolves around this tiny human, sitting across the room from me in his overalls, ignoring his block toys and glaring at me with a look that can only be described as skeptical.

Like: This is what you got? This is *it*?

Scott comes home every day to find the cliché of the haggard housewife mom with throw-up in her hair, holding a screaming baby, hating her husband for being allowed to leave.

Tariku and I have to do something—something outside the house—or we're both going to go crazy. Or maybe it's just me, but still. One morning, after Scott leaves for work, I breach the cocoon.

It's February and cold for L.A., which is not very cold at all, but still I bundle him up in his handmade sweater and hat-with-ears. I don my running shoes, yoga pants, and a sweater and hat of my own. I might as well be dressed to go to the opera on a Saturday night, so invigorated and alive and proud am I to be walking my adorable baby, *my* baby, down the street, cocoon be damned. I nestle T into his new green jogging stroller.

"We're going out to see the world, little man. We're going to experience the foreign culture of Colorado Boulevard and smell the exotic smells of Pete's Blue Chip Burgers."

Suzanne, who has been entirely pissed off at me for not showing her the baby immediately, spots me out the window and dashes out of the house, as much as dashing is possible in her hugely pregnant state. She even springs a little tear, before enveloping me in a bear hug. I smile and walk on, but tell her that I'm modifying the cocoon, and maybe we can walk together the following day.

Someone has lit a fire and it smells fantastic. A few of the leaves have turned and fallen. The sky has been scrubbed clean by the rain the previous day and the wind rattles the shining fronds of the tall palms. We walk and walk. Tariku cooperates more than usual, quietly chewing on his squeaky giraffe and squinting up at the sky. The respite from his fussing is a small miracle.

A friend from a few streets over drives by and is so excited that she pulls over to the wrong side of our quiet street. It isn't the best driving move, surely, and it angers the driver of the beater car behind her, which belongs to the cantankerous drunk who lives in his parents' basement in the house on the corner. Out of the corner of my eye, I see him roll down the window.

I am about to give him a conciliatory wave, when he says, "What the fuck are you doing? Moron." He yells out the window, "Nigger."

His tires squeal as he peels around her car and drives on.

My friend and I stare at each other, silenced.

"Oh," she says. "Oh."

We say good-bye, the celebratory mood dampened. We don't talk about what has just transpired. I plod the rest of the way around the block, deflated and even a little bit frightened.

When I tell Scott later that night, he turns around, marches down the street, knocks on the drunk's door, and confronts him. When the man sheepishly comes by the next day to apologize, I am alone and T is mercifully napping. It upsets me bodily to see his face.

"Okay, okay," I say. And shut the door in his face.

Is this going to happen often? Was it a fluke thing? What should I have said? I just froze. My husband came home and handled it later. Am I now the kind of woman who needs a man's protection? A tingle of misgiving starts at the base of my skull. I have overshot.

~

That night I lie down with T to put him to bed and he won't stop moving, won't stop crying. I'm afraid he's going to crawl off the end of the bed. He doesn't appear to sense the edges of anything, least of all his own body. He screams until he gags, but there is only milk in his stomach and I'm used to this now. I manage to catch the vomit with a towel, which I wad into a ball and throw into the corner. I try holding him. I try letting him go. He rubs his wet, snot-slimed face hard against mine, as if he's trying to scratch a huge itch and nothing works. He bangs his head repeatedly on the headboard. I pull him back and hold him around the elastic on the ankles of his duckie pj's as he thrashes like a baby alligator. Eventually, a numbness washes over me and I can't move my legs anymore, can't move my mouth to say anything soothing. I lie there, restraining him while he cries, staring up at the ceiling with a blank expression on my face. I wonder if his is a normal reaction to such a huge transition. It could be. Or what if he's sick? We have an appointment scheduled with his pediatrician in a few days. Should I call and say it's an emergency?

Scott comes in and turns on the light.

"What the hell?" he says. "What the hell is wrong?"

He picks up T and sings Elton John songs to him. *Someone saved my life tonight, sugar bear.* He walks him around the house and somehow calms him. As he does, I slide to my knees beside the bed, put my face in my hands, and begin to pray. "Please help me," I say, over and over again.

He comes back to the bedroom and finds me on my knees. I get up, startled, self-conscious. He says, "Go. Just go." He's annoyed with me.

Scott lies down with T on the bed, and the baby immediately falls asleep.

The problem isn't the baby, I think. It's me.

~

Tariku hates to be changed or dressed. One night, the fourth time he wakes howling, I change him too abruptly. I grab his arm and maneuver him around and there is a surprised, indignant expression on his face. So much for respectful diaper changing. I lie with him finally asleep on my chest and remember back to that first night, when we watched the inauguration, and I was so fulfilled, so hopeful.

In the shadows in the corner lies the towel full of crusty puke. I forgot to throw it in the wash. I gingerly unwedge myself from between my baby and my husband and cross to the small upstairs bathroom, off the bedroom. I need to rinse my mouth out. I need to turn on the light.

I look in the mirror and see the Duchess from *Alice's Adventures in Wonderland* staring back at me. I loved that book so much as a child that I can quote nearly the whole thing from memory. I was Alice then. How did I become the Duchess, with her giant head, her manly face, her bloodshot eyes, her jowly chin, and her red nose, irritated from all the pepper sneezes? Pepper in everything—in the porridge, in the pies, in the air. The Duchess, who manhandles her baby. The baby, who turns into a pig.

> *Speak roughly to your little boy*
> *and beat him when he sneezes.*

"Just who did you think you were going to be exactly?" says the Duchess. "Julie Andrews? June Cleaver?"

At the guesthouse he slept through the night. What has gone wrong? I grieve for my lost pre-baby life and while I know this is a common thing for new moms, still I'm torn in two by guilt for feeling this way so soon.

Here it is—what I asked for.

Chapter 14

I tell our new pediatrician about the rocking, the restlessness, the hours of crying, the hurricane that is my baby boy. He's gentle and reassuring. He says, "He's fine. He's doing great. Give him time to adjust."

He recommends, as did the adoption specialist I consulted with on the phone, that we have a full battery of tests done, to look for common parasites like giardia as well as to double-check for hepatitis and HIV, among other things. So our first real family outing is to the pediatrician, followed by the Children's Hospital. Scott and I pack T into the car and move forward with determination. There is a walk-in lab at the Children's Hospital—the best place to go, our friends have assured us.

The waiting room is crowded, with a delay of almost two hours. We're already here, have made it this far, and so we decide to stay and go through with it. I sit next to an older lady with a face that looks like tightly stretched parchment and huge bloodshot green eyes crowned with thick black liner, like something out of *Valley of the Dolls*. She tells me within five manic minutes that she was the Playmate of the Year in 1965, but now she is retired. Her daughter is apparently very busy with a modeling career (she is Miss Myspace USA, whatever that is), and so the woman spends most of her time running around to various hospitals and specialists with her grandson, who has a rare liver disease. She points to a red-headed boy coloring quietly on the floor, wedged into a corner. His freckled skin is a sickly olive yellow and his legs are emaciated and knock-kneed. Around the room, some kids talk nonstop; some kids have no hair at all; one kid sits up unnaturally straight with his hands folded in his lap, eyes fixed ahead.

"This is Mason's volume," says the grandma. She holds up a stuffed purple three-ring binder. "I have ten more at home."

"Oh."

I feel like a wuss. Ashamed, even. I have one crying baby and I'm in a panic.

"You should be prepared," the grandma says. "You'll have to hold him down for his tests. How old is he?"

"Eleven months now."

Tariku just started crawling a week ago. This is late, but not uncommon among children who have lived in orphanages or other institutions. Such kids are likely to be developmentally delayed. Since he's been home, Tariku has been playing catch-up with a vengeance. Within a few days, he went from barely being able to sit unassisted to crawling like a demon. Every time I turn around, he has acquired some new skill. As I chat with the woman, Scott chases T around the waiting room.

One of Tariku's new habits is banging his head against things, like a battering ram. I wouldn't say he enjoys it, but he does pursue it with a singular concentration. He doesn't bang walls, only things that make loud noises, like cabinet doors or stainless steel trash cans. Scott is pulling him away from just such a trash can now. In this particular room, no one looks askance. No one looks at all.

They finally call us in. The Playmate grandma was right about holding him down. Scott wraps his long, tattooed, bass player's hands around T's skinny legs. I hold his arms and torso. As the phlebotomist guides her needle home, T wails a particularly terrified sound, with a pitch different from anything I've heard from him before. I talk to him soothingly, but if he could hear it over all that racket it would be a miracle. I turn and look toward Scott and notice his eyes welled up with tears. He looks stricken.

The drive home is silent. When we get home, T falls asleep on my chest in the rocker, as I sing him "Sweet Baby James" and rub his back. My voice is hoarse and keeps veering off-key. The day before, I painted my nails crimson because I was sick of feeling so frumpy all the time. I watch these hands, running up and down the back of his striped orange and blue onesie. I almost never wear nail polish. These aren't my hands. These are my mother's hands. I have seen them in a hundred photos, holding me. I only wish they were half as capable as hers.

My mother, who is coming to town in a few weeks, delights in holding any and all babies. Babies are her thing, she says, and she's right. I'm not sure babies are exactly my thing, as it turns out. But my mother, she loves them and they love her, with her cashmere sweaters smelling like Chanel No. 5 and her tireless hands with their cherry red nails.

~

The tests all come back negative. Tariku is fine, says the medical establishment. He is progressing wonderfully, as a matter of fact. He's just having a rocky transition. I hear from my friends that a lot of kids are fussy and don't sleep well. There's no need to make a federal case out of it.

T says: Doggy!

Ball!

Ta-dah!

Outtahere!

Gaga (as in Lady—he's her biggest fan)!

It has been four weeks since he came home, and both Suzanne and Jo hang around pretty often now, although I don't let them hold him or feed him yet, so it's more of a psychic break than an actual break. With the exception of one or two times that I have gone out for a run on my own, I've never been apart from him since we got him.

During the day, T is often hilarious and joyful, banging on his drum or his little piano, a tiny Little Richard. He is so full of spunk and personality, so alive in the eyes. His smile delights me more than anything I have ever seen. And yet, I secretly count the hours until he sleeps again. When he takes one of his two short naps a day, I clean up—that Sisyphean task—while watching some unwatchable trashy Hollywood movie. If there is an extra minute, I spend it draped across the couch like a deboned fish.

T wakes at five every morning, prompting Scott to call him the "future doughnut-maker." Even though the late night and early morning shifts are still mine, Scott has finally finished his album and has more time at home. We basically split the day with Tariku. Scott proves a kick-ass dad, whipping up elaborate breakfasts and hanging out with T for hours in the backyard while I tentatively begin to put pen to paper again. While it is hard to pull myself away from the million undone tasks around the house, it's more apparent to me than ever that I must write. Whenever a few days go by without writing, it is like I am caught under a capsized boat and slowly breathing the last of the oxygen. My chest gets tighter and tighter. When Scott is around, I can find at least a few moments to unspool my thoughts into my journal. I haven't yet begun to delve back into the memoir, but I am percolating. The ability to put a framework of words around my days gives me a sense of purpose. Purpose keeps me sane.

Things move slowly and things move crazy quick. T's favorite word is "doggy." Anything he likes becomes doggy. We read *Brown Bear, Brown Bear, What Do You See?* He gleefully points at the bird, the fish, the cat, and says, *"Doggy!"* Tariku crawls so fast, he's like some sort of animatronic robot. I've never seen anything like it.

Our walk remains the highlight of our day. We both seem to settle when we get out and see the scenery. Even though it isn't in our plan, I venture farther. I take T to the dry cleaner, to the park, to the farmers' market. These mundane tasks are suddenly unreasonably, ecstatically fun and I'm not sure if it's because I'm so starved for any contact at all with the outside world or simply because I'm a mother. It's all I wanted for so long. I schlep around a diaper bag and buckle and unbuckle a car seat and shift Tariku from one hip to the other when he gets heavy in the line at the coffee shop and I love it all, truly.

All of this is so enjoyable, in fact, that I decide to try to take him to Mommy and Me Yoga at Golden Bridge, a trendy Kundalini yoga studio run by a celebrated local Sikh guru. It's a cavernous space with a café and a boutique, always smelling of incense and bustling with smiling people in yoga gear. I have not been seeing friends yet, but figure Golden Bridge is sort of a cheat, as I'll probably run into someone or other.

I blow the dust off my mat, put on a white hippie tunic shirt, and bundle T into the car. I'm nearly skipping as I scoot around to the driver's seat. The whole world sparkles. This is it! This is what having kids is about, man. It makes you appreciate life. I mean, not three months ago I would have been grumbling on my way to class, forcing myself to do it. And now look at me: I am practically floating in the door.

I run into a friend—a tall brunette with one of those animated wide-as-a-pie actress faces. She turns toward me with sparkling eyes, a blinding smile, and a big, pregnant belly. Before I can caution her to keep calm around T, she runs up to me and gives me a hug, smushing Tariku between us. She leans in and puts her face an inch from his, launching into a high-pitched stream of incomprehensible babble. He looks at her, wide-eyed and adorable, then opens his mouth and lets out a shriek that turns every head in the room. He attempts to crawl out of his carrier and straight over my head.

"Hey, sorry," I say.

I bounce him and walk in a tiny circle. He looks at me in a way I can only interpret as appalled. I release him from his imprisonment and put him on the floor, attempting to hold down some sort of polite conversation at the same time. He stops crying and makes a beeline for a class in session. I bring him back and he makes a beeline for the door. I bring him back and he makes a beeline for the stairs.

The edges of my friend's smile falter a bit, the tiniest twitch. Her eyes shift to an imaginary savior over my shoulder. I help her out and bid her a quick good-bye. Yes, we should totally hang out sometime! For sure! Miss you! Call you!

I bring T into the room for our class. I'm relieved that I don't recognize anyone there. This is the first time Tariku and I have been in close proximity to other kids since he's been home. Technically, in terms of the cocooning suggestions, I'm way out of bounds here, but I figure—how bad can it be? He spent all those months rolling around with other babies all day long; he even shared a crib. Even though he's with us all day, still, maybe he's lonely for other children. Maybe that's part of why he's so restless.

Four women with their toddlers have staked out spots in front of the teacher. The kids wait quietly by their mothers on the mats. One of the moms reads *The Very Hungry Caterpillar* in an enthusiastic stage whisper. Another sits in lotus position, her eyes in a meditative half-mast, while her child contentedly plays with some sculptural bead and wire contraption—the kind that is made out of sustainable wood by a commune of Marxist elves in Vermont and then sold for a 1,000 percent markup at stores in Silver Lake. We have a trunk of these toys at home that Tariku has never touched. I try to lay our stuff down gently but the diaper bag awkwardly falls off my shoulder and onto the floor with a clatter. The lights are low and the room smells like nag champa. Tariku crawls immediately over to a Kewpie doll toddler with rosebud lips and wide blue eyes. He doesn't even pause before he steamrolls right over the kid, who tips like a bowling pin, his head making a dull thud on the wooden floorboards.

Shit. I apologize and make one of those exaggerated—I'm sorry! Oops!—faces, as the kid howls and the mother rocks him. I retrieve T before he can get to the next victim, and I bring him back to the mat, where I take *Baby Faces* out of my bag. He couldn't be less interested in the book or in me. He hurls himself into the action again and again. One mother beside us is breast-feeding her toddler and he crawls straight for her boob. The lotus position mom opens her eyes just long enough to shoot me a sideways glance. I am almost ready to give up and dive for the door, when a wave of calm anticipation rolls over the room.

A young teacher with dark hair, darker eyes, and creamy skin, wearing a white kerchief on her head and a long ivory tunic, enters. She glides to the front of the room, where she settles onto a sheepskin and begins to talk. Tariku crawls up to her and sits right at her feet. She looks around, as if seeking his mom, and I try to wave, but her eyes move right over me and I can tell she's confused, unable to locate anyone to whom this child obviously belongs. When I try but cannot get him to return to me, I imagine that the other moms are staring, or effortfully not staring. I pick him up and he struggles. He wants to be next to the beautiful young teacher with the soft voice. So I leave him there, until she looks at me one too many times. Tears hot behind my eyes, I gather my bag and my mat and attempt to juggle the whole unwieldy package. When I drag him out under my arm, we are both crying.

~

"Why did you take him to yoga?" Scott says when I tell him the story with tears in my eyes. "That's not in our plan. He's not ready for that much stimulation. It was too soon."

He's right. It was too soon. I had selfishly wanted to go, and had talked myself into thinking it would be good for Tariku as well.

Scott is testy and short with me, as he is trying to quit smoking and loading on the nicotine patches.

"Is this really the best time to quit?" I say. As soon as it's out of my mouth I want to unsay it. I have spent years nagging him to quit smoking, and now I'm asking him not to because I can't take the edge it puts on him?

Scott looks around the messy kitchen and clucks in a disapproving way. I have never punched anyone in my life, but I would really like to start now. To actually punch him. He dares to judge my housekeeping? A fury prickles in my face—similar to the one I feel almost every day toward T, but don't let myself express. This big target in front of me makes it easier to justify an explosion. In seven years together, we have never once called each other names. Strange, I know, but that's the truth. We've never said, "Fuck you," or, "You're an asshole." Nothing. We agreed on it in the beginning, deciding it would be a good way to carve out a world very different from either of our childhoods. After a while, it just became habit. No time like the present to go and fuck up a good thing.

"Stop being such a prick," I say.

He looks at me like he's seeing something he's never seen before, something he doesn't like. He nods his head, then silently turns around and walks out of the kitchen, crossing the lawn to his backyard studio.

For only the second time in our marriage (the first was when he had doubts about adoption), I wonder if Scott and I will make it through this. If the challenges of parenting are digging a trench that can't be breached. This anxiety vibrates near the surface of my skin. Somewhere deeper, I know that it would take more than this to sever our bond. We've been through so much already. We just need to transition. All of us. It takes a while. Like going from dreaming to waking. I am awake; it's morning.

~

Incrementally, I gain confidence in my mothering. I acclimate to functioning in the strange twilight of no sleep. I fold and unfold the stroller without self-consciousness. I conk out in the rocker next to his crib when he naps. I let things get messier and dirtier. I take a Swiffer and wipe off the surfaces as I pass them, when I can. I leave the rest to entropy. I decide to see selectively.

T and I walk for hours, as long as he'll stand it. Our noses get cold and then warm and then cold again, with the strange microclimates of sunshiny Los Angeles winters. I walk him around the Rose Bowl Stadium, where clusters of African American grandmas out walking together in late morning gather around and coo over him and tell me to put more moisturizer on his legs, to put a dab of shea butter on his scalp. I love these women and the easy intimacy they assume with my son. They adore him, but never get in his face or freak him out. They seem to have an instinctive sense of his need for space.

Tariku stages a consistent and impressive rebellion against having his diaper changed. I become a student of the elaborate architecture of changing a screaming, unwilling baby. I do it with a stoic face. Once and for all, I pull out every cloth diaper and all the accompanying accouterments and bag them up, leaving them at the back door of the Goodwill, with a wry smile for the memory of how pious I was about cloth diapers. About so many things. I beg forgiveness of the earth and buy the recycled-ish compostable-ish diapers from Whole Foods.

Diaper changing aside, eye contact is our biggest concern. T doesn't want to look us in the eye. Not up close. Not, say, when I'm holding him and feeding him his bottle. He looks around; he looks up at the ceiling fan. He looks anywhere but at me.

I play peek-a-boo and other games that encourage eye contact, nine billion times a day. I hold him and rock him and gaze into his eyes, even when he looks away. Slowly, he begins to hold my gaze a bit longer. Every second his eyes meet mine is a great victory. And every victory is incredible, and still, it is not enough to keep me from being bored out of my skull. I talk to a friend on the phone, who is also a new mom.

She says, "I can't believe I ever worried that this would be boring! It is so fascinating!"

Oh, no.

It's not that everyone thinks toddlers are boring. I just feel that way because I'm a selfish monster.

I resolve to lean in and fight my boredom, my irritation, my escape fantasies. Depending on the day, these fantasies range from leaving my family for the guy who runs the trolley at the mall to joining the Peace Corps to faking my own death. If I just try hard enough to stay more present, I will be able to look at this from a different angle and discover that grinding spinach in the food mill *is* fascinating after all.

I devise my own rules about the cocooning at this point. We don't stay in the house all the time; I simply can't do it. But I do abide by not having playdates, not hanging out with other moms I know, not allowing anyone else to hold or nurture him. When my mother argues with me about it, I tell her that it's about him learning who his parents are.

Remembering what Karin said to me once, a lifetime ago, on a couch in Africa, I take him to the mall. I once would have mocked a mom who took her baby to the mall, that locus of mindless mass-market consumerism, but that was before I experienced days on the living room floor with:

Happy!

Sad!

Stinky!

Uh-oh!

I wear him in his carrier and we wander along the bright walkways of the Glendale Galleria. The carrier soothes both of us. We gaze at the shiny surfaces, the well-dressed mannequins, the soaring ceilings, the kiosks of eye pillows and crappy silver jewelry. I'm so happy to be out among humanity that it's as if I am strolling the corridors of the Louvre. Wearing my baby on my chest, I feel both alone and complete at the same time. We are a unit, he and I. We are a team. I hold his chubby hands and smell his sweet hair. I rub his back. I talk to him, a steady stream of consciousness. My own body begins to shape itself to his, even if it's only a mental construct and nothing, I'm sure, compared to the changes in the bodies of my friends who have been pregnant. Still, it's palpable. My wide hips, my strong back, my weathered and capable hands—never any of it very slender or delicate—I like them better now that they have a different function. They are suddenly so useful.

One afternoon, as I hit an exhaustion wall during one of our daily mall treks, I decide to treat myself to a sausage sandwich. It's unlike me, to eat questionable meat products on a big pillow of dreaded carbs. But I have enough trouble without monitoring every gram of starch within a three-mile radius.

I had been having almost no luck trying to get T to eat solid foods. My lovingly prepared organic pureed carrots, rice cereal, applesauce, spinach, have all been a bust. He wants bottle after bottle of formula, will barely eat a mouthful. It has repeatedly inspired a sort of desperate panic in me, followed by a grudging surrender.

With Tariku still in the carrier, we sit at a table in the food court as I begin to stuff the sausage sandwich into my mouth. T cranes his neck toward the sausage.

"This?" I ask him. He nods enthusiastically, showing me his goofy-toothed smile.

"Nope. You don't want this. This is way not organic. This is Mommy having a food fail."

He continues to gesture toward the sausage, openmouthed, like a baby bird.

I take a pinch of the sauce-soaked roll and feed it to him. He scarfs it down and reaches for more. I bite off little pieces of the sausage, chew them, take them out of my mouth, and place them in his. He munches them hungrily, and asks for more. When we finish, he screws his face into a knot of consternation.

"You want more?"

Answer: happiness.

I get up and stand in line for another sausage. A mall-wandering mom in the Jody Maroni's line says to me, snottily, "I saw you feeding him *that*. Isn't that spicy for him?"

"You have a better idea?" I snap. "You want to try to feed this kid?"

It comes out sharper than I mean it, and it surprises me as much as her. I am not usually this confrontational. I get a hit of adrenaline from my outburst; it doesn't feel half-bad. She turns on her heel—decidedly more awkward when you're maneuvering a double stroller—and stalks out of the food court.

In the sausage line, Tariku smiles at me, like: Okay, now, *this* is food. Jesus, that rice cereal was terrible. Can we call this a learning experience and move on?

It takes sitting through so, so many hours of guesswork and frustration and boredom to reach a heartbeat of connection, of understanding.

Chapter 15

"How big is Tariku?" says my mom. "*So* big!" She holds her arms out wide.

He responds with a smile wider than his whole head. It is the eve of his first birthday and he has sprouted four teeth, two in front on the bottom and two incisors on top. We are finally managing to get a little bit of food into him and he's gotten chubby, like a baby should be, instead of looking like a shrunken old man. He's ridiculously adorable.

"Peekaboo!"

She never tires of it. He stands—he can stand now—his chubby fingers gripping the edge of the coffee table, bouncing up and down and giggling like a deranged clown. He also has learned a bit of basic sign language: airplane, milk, more, hungry, ouch.

"Doggy," he says and makes the sign for milk. Scott looks at me for a clue.

"Anyone's guess," I say.

My mother gets him to clap his hands and say *yay!*

My father and my aunt sit on opposite sides of the living room, utterly charmed. T likes them just fine, but my mother is the star of the show.

Tariku immediately takes to having family in the house. I

wondered how it would be for him, seeing as he hadn't had close interactions with anyone other than Scott or me for the first six weeks of his American life. He doesn't miss a step. It's almost as if he doesn't notice. Either that or he's relieved. Finally, someone new to play with. Jo and Anne show up as well. All at once he's being passed around the living room. It's harder for me than it is for him. With each new set of hands holding him, I wonder if some invisible thread that connects us is fraying and we'll be sacrificing the progress we've made—the eye contact and the slightly improved sleep habits and the fact that he's actually eating occasionally.

In spite of my worries, my instinct is that it's probably fine. I'm relieved to have loosened the reins. I'm almost too exhausted, even, to feel the edge of discomfort that I generally have with my family around. I wonder if this is how family wounds are healed—everyone eventually gets too damn tired to cling to them. Usually I have an almost physical reaction to my parents' perpetual disappointment in me. In all fairness, they don't reserve this disappointment just for me—the entire world has fallen so far short of its promises to them. Still they soldier on, but it's with a deep sense of injustice.

I take Tariku out of my mother's hands and bring him into his room to change him. I am so proud of him. I think of the girl I was when my parents, my father in particular, were still so proud of me. An eleven-year-old with my hair in two French braids so tight they raised the skin on my forehead, wearing a tennis skirt, a mint green Lacoste shirt, and a tiny gold tennis racket charm around my neck. I was strung as tightly as my racket, merciless with myself about my weak serve, my thick thighs, my B in science class. This is the girl that speaks to me when my parents are around. The voice that tells me they are right to be so disappointed in how I turned out. After all—just look at my beautiful baby. How will I feel if he turns out as sloppy and lazy and ungrateful and messed up as I did? Though years of therapy have taught me to recognize this voice as not accurate, just one version of the story, it's still pretty convincing to me in weak moments.

I begin the circusworthy contortions that it takes to change a baby who doesn't want to be changed. He screams and screams and I imagine my mother in the next room, sitting on her hands, trying not to come in and show me that she can do it better.

~

That evening we hang out on the front lawn in the chilly spring twilight. The sunset lights the sky a thousand shades of salmon and apricot, with purple brushstrokes of clouds that look like signposts for Valhalla. My mother sits on the lawn, slumped forward slightly, looking fatigued, as my aunt crawls around with T in a fabric tunnel I got at Ikea on one of our many mall outings. There is a placidity to the nowhere to be and nothing to do, because in order to actually *do* something, I'd have to take my eyes off Tariku, and that isn't going to happen. My vigilance doubles now that there are people other than Scott near the baby.

It's impossible for me to trust that anyone else will keep him from danger. I barely have faith that I'll be able to protect him, but at least I can be assured of my own attentiveness. Until now, I have always been reasonably sure that in the face of most tragedy, I would still land on my feet. I have been through my share of trying times and it's given me a confidence in my survival instinct. Even if something should happen to Scott, I would be devastated, but I would recover and live again. I'm a fighter. I know this about myself. But the fragile being toddling around on my front lawn, with his pillowy lips, his one lazy eye that wanders just a hair, his voice that makes him sound like Pebbles from *The Flintstones*. If anything should happen to this child, I would be undone.

Scott and my father and I sit on the porch in Adirondack chairs, noshing on my first attempt at baking rugelach (the consensus is *meh*), as my father unfurls some disturbing family news. I've heard rumblings of it during our recent phone conversations. My father is a stockbroker and the financial crisis has knocked him sideways. His savings have taken a significant hit and he has been railroaded into an early retirement. Scott sits quietly, a somewhat detached witness, a solid guy. This is the beauty of Scott. He doesn't need to say anything; I just know he's there for me.

There's almost a sort of satisfaction underlying the despair in my father's voice. I get it. I know that it can feel oddly liberating to have the universe give you a carte blanche for self-pity. Not only is his business collapsing but my mother's health is failing. She has a rare autoimmune disease and can barely walk a block these days. A cream-colored turtleneck conceals the rash on her neck.

Though I don't feel responsible for their problems, somehow I do feel responsible for their unhappiness. Whether or not this sentiment is justified, it's deep-seated and I have never managed to fully exorcise it. It breaks my heart to think of my father's closet, full of suits and shiny shoes. He always hated his job, but the very hatred itself had a certain swagger to it. I imagine him putting on one of those suits and going in to work, a round man now, nose covered in broken capillaries, wearing thick glasses from the pharmacy because he's too stubborn to get a nice pair. He walks into his office with the Monet at Giverny poster on the wall, the pictures of his children and grandchildren on his desk. A small rustle of whispers moves down the corridor as his boss strides to his office door, steps in, and closes it behind him.

Faced with my sometimes-disastrous money problems over the years, my father has been unflaggingly generous and forgiving. When I was reckless and partying and blew my whole college fund, he still paid for me to finish college years later when I finally got my shit together.

He coached every soccer and softball team. He passed on to me his love of theater and music.

I think back on the endless theater classes that my father paid for, in which I read *Death of a Salesman* time and time again. And here he is on my front porch: Willy Loman with a briefcase full of worthless stock. He tells anyone who will listen about his worries, in fact. He tells Jo and Anne. He tells Suzanne when she stops by. He's trying out a new role. Before he was the reluctant success story; now he is the recession victim, with an ailing business and a sick wife.

They've spent twenty years waiting for my return to the fold. Look at them—they're getting older. Time is running out. It may be now or never to finally become the prodigal daughter they've been waiting for. I don't know how I would do that exactly, but I feel the weight of this expectation grow heavier by the year.

I watch as Tariku plays on the lawn. He keeps rubbernecking, looking back at me, checking if I'm there. We make eye contact and he speed-crawls up the stairs and into my lap. No one else sees it. No one else knows the momentous nature of this interaction, except maybe Scott, and even he is not as sensitized to it as I am. Strangers have entered our world, and Tariku keeps looking over and checking with me. He has crawled to my lap for security. He's making eye contact. He's connecting with me. He is recognizing me as his mother.

~

I buy a tiny gold crown with an elastic chin strap. I buy balloons and enough chocolate cake to feed my parents; Jo and Anne; Suzanne, her husband, and their son, Hank; and a handful of neighbors. I wear a long hippie dress and a silver necklace I bought in Ethiopia. T sits in his high chair, wide-eyed and frozen. I worry that I have miscalculated and sent my son into shock with the sudden overstimulation of all these people in the house. In a few minutes he comes back to life and begins to enjoy the attention. I bring out his cake, one candle in it. When everyone in the room sings, the sound could lift

the dining room right off the house's foundation, not b
so loud, but because it is so full of joy and support. T
beams as the song crescendos, and I imagine that he feels loved.
Or maybe I'm projecting and it's me who feels loved, in our little
crooked house, in our neighborhood that time forgot, sandwiched
between sixty freeways. I hold the small, warm flame of this feeling
in my chest.

Then I breeze by with a pile of dirty dishes in my hand and hear
my father talking to Suzanne.

He says, "Jillian has always been so *different*. Do you know that
when she was little she used to pretend not to know who we even
were?"

Ah yes. Different. There it is. And just when I was feeling like I
fit so well.

My father uses coded words to describe me: different, unusual,
sensitive, troubled (his fave), nonlinear (an in-joke—still quoting a
pretentious paper of mine from high school). All of it is loving as
well as unkind. All of it is said with a grudging sort of respect over-
laying a profound dissatisfaction. All of it describes a child he has
always loved and never understood. He has never stopped punishing me for this painful disconnect.

He is right; I did pretend not to know him. Once.

The thing about stories that diverge from those of your
parents—you spend your life never exactly sure who is right. Here
is my version of the time I pretended not to know my father:

I was six years old and I had a friend named Penelope—a Gen-
tile girl, one of the few at my summer camp, with a peaches-and-
cream complexion framed by windblown platinum sausage curls.
She was one of those girls with whom everyone, male and female
alike, fell in love. She was a tiny beauty queen with a wild streak,
smuggling sugary, fruity sticks of gum in her pockets and doling
them out like papal pardons. Penelope didn't have friends as
much as servants. She didn't have buckteeth and scabby knees like

I did. She never wound up with her gum stuck in her hair. She broke the rules and never got in trouble. I was fiercely loyal to her, cowed by her winning sense of humor and occasional cruel streak. One time she convinced me to steal a carnival prize out of a boy's knapsack and say it was my own. I wound up sitting in the camp office while the director called my mother, but I never snitched.

Penelope wasn't in my group at camp; she was in the other division of girls my age. We huddled together on the bus one morning, our knees up on the seat in front of us, our butts sliding around on the vinyl.

"Group 5A is better. You should come to my group," she said. "You can make up a name and say you're new."

I was enchanted by the idea of becoming someone new, someone much more . . . Jodi.

And that is how Jodi was born. Jodi Feldstein (oh, the glamour of a stage name) was a combination of the names of two of my babysitters. We decided that I was from Morristown and my dad was a doctor like hers, and my mom was a mom like everyone's we knew, even in the progressive seventies.

Jodi got off the bus that day, holding hands with Penelope. I walked up to her counselor and told her that I was new in that group. I informed her of my Jodi identity.

Of course the counselor marched me straight to the camp office, where I stuck to my story.

They were like, "Uh, Jill . . . we *know* you."

I responded, "Who's Jill?"

I was like the possessed girl in *The Exorcist*: I'm not Regan!

I persisted so stubbornly that my parents were called to come pick me up from camp. When they showed up, I said, "I have no idea who those people are; I've never seen them before."

"What the hell is wrong with you?" asked my father. "Are you crazy? Are you ill?"

Eventually they grabbed me by the arm and dragged me home. My mother was less confrontational than my father, as always, but she did give me strange sideways glances and treat me extra sweetly, as if I were a particularly delicate mental patient. I watched cartoons and ate grilled cheese until I finally relented and acknowledged that yes, those were pictures of me on the wall, so this must be my home, I guess. Can I have a Twinkie now?

The next day I gave up on being in Penelope's group and surrendered to my fate of just being me. Boring old me in my lousy old group. I wasn't sick and insane; I just wanted to be someone else. What could be more common?

That is the legendary tale of the Time I Pretended Not to Know Them.

I pass by as my father tells Suzanne his version of the story, in which I am strange, defiant, embarrassing. This is the me he presents to my waspy Yalie friend with beautiful manners and a brilliant mind and a lovely face and fancy china. My modern-day Penelope. I flush with shame.

And then I see a third version of the story—Suzanne's, whom I did not befriend for her choice in china pattern. All of that outside stuff tells you as much about her as my father's set of adjectives does about me: something, certainly, but not everything. And not remotely the most important things. Suzanne is someone who values authenticity above sentiment. She is not easily thrown, nor often embarrassed. I can imagine it from her perspective. I can hear what she'd say to me if I told her the tale.

"Oh, big deal," she'd say. "You were creative. You were curious. You were feeling for the edges of your world. Would it have killed them to be, like, 'Okay, Jodi, welcome to camp,' for a day?"

This rift between my father and me is tragic. We are very much alike, and doomed by our similarities to be distant from one another—forever, I suspect. I was not the only one wishing I was someone else. He was also wishing I was someone else, always. Not this *different* kid. Maybe that person, that someone else, would be able to save him from his current misery. But me, I can't. I thought that maybe things would change now that there's this little fulcrum between us, sitting in his high chair with a crown on his head, trying to put his whole fist into his mouth. I hear my father telling the story to Suzanne and worry that I might be wrong, that Tariku might not be the bridge that will finally cross this chasm between my parents and me.

Then I think: But how could that be possible? Of course he will. Just look at that kid. Just look at him.

~

Three days later, after my parents have left, my phone rings at 5:20 A.M. and my immediate panicked thought, still half-asleep, is that something has happened to my father. I never even realized that I was worried about this until I heard my phone in the early morning hours.

But no, it's Suzanne on the other end of the line. In my haze I forgot that Suzanne put me on baby alert. That's why my ringer was on in the first place. It was meant to be an unnecessary precaution. She had received a confident assurance from her doctor that she was not—no way, no how—going into early labor with her twins. Greg left for a night to argue a case in San Francisco that he has been working on for a year. He didn't want to go, but she insisted. She had the babysitter sleep over. She told me to leave my phone by my head, just in case, but that nothing was going to happen.

The doctor was wrong.

"All right!" I say. "Here we go! We're having some babies!"

I pull on some jeans, grab my purse, and dash across the street, where I find Suzanne pacing the bedroom dressed in a long brown sweater and sweatpants, her socks still wet. Hank and the babysitter perch wide-eyed on the bed.

"Greg is already on his way back," she says. "I'm sure he'll make it."

"Let's change those socks," I say.

I drive her minivan across town like the Mario Andretti of maternity chauffeurs.

"Oh, my God," I say. "There are two tiny babies getting ready to swim out."

"Not if you keep driving like that they won't. They'll crawl right back up."

We reach the hospital safely. The reception desk is empty but the midwife meets us in the hall and shows us to a small room. She doesn't look like the granola crystal-waver I imagined and instead is a tall, capable-looking woman in her midforties, with designer jeans and a powder blue cable-knit sweater. She hooks up the heart monitors and places them on Suzanne's belly. She rubs Suzanne's legs and I rub her shoulders. I watch as the doctor inserts the epidural into her spine, needle after needle. Suzanne sits stoically cross-legged and holds the midwife's hands.

"Welcome, babies," says the midwife. "We wish you a safe journey."

"Welcome, babies," I say. I picture Suzanne surrounded with white light. I try to imagine the same for myself, so that I don't bring any bad vibes or spiritual cooties into the room with me.

"Welcome, little guys," says Suzanne. "But wait an hour or two until your dad gets here."

We're switched to a bigger, sunnier, freezing room where the doctor does a sonogram. I see Waylon's backbone like a chicken spine. I see Violet's butt pressed against the placenta like someone mooning a car window.

"We're about ready to go," says the doctor.

"Oh, shit," says Suzanne. "Greg is still on his way. I can wait."

"No, I don't think you can." He turns to me. "Why don't you go suit up?"

A nurse hands me a set of scrubs. I am just tucking the last of my hair under the cap when I see Greg barreling down the hallway in a suit, his tie flapping behind him like a flag. And just that quickly he puts on a set of scrubs and I am left standing at the door, alone in a shower cap, as they wheel her away.

As soon as the sudden solitude settles in, I am almost doubled over with pangs of missing T. This is the longest I've been away from him since we got him. A panic seizes me. What if something happens and I'm not there?

He could fall down the stairs and break his neck. He could drown in two inches of bathwater. He could suffocate in a carelessly discarded plastic bag. He could fall and break his head open on the fireplace. He could get run over in a driveway. He could get mauled by a loose dog. He could . . .

It's not the first time I've had these overpowering feelings of anxiety about his safety, but it's the most acute. I actually shake my head to try to make it stop; it doesn't work. I run to my car and peel out of the parking lot. I roll down the windows to the warm day and turn the music up loud. I drive straight home and breathlessly enter the house, after a forty-five-minute drive across town, my mind crammed with uncontrollable, ghoulish thoughts. I find my family still in bed, Scott only sort of awake, Tariku watching Lady Gaga videos on Scott's laptop, which is precariously perched on a pillow at the foot of the bed. We don't sit T in front of a screen often, but when we do, it's Gaga. Gaga is our biggest gun. T is entranced with her.

They are safe. My family is safe. Relief breaks over me. I lie down next to them.

Tariku fidgets, as usual, but he's not crawling away, not hollering. He babbles to the screen, to his girl Gaga, in baby talk. I look at him and think, This is the last time he'll ever look quite like this. Soon the baby babbling is going to be replaced with more and more words.

A baby. How strange and beautiful to have a baby. And then my mind travels to plans and schedules—what to make for dinner, the persistent mental chatter. Not five minutes ago, I was terrified for his very life and he is here and safe and all I can think of is meatballs. Tariku nestles into my side, resting his cheek on mine. I am pulled back to the fullness of the moment, the softness of his baby cheek, the sound of his raspy, milky breathing, the feel of his bird heart.

I get a text a few hours later that all is well with Suzanne and the babies. They were born almost immediately after I left.

I call my mother to tell her about the twins.

"Oh, terrific! I'll call her to say mazel tov!" she says.

"Did you ever have a hard time not thinking over and over about every horrible thing that could have happened to David and me?" I ask her.

Even asking the question worries me. I wonder if it will expose me as some kind of a ghoul.

"Sure, sweetheart, of course. That happens to every mother, I think."

"What did you do?"

"I sang. It took my mind off it. I really liked to sing *Hair* but I had to stop once you got old enough to understand the lyrics."

"Thanks, Ma."

I hang up and walk to T, who is sitting in the center of the living room rug attempting to throw his set of plush stacking blocks into the ceiling fan. Mostly he can't reach yet, so they plop back down on him. He did once have some success hitting it with my iPhone.

I pick him up. He squirms, tries to grab the small portable speaker off the sideboard—eager, perhaps, to throw more electronic equipment into the slowly turning blades. I divert him, walking toward the kitchen to start the meatballs, singing him the only song I remember from *Hair*.

Good morning starshine.
The earth says hello.
You twinkle above us.
We twinkle below . . .

He giggles.
"Star," he says. "Gaga!"

~ Chapter 16

TARIKU is eighteen months old when he goes immediately from crawling to sprinting. I get stir-crazy enough to forget the yoga debacle and try Gymboree, Music Together, and Mommy and Me Swimming. I have no idea whether T is ready. Maybe he's challenging because he needs more interesting activities than reading *Mr. Brown Can Moo* and pouring sippy cups full of milk into the Blu-ray player. On the other hand, maybe he's still transitioning and should stay in the house for another three months until he feels safe. But how am I supposed to know if either of these is true? I am so restless myself that I decide to go with the former.

I stride into the classes as if I know what I'm doing. It's a strange thing, to have a one-and-a-half-year-old and have only six months of mothering under my belt. Most of the women walking around with kids this size have a crucial year on me. I am always self-consciously scrambling to catch up. In each class, when I begin to notice that T is markedly different from the other kids his age, I wonder if it's just the result of my lack of experience.

At first, he is just the loudest and most active kid and I take it as a point of secret pride, wondering why all those other kids are such duds. After about a month, he goes from being the kid who inspires laughter that then turns a bit nervous, to the kid the other parents actually scramble to avoid sitting next to because he has no sense of personal space. I stop bothering to smile at the other parents because they avoid eye contact. He knocks kids down in a way that lands somewhere between accidental and intentional. Every room we're in, whether in the coffee shop or the indoor playground, he turns on a dime and makes a daring escape attempt, hurtling toward the door. I have to drop everything where I stand and dash out after him. He makes a break for it again and again, undeterred by how many times I bring him back, squirming like a greased pig and usually hollering to boot. At first I'm painfully embarrassed, but eventually my embarrassment dissolves and is replaced by foreboding. What does this behavior *mean*? Will it just take a little time for him to feel safe, for his neurons to start firing correctly? Or are we looking at a lifetime of struggle?

What the hell is going on with my kid?

With his six brand-new teeth, Tariku begins to bite me. He bites Scott as well, but not with nearly the same frequency and fervor. At first it is tentative and only occasional. Soon his bites break the skin, when I can't dodge them. One night he latches on to the thin skin over my collarbone and tears a hole in it. I have to grab his hair to get him to let go. I have pulled my child's hair. He glares at me with accusation and bawls.

During this time, a major news headline involves an adoptee, a child from Russia, left on a plane by his parents with a note pinned to his shirt. It seems nearly everyone I know wants to talk about it with me, an odd gleam flashing in their eyes, almost wolfish. Did you hear about that adopted kid from Russia who got sent back? Did you hear he threatened to burn their house down? Horrifying!

I can't say for sure, but my sense is that when they say horrifying, they are talking not about the egregiously neglectful parents in the story but about the child. The general perception is that adopted children are expected to immediately and unequivocally acquire a

sense of overwhelming gratitude for not being starving, abandoned, dying of malaria in a developing country. I mean, what the
hell is wrong with that confused and frightened child, abandoned,
alone on an airplane? That little boy, who has lost everything he has
ever known and loved, in many cases repeatedly? How could he
misbehave? Doesn't he know that he is so *lucky*?

I can't talk to any of these friends about the struggles that are
beginning to surface with my son. I want to wall out the world and
protect him from their judgments and their schadenfreude. It is not
that surprising, is it? That it's taking a while for his brain to make
sense of this. That it's taking a minute for him to trust. It's not surprising that he needs some extra help. But this is only really clear to
me in the face of other people's judgments. This is the mama lion
in me. In my darkest moments, when I am not so bold, I hear whispers of the same fears and doubts.

One Wednesday morning, Scott takes T to music class and I
attempt to get some writing done. The hour goes so quickly that
my ass has barely touched my desk chair when Scott reappears at
the doorway of my office.

"I'm not doing that again," he says.

"I know." I sigh. "I know. What are we going to do?"

"Well, I'm definitely not doing kitty ears again."

"What?"

"They made us do the song with the kitty ears."

He holds his hands up behind his head in an approximation of
ears.

"I will change diapers and I will wear him in that chick sack
thing . . ."

"The sling?"

"Whatever. And I will do anything, *anything* for that kid. Except
kitty ears. Kitty ears is all you."

"But did you notice anything about his *behavior*?" I ask.

"Like, anything new? No," he says. He whistles on his way back down the stairs. "How about I do the swimming thing next week instead?" he calls back to me.

Maybe I'm exaggerating. Maybe I'm just a wuss.

The following Wednesday my desk sits empty and I am back in music class, resenting my husband's refusal to go. In all fairness to Scott, he's not the only dad resistant to the wildlife pantomime. One dad shows up, every once in a while, but mostly it is just us moms. How is it that in the hippest neighborhood in one of the most cosmopolitan cities of this country, it's still all women here in the middle of the morning?

I look around and feel a shimmer of apprehension, as if my cover is about to be blown and it'll be discovered that I'm only masquerading. That I'm secretly longing for a few hours of the day during which I'm just me, not strictly defined by being a mom. Maybe this is why I can't get my toddler to sit still and stop whacking everyone over the head.

It's too soon to want out so badly. I look around. These other moms seem happy. Happier than I am, anyway. I wonder if it's the truth.

We all walk in circles and sing the animal song. We make the dreaded kitty ears; we roar like lions; we dangle an arm in front of our nose to make an elephant trunk. We march and sing like champs and everything is going well, until the teacher sets a basket of rhythm instruments in the center of the circle. When Tariku dives for the shaker shaped like a banana, a wiry little girl snags it out from under him. He sinks his half-dozen teeth into her delicate pink flesh. She howls as the blood beads on her arm. I can feel the stink eye from the other moms, as if it has weight and density.

His energetic teacher, with the singsong voice that makes everything she says sound like a Dr. Seuss book, calls me over after class.

"Tariku is such a wonderful, energetic spirit and, of course, we all love him. But you might do better in a different class. It's my responsibility to keep the kids safe," she says with a sad smile that makes me want to pinch her. Hard. "I don't feel that I can do that with him here."

I capitulate, forcing myself to look her in the eye with a smile, as if I'm not devastated. My kid is eighteen months old and has already been expelled. True, it's just from Music Together, which is torture anyway, but still. I had hoped to give him a different childhood from that of my rebellious friends and me, getting into trouble our whole lives.

I bundle Tariku up into his carrier.

"We're going to get through this together," I tell him as we walk home. "I'm going to help you."

More and more we stay home, or we go to the park by ourselves. Maybe he just needs more time to connect with us before we venture out into the wide world. T loves music so much that I decide we'll have our own music class. I open my computer and play his favorite Lady Gaga. He wraps himself around me like a little koala bear, presses his cheek to mine and we sway, we jiggle, we shimmy, we jump up and down, we tango, we cha-cha, we do the mashed potato. We play "Bad Romance" over and over. He loves the gibberish—*rah rah rah-ah-ah, roma, ro-ma-ma, gaga ooh-la-la*. I put him down and demonstrate (poorly) every hip-hop move I can conjure until we're hysterical.

The dancing is sweetness itself. And when we're dancing, I can almost forget the fact that I have thrown out shirt after shirt because he's biting me until I bleed and I can't always get the stains out.

That's not all I forget. My memory seems to be functioning at roughly the capacity of a goldfish. I forget if I've eaten, if I've showered. I repeat everything to Scott so many times that the most common thing I hear these days is, "Hon, you told me that already." I become somehow less aware of the space around my body. I trip on the edge of our carpet, on the uneven stair in the middle of the staircase, on nothing at all. I drop glasses on the kitchen floor and break them. I cut my hands when I go to clean them up.

When I tell Suzanne, she just laughs. "Sleep dep! They use it as actual torture, you know."

And I think, Yes, yes, of course. But maybe it's something more. Maybe I am unable to handle motherhood. Maybe I'm leaving my body little by little, in a subconscious attempt to escape.

Scott finally has a few solid weeks off work and we decide it's time for me to start working in earnest on my albatross of a book. It's due in a couple of months and since we've been back from Africa, I haven't managed to put down on the page anything more than gobbledygook. The shadow of the Memoir is becoming larger and more unwieldy by the day.

At nine A.M. on a Tuesday, I have already been up for four hours. I climb the stairs and enter my sun-dappled office, tucked in the back of the house. I haven't been working here much, instead mostly stealing an hour here and there at the dining room table. I initially recoil. I remind myself that I know this place. I look over it for the thousandth time. There is the hole in the wall I never bothered fixing, from when my bookshelf fell down. There is my new bookshelf, holding a cluster of my favorite books, which I hope will rain down their magic onto my desk somehow. There is my picture of my beloved grandmother Sylvia, her stiff wig, beaklike nose, and wickedly smart eyes. There is my hunk of pink quartz from Sedona. It has been months since I sat in this chair. I light a candle. I realize I forgot to start the laundry so I run downstairs and then come back up again. Scott is at the park with T, and I'm alone in the house, which is a unicorn-rare occurrence. These are the best conditions for writing that I could ask for. An unfamiliar quiet descends and with it a sluggishness, a dense warmth, a lazy cloud of comfort. I could just curl up on the couch and take a nap. I've earned that much, haven't I?

I push back at the nap idea. This is my only time to write. I know how to do this. I've done this before. Just put down one word and then follow it with another and a sentence will get written and then eventually a page.

My eyes wander to the world outside the window. My neighbor unloads camping equipment from his Prius. The gardener blows leaves off Helen's lawn and onto ours. Tomorrow our gardener will come and blow them back. The kicker is that we have the same gardener, performing this futile ritual with the leaves.

Jane Austen wrote at a tiny desk in a house with tons of people running around her, I tell myself.

Jane Austen. As if.

My fingers wander absentmindedly to the raw-looking bite marks on my chest.

Maybe he's angry about not being breast-fed. Maybe I should have listened to the friends of mine who suggested that I nurse Tariku. It's possible. I've known adoptive moms who have, through either medical or herbal methods, stimulated lactation. Even if I didn't want to go that far, people recommended that I let him nurse just for comfort. I tried it a couple of times. I don't think that these people took into account the teeth that were already there even when we first got him. While pregnancy is no longer something I long for, no longer something I even really think about anymore, the fact that I never nursed my son does still sometimes make me sad. I wish I could have fed him, nurtured him, from my own body.

These are the thoughts that consume me. I do not get even one word written that first day.

But I go back up the stairs the next day and back again until the work slowly gets rolling. I don't know if what I'm writing is any good, but at least I'm making a dent.

No sooner do I have a toehold in my work than Scott leaves for Korea for three weeks. We decide to hire Auntie Jo to come on board and help with child care so I can keep writing in the mornings. Every time I hand T over to her he screams and screams and I'm snowed under an avalanche of guilt, even though I know that once the two of them get into their groove they have a blast. Half of my attention is always with the baby. I'm like a broken conduit for an electric current. I begin to pull my story up from the floor, up from the center of the earth (where I imagine the stories all live), and before it reaches my fingers, it's diverted downstairs. The baby is crying. Something falls.

"What's going on down there?" I yell. And whatever thread of a story I had is lost. I struggle to find it again.

In the end, it's Jo's fierce commitment to T that allows me to ease up and actually smile when I watch the two of them holding hands, heading to the car. I do get a few words written when they go on their "auntie" adventures, to the zoo and the aquarium and the pony rides. I recognize that there's something self-important to this guilt I swim in every second T spends with someone else. A kid needs more than just one doting person. Everyone needs an auntie.

When T goes down for his afternoon nap, Jo leaves the baby monitor on the corner of my desk, kisses me on the cheek, and goes home for the day. I watch obsessively, straining my eyes at the little lump on the black-and-white screen to make sure he is still breathing. At the same time, I dread the stirrings of wakefulness that signal the end of my work and the beginning of our long afternoon together.

~

One afternoon, I take him for a walk at the Americana at Brand, an outdoor mall with a big, impossibly green lawn, where families spread out in the sun with strollers and slices of pizza. Kids run around chasing bubbles blowing over from the kiosk that sells crappy, overpriced battery-operated toys. I follow T as he trucks around the winding sidewalks. We watch the dancing fountain. We ride the trolley. It's not a bad place, if you don't mind a certain Vegas-y, overgroomed, forced serenity.

We draw stares, as we always do. A white mom with a black baby is an irresistible magnet for people's eyes. For the most part, I'm sure it's not malicious and it doesn't bother me all that much. Tariku is absurdly cute and people can't help but gawk. I imagine they're just trying to piece it together—this tableau that challenges their assumptions. It only starts to make me self-conscious when the tantrums start. Because then I am not just the visible mom with the super-cute black baby; I am the bad mom with the super-cute *freaking-out* black baby.

I put off leaving for as long as I possibly can, knowing what will come along with the transition. When it is time to go, I give him a ten- and then a five-minute warning and set the timer on my phone. When he hears it go off he looks at me with indignation. His face shatters; his limbs go stiff; he begins to thrash and wail. Scott and I have decided that he looks less like an alligator, as I used to say, and more like the honey badger in those YouTube videos. We call it, jokingly, *When Babies Attack,* after the Discovery Channel show *When Animals Attack.* If you try to walk away, he'll crawl toward you at a shocking speed and latch on to you with his teeth. We have worked out a relatively dependable method of what the websites call "containing" him. I lie down next to my son on the ground and wrap one arm around him from behind, pinning his arms to his body. I hold his forehead with the other, then secure his legs between mine and lie there while he hollers. Eventually he tires himself out and sobs pitifully, his face wet with tears.

"Hurt!" he says. "No hurt Ta-ku!"

I tell him that I can't let him go until he calms down because I'm here to keep him safe. The eyes of every person on the lawn are on us. I have never before in my life wished quite so fervently for invisibility.

A security guard crosses the green and approaches us with a purposeful gait.

"Ma'am, what is going on here? Whose child is this?"

I'm on the ground looking up at him in his wide-brimmed hat, backlit by the sun.

"This is my child. We're having sort of a hard time here. Could you please give us a little space?"

"I'm afraid I'm going to need to see some ID, just in case."

"In case what?"

"Show me your ID, ma'am."

I release Tariku, half hoping he'll fasten his teeth to the officer. Instead, he tears off. I chase after him and ignore the security guard, who is too confused or just too lazy to pursue us.

When I catch T, I have to start all over again.

It's been a week since Scott left for Korea. I can barely even Skype with him, I'm so pissed at him for leaving. Logically I know that tour money pays for our house, our babysitter, our food, our clothes. Still, I resent him for being on tour while I'm at home with the Honey Badger. I know what rock tours are like; I used to go along. They are work, certainly, but they are also fun, with music and fans and first-class travel and foreign skylines and nice hotels and room service. Rock tours do not suck. Containing a toddler at the mall most surely sucks.

~ Chapter 17

As he approaches two years old, T's violent and prolonged screaming biting crying Honey Badger tantrums happen at least ten times a day, usually whenever a transition occurs: putting him in the car seat, taking him out of the car seat, feeding him, changing his diaper, saying no to him. The fat tears that roll down his cheeks are far worse than the high-decibel assault on my ears. My child is suffering and I can't seem to find one thing that helps him, with the exception, sometimes, of a bottle of milk. He sucks on it as if he is suffocating and it contains not milk but air.

People are constantly saying:

Oh, it's a boy thing.

Oh, it's a stage.

Oh, everyone goes through that.

They mean to be helpful, but I am left feeling lonely and inadequate. If everyone goes through this, why does it feel so insurmountable? If everyone goes through this, why am I the only mom I know who can't take my child out in public without a dramatic scene? Is every mother really sitting at home Googling "how to safely restrain a child"?

I do some other searching, too, but can hardly bear the results that come up when I begin stringing together search words like "attachment, adoption, aggression." I look at websites about "attachment challenges" and am so scared out of my wits that I have to stop myself, knowing from experience that falling down a self-diagnosing Internet rabbit hole rarely turns up anything productive. I once spent an afternoon in the emergency room with Scott, convinced I was in the process of being widowed by an aneurysm when really he had just put eyedrops in one eye and not the other. I don't trust myself not to be alarmist.

I call our pediatrician, who is still confident that T is just adjusting.

"But it's been a year," I tell him.

"Maybe it would be helpful for you to have some extra support," he tells me.

He gives me the number of a counselor named Ruth Beaglehole, who founded an organization called Echo Parenting and Education. She is something of a Los Angeles parenting guru, and I've heard raves about her from friends. The therapy would be for me, not for Tariku. I don't feel like I have either the time or the extra money for therapy, so I file the number.

That night, I give T a bath. He colors with his bath crayons all over the walls and I snap pictures of the masterpiece, charmed by his exuberant creativity. Except he uses up the last of his favorite red crayon and I don't have another. He screams, "Hate you!" and begins to splash like crazy, displacing most of the water onto the bathroom floor. When he won't listen to my admonitions, I eventually pull up the drain and let out whatever little water remains. He is none too pleased with this turn of events, so he leans over and fastens his teeth on my arm.

With the hand at the end of the arm that's not in a teeth-vise, I smack my child across the face.

Chubby arms, twinkling eyes, swirl of soft curly hair, the love of my life. I hit him hard enough that my palm stings.

"God damn it, Tariku, stop biting me."

He looks at me, stunned and betrayed, silent for a heartbeat before he sobs. He calls out for Daddy over and over.

Unnaturally calm, I pick him up and wrap him with a towel into what I like to call the "bath burrito." I rock him there in my arms, sitting in a puddle of water on the floor, and say, "I'm sorry. Mommy is sorry, honey."

"Daddy. I want Daddy."

He is over it within minutes. I robotically move through the rest of our routine. Book. Bed. I lie with him until he falls asleep. When I hear his breathing deepen, punctuated by little snores, I get up and go into the dining room, where I sit at the table and put my head into my hands. I want to vomit up the black ball that is swirling in my chest gaining density, gravity. Vomit it up or just sink into it like tar.

My father hit my brother and me. Not all the time, but enough for us to be frightened of him. In all my years of wanting a baby so badly that my body memorized a whole new experience of longing, it never occurred to me that I would ever be violent toward my own child. Ever. I could never summon any compassion for people who hit their kids. How could you? I'd think. What kind of monster are you?

Now I know exactly what kind of monster.

I think of the many times I have heard in my life, from frustrated family, friends, lovers, in response to my mercurial desires, my famous capriciousness:

You don't know what you want. You don't know who you are.

They were right. I don't know myself at all. Look at what I'm capable of.

I'm not capable of making my son feel secure, or he wouldn't be in such a panicked rage all the time. I'm not even capable of keeping him safe from me, which, in all the things I have read about and planned for, I never dreamed would be necessary.

I lay my head on the table and push my fingertips into my

stomach, trying to knead out the poison. I am pretty sure my child would be better off without me. I should leave and let his father find a better wife. A good wife. A good mother.

I don't bother to fall to my knees. I just pray with my head on the table.

"Please, God, help me be a better mother. Please, God or Jesus or Krishna or Allah or Mary or Moses or Grandma or whoever is on the other end of this line right now. Please throw me a bone here. I need help."

I call Suzanne.

"I hit my kid," I say. I sob. "I want to kill myself."

"Oh, for God's sake," she says. "Most people snap and do it sometime, you know. Stop being so dramatic. I'm coming over."

She sits beside me on the couch, opening a dark chocolate bar the size of a small country. I cry until I don't. We are silent for a while.

"All kids have some shit to deal with, you know. All of them. One time or another. You're just getting all yours at the front end. This won't last forever."

It might be an answered prayer—the friend, the chocolate bar— because when she leaves I don't feel okay exactly, but I am no longer ready to buy a plane ticket to China. When I close the door behind her, I walk back to the bedroom, kneel next to the bed, and place my palm on the rise and fall of his back. Still breathing, still hope.

~

The next day, while Auntie Jo is on child-care duty, I decide that I badly need a break. I skip work and go to a yoga class. It isn't my regular class and the teacher is a woman I haven't seen before. During the opening meditation at the beginning of the class, she tells us to set an intention for the day. Mine is less of an intention and more of a promise to God himself: I will never hit my child again.

During the final meditation, the teacher gives us a mantra.

I love you. I'm sorry. Forgive me. Thank you.

She instructs us to use it for our enemies, but who has enemies? I'm not a politician or a gangster or even the president of the PTA.

There is someone who has been on my mind all week, however: Grandpa Jack. I'm trying to figure out what Tariku's Hebrew name should be, as my mother is insisting we have a naming ceremony, in case I should ever feel compelled to take my commitment to Judaism further than a love of pickled fish products and a tendency to say *"Oy!"* I have chosen Sippur Ya'akov, but I am waffling. My mother presses me to commit, doubtless because she has plans to needlepoint the name onto every pillow in the tristate area.

Sippur is for my beloved grandmother Sylvia. It also means "story" in Hebrew, which is close to the meaning of Tariku's name in Amharic: his story. It is not the Sippur part of the name that I am stuck on; it is the Ya'akov part.

Ya'akov means Jacob, after my paternal grandfather, Jack, whom I adored as a girl. Only later did I learn that throughout my father's childhood, while Jack was a much-loved physician out in the world, he was a tyrannical and unforgiving man at home. Jacob's violence cut a swath through my family that has spanned generations. Stopping with me, I always thought. Or maybe not.

Jacob and I share initials. Or we did, before my name changed with my marriage. As a child, these initials were a point of pride. I was the firstborn, sharing initials with both my father and my grandfather. What if I name my son this, and some savage essence leaks through the cracks in the generations? What if it already has?

Jacob, I think. Jack. Grandpa Jack.

I love you. I'm sorry. Forgive me. Thank you.

Okay, here goes.

I love you.

This is an easy one. This has always been true. I never knew him the way the older generation knew him. He died when I was five and I still remember him, bespectacled and sitting up ramrod straight, hand on his gold-topped cane, always smiling. I'm sure many of these memories are conflations of real life and photographs, but I do know this—he doted on me. He visited all the time, even though he was almost completely crippled. He would invent all kinds of games that he could play from the couch. I would take his cane and play Bo Peep, searching the house for the elusive lost sheep. My mother has told me that he was different with me—his best and softest self. This is the man I knew. The man who gave me my initials, the armature on which my name was built. After he died, for years I drew pictures and made my father carry me on his shoulders so I could hold them to the ceiling, so Grandpa Jack could see them.

I'm sorry.

This one is harder. For what am I sorry? I'm sorry for how it all turned out, I guess. For the legacy I'm sure Jack never intended. No one sets out aiming to brutalize their family. I'm sorry that I haven't been able to turn it all around yet. I'm sorry that I am too much like you. I'm trying to change.

I forgive you.

This one is the hardest yet. Is it for me to forgive? My aunt has told me that my father had a facial tic as a child. With each involuntary contraction of the muscles around his left eye, my grandfather would throw food at him at the dinner table, calling him a mental retard. Forgiveness is a tricky thing and I'm not sure it can be manufactured, but for the purposes of the exercise I decide that I will. That I do. Forgive him.

Thank you.

This one is easy. Because after everything, I know I was loved. I have always known this. And for this, I'm grateful. People are often surprised to hear about my history and find me relatively intact, generally goofy and optimistic, at least among friends. I count the love I received as the reason. There were so many failings in my house, and also so much love.

I understand now, more than I ever could, that you can love someone and still smack them in the face. You can try and try and still be unknowable to yourself.

Maybe someday I will tell my father this.

By the time we press our palms together in front of our chests and close out the class, I have brokered an accord with the name. I call my mother from the car and tell her to go ahead and pull out the needlepoint.

Chapter 18

THE morning of Tariku's final adoption hearing in Monterey Park, I arrive home late from my hike-turned-bushwhacking, fence-scaling expedition to find Scott worried and pissed and panicking.

"We have to be out of here in twenty minutes!" he says. "Can you leave a note next time at least?"

There is no time to tell him about my experience on the trail. There never is anymore. We're in survival mode lately and every interaction centers around Tariku, the worst cliché of a married couple with a new kid. I remember the couple who took the romantic road trip through the American West, with no destination in mind. We pulled the car over to make love on deserted desert highways. We almost got married on the spur of the moment in a casino in Reno. Now I find it hard to imagine that we ever did anything on the spur of the moment.

I take a cursory shower, bolt up the stairs, and look for the suit I bought to wear to court. As I open my closet door, a compulsion to see one of my old family photographs overtakes me. I definitely do not have time to dig for the picture I'm thinking of, but I search anyway. I know it's in my keepsake box, behind the purses in my closet. I find it, next to my Holly Hobbie charm necklace and a dried flower from the lei I wore at my wedding. The picture is square, taken in the seventies, the kind it's hard to find a frame for now. My mother and father and I squish together into a blue plastic baby pool, in front of the understated brick apartment complex we lived in for the first couple of years of my life. Maybe I'm one year old, maybe a little older. My parents look attractive, young, with no hint of the dissolution that's to come. In the pictures my father looks like a normal guy, happy even, not chronically angry or overweight. There's an odd darkness around my eyes. My father has the same darkness. Maybe it's just the lighting, the old cameras. I wonder who was taking the picture. We look like such an isolated and complete unit.

I put it in my purse and slip on my suit. The skirt is cream colored, knee length, with olive horizontal stripes on it. I wear it with a white button-down shirt, a navy blazer, and the shiny patent nude-colored shoes that all the stores are showing. It's a smart little outfit. I feel put together, like I'm playing a part.

My father only ever wanted to buy me clothes from J. Crew when I was in high school. All I wanted to wear were kilts, ripped fishnets, and Sex Pistols T-shirts. It ate him alive that I dressed like a punk. My father interpreted this choice as a personal assault on him, rather than an attempt at self-expression, an adolescent casting-about for identity. To my mother, it was simply perplexing—why would you not want to fit in? My fashion choices inspired manifold tirades of you-look-like-a-whore and you-make-yourself-ugly and you-intentionally-shame-me. Here I am now, all he wanted me to be. A girl who can zip herself into a fitting-in costume at a moment's notice. Too late.

~

When I get downstairs, everyone is dressed to go and waiting for me on the couch. Auntie Anne and Auntie Jo entertain Tariku, while Scott seethes with anger, his jaw muscles flexing. I abandoned him on this of all mornings.

"Hey, hon," I say. "Can we move forward?"

Always forward. Later than I'd like, and still pulling twigs out of my hair, we drive to the court and arrive in plenty of time. By the time we're walking through the parking lot, T a bundle in Scott's arms, all is forgiven. I can tell by how Scott holds his shoulders, thrown back and proud. This is the last hurdle. Tariku is nearly two years old and while he has always been Scott's boy in his heart, it will finally be official in the eyes of the law.

The Children's Court is in a large, nondescript concrete building. The waiting area on the fourth floor is lined on one side with east-facing windows. The clouds shift in shades of gray and the filtered light falls on a conflicted scene, where a small percentage of beaming adults carry celebratory balloons and the rest sit with bad posture while kids zoom back and forth between one family member at one side of the room and another family member at the other. A few kids sit and talk with attorneys.

Tariku toddles down every hallway, with me close behind. This is what he likes to do—walk, explore. My role is most often to just follow him until I have to jump in front of him and stop him from going where he's not supposed to go. He tries to get into every door and hugs every kid in the room. I have to monitor the hugging. I've learned from our doomed attempts at various classes that sometimes he clings to kids with a vengeance and won't let them go. If they don't hug him back, he shoves them down.

I think of the room he was in when we first met him in the orphanage. All of those babies rolled over each other on the floor, all day long. He shared a crib. He was always hugging someone, never alone.

Tariku crawls into Scott's lap. "Dee-Doo," he says. "Dee-Dee." This is what he calls Scott. Tariku kisses him and kisses him.

Auntie Jo and Auntie Anne take turns chasing him around, until we're called into a courtroom, where the proceedings are short and sweet. We answer a few questions and sign the final documents.

The judge says, "Congratulations, Scott and Jillian. Tariku Moon Shriner is now your legal son with all corresponding rights and privileges."

We all cry and laugh at the same time.

Afterward, we go home to a small party—a neighbor or two and a few friends with kids his age. We have submarine sandwiches and cake and water toys in the backyard. The party is sun drenched and laughter filled and idyllic. I'm still vigilant, still holding my breath and waiting for a tantrum, like I always do behind my smile.

Twenty minutes in, Tariku's friend reaches for the blue shovel in the sandbox. I guess Tariku wants that shovel, because he rips it from the kid's hand and uses it to hit him over the head. There is gasping, a mad rush, tears.

Two things are clear to me: that I have never loved anything or anyone in this world the way I love my son; and that love simply isn't enough to guide me. I need help.

~

The day after the adoption is finalized, I call the number my pediatrician gave me for Echo Parenting and Education, where I set up a counseling session with Ruth Beaglehole, a teacher and therapist who has been cultivating her ideas about child development and family dynamics since the late 1970s. Ruth is legendary to many parents looking for a different model from the way we were raised. Her philosophy is based around empathy, "connecting language," and the understanding of a child's emotional, physical, and brain development.

Seeking help in L.A., you never know what you're going to get. My last outing was to a slick and intimidating Beverly Hills psychiatrist. I had thought that all my recent crying might warrant some antidepressants. I lost my child care at the last minute and brought T with me as an emergency measure. When T licked his spotless floor-to-ceiling windows, the doctor nearly had a nervous collapse (strike one against a psychiatrist). The doctor handed me a bottle of Windex and insisted I clean the windows myself.

There are no floor-to-ceiling windows at the Echo Center. It's run out of the basement of a Methodist church in Echo Park. Ruth meets Scott and me in the office and leads us into what was probably once a storage room, with industrial carpet and high, narrow windows that look out on people's feet walking by. We sit in three straight-backed chairs facing each other. Extra chairs and reams of printer paper are stacked in the corner. The low-key surroundings comfort me. Ruth and her staff teach parenting classes to people sentenced to anger management and to teen parents, among others. They certify caregivers for day cares and schools. They don't turn anyone away for lack of funds. These people are for real.

Scott does most of the talking, explaining Tariku's excessive amounts of energy, as well as the aggression, the sleeplessness, the contrariness, the biting. I sit silently crying the whole time. I don't admit that I've hit him. I haven't even admitted it to Scott. But I tell her that I yell too much. That I have grabbed him and handled him in ways that were quick and angry.

She listens so respectfully that I feel heard for the first time in years. Finally, here is someone who isn't saying:

Oh, he's just a boy.

Oh, my kid was just like that.

Oh, he'll grow out of it.

Instead, Ruth says the word "trauma" and it's the first time I hear it in relation to my child. Recognition shimmers up and down my spine. Trauma. It feels like the first time I've ever heard the word.

"Anyone caring for Tariku will need to be educated in trauma-informed care."

"What do you mean? What trauma?" I croak.

But I already know the answer. Of course he's traumatized. But I had thought that we'd take him home and snuggle and kiss him and that we would eventually hug it right out of him—the malnutrition and illness and separation he suffered when his brain was at its most malleable and most vulnerable, during his first months of life.

"But everyone thinks we don't discipline him," I say, suddenly always worried about what other people think. What happened to the girl in the Sex Pistols T-shirt?

"It's never about discipline," she says. "It's always about connection."

"But won't we raise a spoiled brat if we don't figure out how to discipline him?" I ask. I feel desperate. I wanted a list of things to *do* to help manage his behavior. "He's so controlling."

"Ask yourself in any situation if there's a way you can gather him to you. Can you make him feel safe?"

For the rest of the hour, she talks about raising an empathetic child by modeling empathy, compassion, and respect.

"You get that we need to *restrain* this kid, right?" my husband asks, still skeptical about the gentleness of her language.

"You may need to contain him, to keep everybody safe," she says. "But if at all possible, strive to do it without anger, without electricity in your arms."

This makes sense to me. I know what she's talking about—the angry electricity. It courses through me a hundred times a day.

Ruth goes on to say that we have to build a strong scaffold around him, provide him with structure and routine. Not exactly my strong points, but I can learn.

We get back to the car armed with some helpful tools. Scott looks lit up from inside, newly hopeful.

He says, "That woman is righteous. She can sure listen."

I write the suggestions down. I repeat them to myself.

Locate the need behind the behavior.

Give him words for his feelings.

I am buoyed by our new information. I'm a great researcher, a determined problem-solver. We have identified the problem. Now all we have to do is fix it. How hard can it be?

~ Chapter 19

I have finished my memoir, final edits, everything. I scrambled and crammed before the deadline, with Jo babysitting extra hours and me working all day long and heading back upstairs to the office every night after T was in bed. Pressure makes diamonds, my grandmother used to say. I wrote that into the memoir, somewhere, though I can't remember where anymore, my brain is such a churning jumble of words.

I sit on the bench in the backyard, late summer afternoon, with Tariku and the dogs rolling around on the grass. The figs and late tomatoes are in bloom, the sunlight filtering through the leaves. It is quiet inside me, finally, in a summer day kind of way. Not three days ago I was truly unsure if I could finish the book. And here I am: finished. That is something. At the same time I'm learning to care for someone else, I'm also becoming more my own person. I'm bone tired, but this has been a thrilling time. On the other side of it, I find a deep placidity.

Later that night, I pack our bags. So much for placidity. T and I are going along on the Weezer and Blink-182 summer tour, which will take us from Toronto to Irvine, with fourteen stops in between.

Touring always used to be such a fun and selfish time for me, with no obligations other than showing up at lobby call and putting on a pair of nice shoes for the show every once in a while. I could kill entire afternoons reading and writing in the back of buses, the corners of dressing rooms, street-side tables in foreign cafés. What will it look like now? I have no idea and yet I'm trying to pack for it.

I tick each item off the list, the endless list, which has only gotten longer and longer. When does life stop feeling like one endless list? I schlep the suitcase, half-packed, downstairs. It's already eleven P.M. and we're leaving the next morning. I stare at T's disorganized closet with nothing less than despair. Where is his other shoe? How did it get this messy?

C'mon, pull it together. What would Gwyneth Paltrow do? Besides write a cookbook with nothing in it my son will eat. But that's his fault, not hers. I mean, just look at her.

I imagine I am GP herself, straight blond hair casually pulled into a ponytail, clothes hanging off me perfectly, like a fashion model, blue eyes sparkling as if lit from within, house arranged just so, like something from the cover of *Real Simple* magazine. *So* busy these days! After Mommy and Me Mandarin I gotta stop over for a quick lunch at Beyoncé's before running off to Cannes.

This is my chance to prove that all those people I grew up with were wrong about me all along. I can be just like my girl Gwyneth—invincible! I mean, obviously not quite, but close enough.

~

Sky. Blue. Airplane.

Tariku says these words over and over. As long as there are wide windows looking out over a tarmac, a view of the hulking steel beasts in their dance with each other and the earth and sky, he is happy. I'm still infused with my imagined Gwyneth-dom, relaxed and confident at the airport. I'm excited to be off on an adventure, in my skinny jeans that almost still fit, sunglasses pushing the hair off my forehead.

I have always loved the liminal space of airports, the soaring ceilings, the moving walkways, the visual white noise of people coming and going. More than anything, I love the moment that the plane leaves the ground and whatever was left behind is irretrievable.

T has his own seat for the first time. He clutches his Animal Muppet doll, which was given to his father by Animal himself during a music video shoot. He lets me hold his hand. Until this point in his life, he hasn't watched much TV, with the exception of Lady Gaga, and the Muppet Weezer video, but we have experimentally brought some Baby Einstein videos. Maybe our real problem is that we haven't yet tried the opiate of the toddler masses—the iPad.

I am wrong. The plane ride seems the length of a screening of *Shoah*, and about as fun. He only wails for a couple of hours, but for the remaining time he's just not *into* anything much yet, so entertaining him is a nonstop tap dance. And he couldn't care less about Baby Einstein. That's what you get for weaning your kid on Gaga—everything else pales.

There are some peaceful moments, mostly when he's gazing out the window.

Clouds, he says. Sky. Blue. Airplane.

When we finally arrive, Toronto is bathed in watery light, all shiny silver buildings and wide blue-gray sky. It feels modern and windblown and clean. From outside the venue, we can see the whole skyline across the harbor. Inside, there is a big playroom set up, with kids driving little pink electric Cadillacs around, pursued by nannies in baggy jeans and track shoes. All of the guys from Blink-182 are traveling with their families. When we get there, two of the sexy Blink rock wives nonchalantly lounge on a couch in the corner, heads inclined toward each other, nursing sparkling waters. None of the Weezer wives have showed up yet.

So it's just me and T, in the rock-life deep end, hanging out with a bunch of kids who are already reality TV stars at seven years old.

Everything goes great for about an hour. T toddles around, trying to get in on the action, knocking everything over and grabbing stuff as usual. The other kids are older and turn out to be nice kids, who tolerate him admirably, if occasionally nudging him aside. One of the girls even coos over Tariku, stacking blocks with him and calling him adorable. I hover a few feet from T as always, ready to prevent a shove or a right hook. I'm self-conscious in front of these beautiful, confident wives. They must think I'm neurotic, lurking by him. Why don't I just go sit down and gossip with them? They have no idea how much I wish I could.

Still photographers and one videographer float around the edges of the room. I'm not sure who they are—is someone making a documentary? A reality show? Are they press? Their presence adds exponentially to my discomfort.

I'm vigilant, constantly scanning the room, and still it's a complete mystery to me why T begins to cry. Nothing has happened; nothing has been taken from him; nothing has changed. His crying quickly escalates in pitch until he's in hysterics, face contorted, fat tears rolling down his cheeks. I pick him up and bring him over to one of the empty couches. I'm baffled. He isn't having a tantrum exactly, not angry or aggressive. I ask him what happened. I ask him if anything hurts. He has lost his words and only responds with more sobbing. I rock him. I pick him up and walk him around the hallways. Then I go outside and walk around the parking lot. I bring him in to listen to the sound check, hoping the sight of Daddy might cheer him up. I quickly take him away from the sound check when the crying doesn't abate. I try to feed him. I try to give him milk. I give him homeopathics. I bust out the Orajel and the Motrin. I bounce him. I sing to him. Concerned security guards bring us stuffed Toronto Blue Jays bears and glow-in-the-dark yo-yos.

After an hour of this, I finally ask for a van to take us back to the hotel. Still he screams like someone is prodding him with a hot poker. I'm beside myself, ready to tell the driver to take us to the nearest emergency room, when, for some reason, I think to take off his shoes. I discover that he has a toenail falling off, after a particularly nasty stub a few days ago. The edge of it got wedged wrong in his sandal. Essentially, his toenail was being ripped off. He stops crying almost immediately, looks up at me, and says, "Airplane," then falls off to sleep in my arms. I'm crestfallen. Why wouldn't he at least have pointed to his foot? Why didn't he indicate that he was in pain? Are his neural connections so haywire that he's unable to identify what's going on with his body? Or am I just blind to his needs? That night he sleeps better than he ever has, exhausted by his ordeal. The first night in a year that I could have actually gotten some sleep and not had to wake up with him five times, and I keep startling awake, consumed with worry.

The next day, we arrive in New York and I'm sure things are about to look up. Even if things get rough, I know this city. This used to be my city. We drive through the streets from JFK in the pouring rain, the tops of the buildings obscured with gray mist. I rest my head back against the seat, relieved to have finally arrived. If pressed, I'll admit that I prefer my garden and my house and my slow, sunshiny L.A. life, but the pace of the sidewalk here mirrors something inside me and New York will never stop feeling like home.

I keep whipping my head around, thinking I see people I recognize. This is a common experience for me in New York. Everyone is a doppelgänger of someone from my past.

We dig in for a weeklong stay at a hotel four blocks from Central Park. Scott gets picked up in a van to do some publicity and I'm left staring across the room at T.

"All right. This is the greatest city in the world. Where should we start?"

"Taxi!" T says.

"You're not gonna believe your luck, but there are funner things even than taxis here."

I strap him into the stroller I'm schlepping across the country and pretend that I'm a New York mom, unfazed by the prospect of somehow getting said stroller down and up the stairs, on and off the subway. This little game lends purpose to my step. I imagine the apartment we would live in. Are we Upper East Side socialites today? Or have we come from our brownstone in Spanish Harlem? Are we uptown visiting the museum from our loft in Bushwick? I can imagine being all of these women—what they might be wearing, where they shop for groceries. Later, we'll meet my parents at the Natural History Museum and I'll become boring old me, the girl who once lied and pretended I didn't know them. The girl who tried to step into a different skin and failed. Until then, I could be anyone.

I decide we'll walk to the park. The rain has blown over, though the humidity still hangs heavy and low over the streets. We pass the front of the Plaza Hotel. I remember when my parents took me to the Palm Court. It was around Christmas, I think, a Sunday afternoon. A bright gray winter light infused the room, filtering down from the wide atrium. We had been ice skating at Wollman Rink and my hair was slightly damp, smelled like sweat when I took off my hat. I loved New York so fiercely then.

Once we're in the park, Tariku points and gasps and howls with joy again and again.

Horsey!

Bus!

Taxi!

Airplane!

Also flowers, swing sets, boats, fountains, meadows, hot dogs, street musicians, break dancers, a sketchy-looking guy making giant bubbles with a rope contraption and a bucket of detergent. Tariku takes off his shoes and dances under the bubbles. I look around at the other mothers, who seem not to worry about the kids getting staph infections from running around barefoot in Central Park, so I choose to be similarly unconcerned.

Each of these park delights alone could fill an entire afternoon. My heart contracts, sending a rush of blood to my face. Of course. New York. How could I have settled for pacing in circles around a mall? How had I ever even considered living anywhere but here?

The morning sails by faster and more easily than any in recent memory. We go back to the hotel for his nap and, afterward, trek the twenty blocks back uptown to the Museum of Natural History, because I am still reluctant to negotiate the whole stroller-on-the-subway thing.

My parents make little jumping motions and wave their arms when they catch sight of us. They look smaller than I remember, like harmless older people now. Maybe they are actually shrinking or maybe they just tower over me less emotionally. Tariku lights up at the sight of them. They're sweet and well behaved, in spite of some characteristic fussing and grunting from my father at the ticket counter. In short order we all wind up inside, properly be-stickered.

I loose T from his stroller and he takes off running, of course. We follow as he blows past the exhibits of taxidermied animals, dusty and gruesome—all those animals still frozen in time since I last was there a million years ago. The dinosaur fossils are as magnificent as I remember.

"He should slow down," says my mother, her breathing slightly labored.

"Tell *him* that," I say.

Tariku runs and points and runs some more.

"Felephant! Tiger! Tiger says, *Roar!*"

When he roars, the whole room turns to look at us.

"There is no yelling," yells the guard. "And no running."

But we are already gone. We take in whole cultures, ecosystems, continents, in furiously fast glances.

While we walk, my mother asks about another baby.

"So?"

"I don't know. I just don't know."

"Don't know if you want one?"

"I know that I want one. I just don't know if I'm cut out for this."

"Oh, who's cut out for it?"

"But I am so exhausted."

"Oh, we're all exhausted. That's just living."

I almost tell her about the struggles we've been facing. I want to tell her what I'm learning about trauma, but I decide against it. I think of her reaction to my cocooning plan, and I'm sure she'll dismiss this trauma thing as just another of my silly hippie ideas. I can imagine her saying again, "You just need to show him who's boss."

I keep my mouth shut. Maybe I do this too often, opting just to stay silent rather than have a real discussion. Maybe I should give her more of a chance.

We take T to the ocean room. He looks up at the massive blue whale hanging from the ceiling and squeals with glee.

"Airplane!" he says.

~

The rest of the week in New York is tiring as usual, but it's also a reprieve from much of the judgment we usually experience. After T has had two epic tantrums, one in Rockefeller Center and one at the Coney Island stop on the F train, I realize that no one really cares if your kid is screaming bloody murder on a New York street. They glance over to make sure you're not strangling him or something, but they look away quickly. Here's another thing I learn about New Yorkers—they don't stare at a white mom walking around with a black kid. The anonymity is refreshing, a luxury we don't have in Los Angeles. How could the two cities be so different in this way?

This idyllic New York fantasy life ends abruptly when we again take to the road. The band is divided between two buses, and in these little rolling hotel rooms we traverse the country together. We watch documentaries and eat crap, while a bus driver with turquoise rings on every finger regales us with stories about how he drove Dylan on the Rolling Thunder tour. Scott sits in the passenger seat with Tariku on his lap, because T quiets down when he gets to look out the front windows. It's something like I always dreamed, our little circus family . . . except it's so hard I can't believe it.

I spend every minute of every festival date trying to keep Tariku from chewing on electrical wires or blindsiding the other kids with his fist or eating smooshed french fries out of the dirt or playing with used beer cups. I try to discourage his new habit of meeting teenage girls in shorts by pointing out airplanes, then lunging to bite their thighs. I wear him in his carrier and walk in circle after circle, in spite of his impressive heft. He has no time for toys. He's interested only in conquering the world. Every time I let his feet touch the ground, he pursues this goal in earnest, stomping everything and everyone in his path, as if he's Godzilla and the world in front of him is Tokyo.

In Cleveland we meet up with Scott's parents and go to the Rock and Roll Hall of Fame. I expect it to be cheesy, but it's actually great, with room after room of fantastic costumes and intriguing memorabilia. There is even a huge lit-up Weezer "W" sign hanging over the gift shop, famous for its appearance in their videos and live stage shows.

Tariku runs through the place, as usual, and dances to the music. A small pack of security guards begins following us from room to room. The guards' efforts are not in vain. When we reach the room with John Lennon's piano, Tariku turns on a dime, runs under the red velvet rope, climbs onto the platform, and wildly begins to play, banging away with abandon. Scott and I see it happening, but not fast enough. I dive under the rope and pry his little fingers off the ivories, throwing him over my shoulder in a fireman's carry as he screams. He sinks his teeth into my back, but I keep walking. I hardly feel the bites anymore. Scott positions him-self between us and the approaching swarm of security guards, who both yell at us and into their walkie-talkies for reinforcements.

"We're leaving, okay?" he explains, hands out in front of him. "Just calm down. We're leaving."

We exit, in front of an escort of dour-faced guards, with T still slung over my shoulder. Scott's parents follow behind, in a confused haze. Eighty-sixed, our little procession plods right under the Wee-zer sign.

"Good thing we got a picture of it on the way in," I say.

Scott takes his parents out for dinner that night and T and I stay home in the hotel room, while T hollers to go out and I pretty much lie on the floor in a stupor. While *The Muppet Show* plays on repeat in the background, I look up at the cottage cheese ceiling, feeling like I have a hundred-pound weight on my chest.

I am no Gwyneth Paltrow after all, I guess. I just want to be home. I don't want any more public meltdowns. I don't want any more pictures of us. I want to slide quietly into invisibility.

~

For the rest of the tour, I face into the wind and keep my head down and decide that my entire mission in life is just to keep Tariku alive and healthy until we can get home. It's a game of survival.

T wakes earlier and earlier, as we peel back the time zones, winding our way through the country, back to the west coast. He has figured out how to pull the curtain on his bunk and climb out, and I'm preternaturally attuned to the sounds, afraid that he'll wake one of the band members, who badly need their sleep. Somewhere outside of Denver, I hear the sound of the rings on the brass curtain rod and turn over to find him looking at me. I blearily bundle both of us off to the lounge at the back of the bus.

I'm unsure of what time it is, other than pretty fucking early. I lift the shades to a brightening sky smudged with clouds the color of Creamsicles and a full moon hanging over a little white farm-house. Green and gold fields of sunflowers turn their expectant faces to the horizon. This kind of sunrise is a gift to baristas, farm-ers, insomniacs, and mothers.

I had a good dream last night. My grandmother showed up to tell me what my secret powers are. I can't remember them, though. I'm left with a feeling of loss, and a hope that I'll dream it again someday and will finally know. Whatever my powers are, I could sure use them now. This is not the tour life as I loved it before—a meditative drift through the world. This is confinement and chaos and all of our messiest bits on the most public display. And yet, there are these moments of something bordering on understand-ing, on acceptance. I'm not quite there yet, but I can feel the possi-bility hovering.

We pass a red barn, like something out of a pastoral painting, and on the side, for no discernible reason, is painted *August 16*. My birthday. It feels like a signal, a nod. This is not a dream. I'm not in the wrong place after all.

Chapter 20

IN a one-bedroom apartment in West Orange, New Jersey, late winter 1973, my mother, Helene, is home in the middle of the day, dancing to the *Hair* soundtrack while cleaning the house, when she gets a call from an old college friend named Jillian. Jillian married a fertility specialist after graduation and lives in Chicago now. My mother called her years before, seeking advice. Helene is on a list for a study in experimental fertility drugs, but the process seems to be dragging on forever. After nearly four years of trying to conceive, her diagnosis is unexplained infertility.

Jillian says, "Look, Helene, I don't know if you've considered this yet. I don't want to overstep my bounds, but we have some friends who just used this lawyer out here to adopt a healthy white baby and it was fast and relatively painless. I just saw them at temple and that baby is so cute and I thought of you. I got the lawyer's name, in case you're interested."

My mother prepares a special dinner that night. She's been doing that a lot lately to cheer my father up, since the stock market has been lousy and he's been coming home dejected, dissatisfied, looking like a trapped animal. She doesn't bring up the lawyer until after dessert. He is surprisingly amenable to the idea. Sure, what the hell. Let's adopt a baby. We want a family, right? What's the difference how you get one?

There are the interviews and the paperwork and the planning. My mother is good at this; she's meticulous and organized and likes to color-code and label. It gives her something to take her mind off the wait.

My parents finally receive the call. Your daughter has been born. They board a flight to Chicago. The lawyer hands my mother the baby, sweet and perfect and pink, in the waiting room of the hospital. It's a closed adoption, meaning that the records will be permanently sealed, my birth mother Sherri's name expunged from any documents as if she never existed.

They fly home from Chicago and the stewardess offers my mother a bassinet but she declines. She doesn't want to put the baby down. Ever. She never will put this little girl down.

I'm a pretty baby, with steady brown eyes that are melancholy from the get-go. When my mother walks through town with me, she's instantly the most blessed and shining of things: a new mother. In 1973, the birth mother in an adoption agreement legally has six months to change her mind and reverse the adoption. Every single time the phone rings, my mother's stomach drops and she has a sense of vertigo on her way to the phone, as if, on the other side of the kitchen wall with the tiny blue flower wallpaper, there is a precipice. If, by chance, it is the lawyer's voice on the other end (there are little things he has to call her about now and then) her mouth becomes immediately parched and her hands tremble.

My mother keeps a suitcase packed and hidden away in the back of the closet. In it are a couple of changes of clothes for herself and for me, diapers and bottles and formula, travel toiletries, and five thousand dollars in cash. If the call ever comes informing her that she has to give me back, she's taking me to Mexico. This nice, accommodating, middle-class woman would rather be a fugitive in exile than give me up.

It is a grand and powerful thing, the love my mother has for me. And yet. It has its limits.

~

Scott and I face my parents across the office of a highly recommended New York therapist, decorated with the requisite leather chairs, potted plants, erudite books, and tasteful paintings. My mother's hand shakes as she lifts a glass of water from a Moroccan end table, inlaid with mother of pearl.

I've brought them here to tell them about my memoir. I've made a list of every single point in the book, both related to them and not, and my plan is to run through them in a safe and neutral space, with a mediator present. Two hours have gone by and I'm near the end of the list. It's been abysmal.

"Why can't you just get over this stuff?" they ask, again and again.

"I think it's really sad that you can't shut the door on the past," says my father. "You dwell. You're obsessed."

"I'm not obsessed. I'm a writer."

Which is not strictly true. I am also an obsessive dweller, of course. That's why I'm a memoirist. My past is the vein of gold that I mine every day when I sit down to work. It's just not true in the sense that he means it. It doesn't indicate the emotional reality in my present life. It's not like I sit around angry at my parents all day long. Just when they vote Republican.

"We give and give and give and all you have ever done is take. I don't see any love from you. Any caring," he says.

"Wait, wait," says the therapist. "You're misunderstanding. There is a lot of love for you in the book."

I tell my father about a passage in the book in which I fondly recall going with him to buy cinnamon doughnuts in the early morning, during our yearly trips to the Jersey Shore. It was something we'd do just the two of us, when the rest of the world was still asleep.

"After everything," says my father, deeply hurt, stammering, quietly now. "After everything, the doughnuts are what you remember?"

"The doughnuts," I say, "weren't doughnuts. The doughnuts were you and me."

I'm asking the impossible—for a crushed and enraged man to understand a metaphor.

Months of negotiating and wheedling and cajoling and threatening and crying follow the therapy session. When none of that works, my parents disown me, emotionally holing themselves up in a storm cellar until this whole book thing passes them by.

"I cannot deal with this," says my mother in a sort of hysterical wheeze, during our final conversation.

It's nap time and I'm lying on my living room floor in a bra and a pair of sweat shorts that say *Hanalei Bay* across the butt, a relic from the Kauai honeymoon that seems a thousand years ago. Her phone call catches me in the middle of changing clothes.

"You have always been so ungrateful. I need time away from you. I do not want to hear from you anymore."

Like Chava, the daughter of the Jewish patriarch, Tevye, in my father's beloved musical *Fiddler on the Roof*, I committed a sin that caused my family to respond by killing me off, in spirit at least. By writing a book that portrayed the clan as less than perfect, suffering from the same dysfunctions, violence, addictions as our neighbors, I perpetrated an unforgivable betrayal, not just of my parents but also of the entire community. When my mother tells me that they have taken down my pictures, rewritten the will, want no further contact with me, I think of Tevye's famous debates with himself, repeated over and over again throughout the course of *Fiddler*, like a mantra. *On the other hand . . . On the other hand . . .* Ending, finally, tragically, with his rejection of Chava for marrying out of the tribe. *NO. There is no other hand.*

I hang up the phone and imagine my father, like Tevye, going back and forth between his love for me (*Little bird, little Chaveleh . . .*)

and the deep hurt I have caused him, and siding, eventually, with the hurt.

Write a book about an unsavory past, about an imperfect family?

NO. There is no other hand.

I don't argue. I don't protest. I'm grateful to put the phone down. The silence that follows has a new sort of texture to it—this silence in which I no longer have parents. I'm sad and have a hollow sickness in my gut, yes, but I'm also relieved. An enormous burden immediately lifts when I realize that I will have a reprieve from hearing myself described as ungrateful no matter how many times I say thank you.

Just how grateful are we supposed to be to our parents exactly? Grateful enough to never pursue our own dreams? Grateful enough not to tell our own stories?

"He is so *lucky!*" is one of the most irritating things that people say to me about Tariku. I get it at least once a day.

This "lucky" is laden with multiple shades of meaning. It's meant to be congratulatory to Scott and me. He is lucky because we're so very benevolent, because we're so very generous. Oh, and also because he's not dying from malaria in a developing country. Lucky little guy. The implication always seems to be that he's indebted to us, that he owes us some sort of obeisance. Gratitude isn't as simple as it sounds.

When I was a kid, my father used to say to me (usually when I was tearfully begging for a pair of Jordache jeans or a Joan Jett cassette tape), "I cried when I had no shoes, until I saw the man who had no feet."

"Why should I stop crying because of some poor footless schmuck? What kind of shitty way is that to think? I should cry harder."

"Ach. Do-gooder." This was meant as a sort of insult, as if having a bleeding heart made you a fool.

If I argued cleverly enough, sometimes I'd get the jeans. Not because he agreed with me, but because my dad liked a good debate.

When people tell us how lucky T is, we say, *"We're* lucky." It is both a memorized response and the absolute truth.

There was a time my parents felt truly lucky, too. Now, they have assured me of radio silence. It's not an idle threat. They'll stick to their guns. As I lie with the now-quiet phone next to me, my feeling is twofold. First, how sad it is that my parents and I never manage to meet emotionally. It's not for lack of trying on either of our parts. I do love my parents. If they never talk to me another day in my life, still I would not trade them. But I also feel relieved to stop living in a story in which I am different, selfish, troubled, and, above all, ungrateful.

My arm and shoulder ache from carrying my toddler around. My head is full of too much hot and heavy static. I go stand blankly in front of the fridge, as if the answer is inside a frozen York Peppermint Pattie. I stick a piece of cheese in the mayo and shove it in my mouth, like my father in so many ways, including our fondness for stuffing our emotions by shoveling food down our gullets.

Grunting and rustling come from the baby monitor. I forgot about the monitor for a minute, while I was being flattened by this latest emotional steamroller. Usually I have the monitor volume turned way, way up, so that T's breathing creates a rhythmic soundtrack for whatever else I'm doing. Panic washes over me. I stopped paying attention to it for a heartbeat. What if he stopped breathing—I wouldn't even have heard. I know that this is not exactly the healthiest of behavior—my running fixation with every possible horrible thing that could go wrong with him—but I can't help myself. Scott has suggested I see a therapist about this ghoulish brain chatter, but I haven't done it yet. No time, I tell him. Maybe I am wary of letting it go. This is my equivalent of the suitcase my mother kept in the closet when I was an infant. The anxiety that is also a badge of honor in some ways. See—I have a love so profound it is driving me crazy. I run in to pick him up out of the crib and cling to him for dear life, like some deranged mother from a Philip Roth novel. He hangs on me like a little monkey for a heartbeat, before squirming, demanding to stand on his own two feet, ready to greet the remainder of the day at 120 mph, as he always does.

T and I go to the Long Beach aquarium that afternoon. It's soothing for him. He likes to watch the octopus, the penguins, especially the sharks. I follow him as he runs from tank to tank, shafts of sunlight hitting the water and shattering into a wavy grid. I'm so attuned to the edges of his little form, so hawkeyed and intent on not losing sight of him, that my own edges are almost nonexistent.

I wonder if this is the fate of mothers: to dissolve ourselves into the needs of others. Is this why my own mother is so furious? Somewhere deep inside are we moms inevitably keeping tabs, expecting payback for our sacrifices?

When I'm out in public with T, I don't just have to watch him to make sure he's not escaping; I must also be within range of intercepting the surprise right hook he could throw at any moment, for the most invisible of offenses. I watch the other mothers with envy and a measure of self-pity. How come they get to sit there and drink an iced tea and chat with a friend while their kid happily plays in the fountain? There's no iced tea for me, just constant vigilance.

Scott and I have been going for regular counseling and parenting classes at the Echo Center and it has at least given us some language to talk about what's going on with T. The problem is, it doesn't seem to be changing anything. Much like the cocooning, many things about the philosophy are helpful, even essential, but it's not a panacea. The Echo Center is a good start, but it's becoming clear that we have to look further and pursue more specialized help.

I have the same thought at least five times a day—I wonder if I should quit working. Would his behavior be less extreme if I quit any pretense of writing and threw myself, every minute of my every day, into being with T? Nearly every night, I talk to Scott about putting my writing on hold for a while. A year, two years. True, I have a book coming out, but that can be the last for a while. I can go back to writing someday.

"Why do you keep bringing this up?" he says. "It's not just that you shouldn't quit; you *can't* quit. You are psychically incapable of stopping."

He is probably right. I write and it draws a thick black line around all of these dissolving, hazy edges; it delineates me. Then the day with Tariku begins the process of eroding that line again. And so we continue.

I know what's the best choice for me, but I am honestly not sure what's the best choice for him. How is a mother ever supposed to know that?

In front of us, a mom yanks her whining little girl by the arm too hard. The girl drops to the ground screaming. With an embarrassed tuck of her hair, the woman leans down toward the girl, speaks in her ear, sets her on her feet again, and they continue on toward the turtle tank, both looking a little weary. Her palm lingers behind the girl's blond curls with tenderness; I can feel the apology in her hand. It never ends, the stuff to be sorry for.

Chapter 21

My memoir about the harem is released and everyone I know finds out everything, all at once. I am on *The View* and *Howard Stern* and *Good Morning America* and there's not a neighbor or a mother in Gymboree or a barista at the local coffee shop who doesn't comment on it to me. I feared I'd be embarrassed but instead it's a relief. After I walked around for years with my insides sorted into compartments, now everything is in one box with an open lid.

Most people just think it's neat that I wrote a book, even if it is kind of a slutty book. Or at least to my face they do. My Christian friends see it as a redemption narrative and my feminist friends see it as a stand against shame. Hundreds of women across the country write me supportive e-mails and tell me that this is, in spirit at least, their story, too, and they are grateful I told it. From strangers, the love pours in. From my parents, nothing.

The slut-shamers come out of their holes. Or rather stay in their holes, typing away in the darkness. The hateful e-mails and comments inform the darkness: "You should be ashamed of yourself." "You are a talentless opportunistic whore and this book proves that you always will be." "Social services should come and take away that child, you fat, middle-aged skank."

It's easy to summon my feminist ire about most of the comments, but the attacks on me as a mother are harder to weather. This coincides with Tariku's starting preschool, so I'm particularly tender, on the brink of a huge transition. The tricky thing about shitty Internet comments is that they always echo the demons that live in your own head.

T is now two and a half. The night before his first day of school, I dress him in his rocket ship jammies and we cuddle in the bed watching *Dinosaur Train* while Scott putters around the house, finishing the last of the chores. Tariku puts his arms around my neck and squeezes, pressing his silky cheek to mine. He pulls back and gives me that incredible smile that pours liquid sunshine into any room.

He says, "Mama, I love you."

Then he winds up like Mike Tyson, stealthily enough that I don't even have time to react, and socks me in the nose. Hard. I leap backward, stumbling off the bed. I hold my face protectively, eyes tearing, and go to the bathroom to see the damage. There is none. Except that I look worn and bloated and a hundred years older than I did a year ago. My eyes water and keep watering. I walk back in and he begins to cry when he sees me.

"Mama, what happened?"

This is the dance lately, and I can't find the switch to turn off the music. We're either unbearably sweet and snuggly or in an all-out war, and there's very little rhyme or reason to it. Tariku insists on repeatedly doing every dangerous thing I tell him not to do, including dashing out into the middle of bike paths and parking lots. Yesterday at the beach, he responded to my entreaty not to touch anything in the public bathrooms by licking the wall. After much debate and an extensive polling of both friends and our parenting counselor, Scott and I have decided that preschool might actually be a great socializing influence for him. Maybe he'll behave differently in a new environment. The director runs this preschool out of her home. Her mother makes the kids organic snacks and they eat them under a pomegranate tree in the yard. I hope T will learn to feel safe there. They're gentle. They sing little anachronistic songs about blacksmiths and stuff. Scott thinks the place looks awesome. Honestly, I'm scared shitless.

~

The next morning, dressed in a rainbow-striped hoodie, tiny cargo pants, and blue soft-soled shoes with airplanes on them, Tariku takes my hand and we head off to his first day of school. Scott is working in the studio all day, and he waves good-bye from the porch, camera in hand. So far, so good.

It really is an adorable school. I loved the tour. The owner is named Wacera and she is a dulcet-voiced woman with a loose Afro that always looks gilded by the sun behind her. She wears long skirts and aprons that look like something out of a pioneer novel. The school is essentially her backyard. I anticipate Tariku will like the hominess and smallness of it.

Wacera and I have spent what seems like about twenty hours discussing possible "trajectories" for Tariku at the school. They have surely let people spy for the CIA with less scrutiny. She understands his challenges and seems unruffled and hopeful. She is aware of trauma-informed care and assures me that she's committed to Tariku and is touched by his story. She says that he should come every day for three hours a day and that I'll have to attend school with him until he learns to "contract when the group contracts," which I think in hippie language means sit still for snack and story time.

It does not take a child development specialist to see that T is more of an expander than a contractor. Still, I am hoping that he will take to it and I won't have to attend with him for too long. I'm dying to start having some regular time to myself that doesn't require paying a nanny.

Tariku and I walk through the creaky wooden gate to a yard

where everything, down to the hay bales, is dripping with farmy charm. T is deeply excited about starting school. In spite of his impulse control problems, he loves being around other children. He opens his mouth wide and puts his hands in the air in a victory pose as we walk in the gate.

"School!" he says, triumphantly. "Yes!"

For the next three hours, I hover awkwardly, not sure what my role is. Am I supposed to jump in when there's conflict? Am I meant to participate in the circle dances and gallop like a horse and all that? Or am I meant to lurk invisibly at the borders of his experience, there for emergencies only? I decide to hang back as much as possible, wait for a cue from the teacher.

This is how the morning goes . . . Tariku wants every toy that everyone else has. He cannot—I mean, cannot—sit still on his pillow for story time. He won't eat at snack time. Instead, he crawls under the table and won't come out. It's the longest three hours of my life. I imagine that preschool would be kind of boring under the best of circumstances, but this is unbearable. I'd rather be at an insurance seminar.

I try to be enlightenedly hands-off. Until I get an unmistakable stink eye from one of the teachers and then I get very hands-on. The whole time I'm watching the other children sit still with napkins in their laps and wondering, Is it me? Is it him? What's wrong with us?

We go home scattered and a bit in shock.

The third day of school, I have to pull a thrashing Tariku off a boy who takes a truck from him. When T learns he will not be getting this truck back, I grimly, jaw set, physically restrain him on an itchy bale of hay for a full twenty minutes. I talk to him quietly, trying to calm him.

"I see that you're sad and angry about that truck," I say. "But we don't hurt other people's bodies. You have to calm down before I let you go because I'm here to keep you safe."

A few members of the school staff are African American. As I hunch there with T in a dusty corner—goose bumps rising on my arms, a lump in my throat that feels like a tennis ball—I become hyperconscious of my tattoos, of the different color of my skin against my son's. I'm some member of the Hell's Angels who has kidnapped a poor orphaned black child and am ritually abusing him in public.

When later we get the call from Wacera, in which she gently tells me this school isn't the right fit for our family, Auntie Jo has T out at the park. I tell Scott. He sits on the edge of the bed with his head in his hands and begins to ask for help, almost like an incantation.

"I need help, man," he says. "I need a class. I need a book. I need a meeting.

"I need Jesus. I need Fred Rogers. I need Tony Soprano. I need Marlon Brando. Listen.

"I'm just trying to say to you. I need help, man. We need help."

~ Chapter 22

DURING one of T's naps, Auntie Jo climbs the stairs and knocks gently on the doorjamb.

"Can I come in?"

"Sure."

"Actually, can you come out? Suzanne is downstairs."

Both Suzanne and Jo know my work time is precious, so I know that something must be serious if they're calling me down for a conference.

Twenty years and twenty pounds ago I never would have believed it possible, that we'd be here tiptoeing past my baby's room. Or that I'd be wearing glasses and threadbare velour sweatpants, while the smell of my orange juice olive oil cake (it's better than it sounds) wafts into the living room. How strange, these ten thousand miles of road behind us. I know the look on my friend's face and I know what's coming is not good.

Suzanne is perched on the edge of our couch, one hand on each knee, as if braced to do something unpleasant. She looks determined and unhappy, always a terrible combination.

Jo sits next to Suzanne on the couch, with her hands in her lap.

"Suzanne and I have been talking," says Jo. "T hit Violet again today."

"T hits Violet every day," says Suzanne. "He doesn't mean to hurt her. He's a love. I know he is. He goes in to hug her, but then she doesn't hug him back enough or who knows what the problem is, but he clocks her. It's just not always possible to get in between them. I'm afraid he's going to accidentally take one of the twins' eyes out. I have got to keep my kids safe. This has got to be the last time."

"Okay," I start, flummoxed, "I've been reading books and we're going to counseling and—"

"It's not enough," says Jo. "T is getting stronger every day. Someone could really get hurt now. One shove the wrong way? Suzanne and I have decided that we're going to keep the kids apart for a while."

I feel nauseated. I fear their judgment, but mine is worse: if I were just around more, if I didn't have a babysitter, if I never yelled at him, if, if, if . . . Tears prick my eyes. Did I think that motherhood was going to make me feel a part of something? It has done exactly the opposite. I'm more isolated than I've ever been.

"Don't worry," says Suzanne. "This isn't going to last forever."

"That's how it feels," I say. "It feels exactly like it's going to last forever."

"Why don't you call Eastern L.A. Regional Center, where they can assess him and see if he qualifies for early intervention?"

"What does that mean?" I ask.

"Free therapy. There's no reason not to do it. Just do it."

I have done enough research to have a rough sense of T's situation. I'm sure he is not autistic. I suspect that he fits what's called "insecure attachment." This is what a combination of Ruth Beaglehole and our pediatrician and mom bloggers and Google has led me to believe.

Attachment challenges—reactive attachment disorder, in particular—are scary things for me to Google. This is what all the coded talk about violent Russian adoptees is about. Reactive attachment disorder is the stuff of horror movies about bad seeds and demonic toddlers.

The name alone sounds like an indictment: attachment disorder. An indictment of him, of us, of adoption itself. Because if he isn't attaching perfectly and immediately, is it because there's some love lacking? Are you something less than a "real" family? Are you simply not quite as good as the sweet family next door with the adorable, well-behaved, pony-obsessed, princess-dress-wearing little girl?

In a culture obsessed with the orphan narrative (see: every Disney movie since the beginning of time) there really is only one possible correct outcome: happily ever after. Orphan narratives let us know that even when you have a hard-knock life, the sun will come out tomorrow. Kabam. Just like that.

From what I'm reading, attachment challenges are the perfect opposite. They're hard to identify and can be treated only through a patient, long-term commitment to trauma-informed parenting. It's a slow thing. No quick and satisfying happy ending about it.

I read and reread the Helpguide.org website. As listed there, here are some things that can cause attachment challenges:

- A baby cries and no one responds or offers comfort.
- A baby is hungry or wet, and isn't attended to for hours.
- No one looks at, talks to, or smiles at the baby, so the baby feels alone.
- A young child gets attention only by acting out or displaying other extreme behaviors.
- A young child or baby is mistreated or abused.
- Sometimes the child's needs are met and sometimes they aren't. The child never knows what to expect.
- The infant or young child is hospitalized or separated from his or her parents.

- A baby or young child is moved from one careg
  another (can be the result of adoption, foster c
  loss of a parent).
- The parent is emotionally unavailable because of depression, an illness, or a substance abuse problem.

Tariku was in an orphanage in a developing country. Many of these conditions apply.

From the same source, here are some signs and symptoms of insecure attachment in an infant:

- Avoids eye contact
- Doesn't smile
- Doesn't reach out to be picked up
- Rejects your efforts to calm, soothe, and connect
- Doesn't seem to notice or care when you leave him or her alone
- Cries inconsolably
- Doesn't coo or make sounds
- Doesn't follow you with his or her eyes
- Isn't interested in playing interactive games or playing with toys
- Spends a lot of time rocking or comforting him- or herself

And here are the listed signs and symptoms of reactive attach-ment disorder, an extreme manifestation of insecure attachment:

- **An aversion to touch and physical affection.** Children with reactive attachment disorder often flinch, laugh, or even say "Ouch" when touched. Rather than producing positive feelings, touch and affection are perceived as a threat.
- **Control issues.** Most children with reactive attachment

disorder go to great lengths to remain in control and avoid feeling helpless. They are often disobedient, defiant, and argumentative.

- **Anger problems.** Anger may be expressed directly, in tantrums or acting out, or through manipulative, passive-aggressive behavior. Children with reactive attachment disorder may hide their anger in socially acceptable actions, like giving a high-five that hurts or hugging someone too hard.
- **Difficulty showing genuine care and affection.** For example, children with reactive attachment disorder may act inappropriately affectionate with strangers while displaying little or no affection toward their parents.
- **An underdeveloped conscience.** Children with reactive attachment disorder may act like they don't have a conscience and fail to show guilt, regret, or remorse after behaving badly.

Yes, no, yes, no . . . I don't know. Read anything long enough and you'll find reasons it applies and reasons it doesn't. It's like the classic problem of the med student self-diagnosing every rare illness she comes across in her studies. I try to sift through my feelings and fears, try to separate reality from being reactionary.

I would say that we're definitely living in a world of control issues and anger problems and hugs that are too hard and high-fives that hurt. But Tariku is also an affectionate child who does display a conscience.

I hunker down and call the Regional Center, ready to wade through the chest-high bureaucracy. It isn't half as bad as I feared. A cheerful (yes, cheerful!) and helpful (really! helpful!) voice answers the phone and takes our information.

And she seems genuinely interested. She is makes those active-listening noises: oohs and mm-hms and that-sounds-hards.

From the next room I hear a conversation between T and Scott, who are heading outside to walk the dogs.

"Do you want to wear your black shoes or your Brobee shoes?"

"Brobee shoes!"

"Okay, great. Let's put on your Brobee shoes."

A high-pitched scream that fades to an extended whine: "*Noooooooo!!* Noooooooooooooo Brobeeeeeee shooooooooooes."

"Please," I say to the woman, "will you help us?"

The paperwork arrives in the mail the next day and I spend hours with it, send it back, and, to my surprise, we have appointments for our first assessment within the month. We decide to put off preschool for another six months before we try again. Maybe he's just too young. I go back to leaning on Jo and writing for a few hours in the morning—struggling to put down scraps of thought, form complete sentences, string paragraphs together. I fall in love with working in my neighborhood coffee shop and learn to appreciate the white noise of public spaces. Working in public also assures that I won't just cry the whole time or fall asleep.

When the assessment dates come, we ferry T around to child psychologists and occupational therapists and speech pathologists. I stand by while he points at pictures and stacks blocks and does basic physical tasks, like standing on one leg and touching his nose. He answers questions about pictures of a boy pulling a wagon, a girl playing baseball, a dog with a bone. Which one of these things is not like the other?

I'm torn again. On the one hand, I want them to find something, to tell me that something specific is wrong and to give me something to *do* about it. But I'm also illogically angry at the therapists for daring to evaluate him. I want to jump in and fix it every time he gets something wrong and feels frustrated.

Two weeks later we get a call telling us that we've been rejected, mostly because he's aging out of the program in a few months but also because he's too smart.

"He's exceptionally intelligent," the woman tells us, with a hint of criticism in her voice, as if she thinks I've been trying to get one over on her. "He's three and his cognitive processing is that of a *five*-year-old, Mrs. Shriner. You should have him tested for being gifted."

I never realized how off-the-charts smart he is, because I never had anyone to compare him to. Also, it hasn't been my primary concern.

"What about developmentally? What about emotionally?" I say.

"He is significantly delayed."

"What does that mean?"

"It means you can wait another year and apply for an IEP, when he's ready for public school."

Great. He's a gifted child with significant emotional delays. He wants everything in the world and he wants it now. He has the psychological profile of Lex Luthor.

We pursue more testing on our own. A highly recommended pediatric neurologist suggests a whole new battery of tests. We wait around in a posh Santa Monica office, the walls covered with black-and-white photographs of babies and pregnant mothers—the beautiful curves of bellies, the universal irresistibility of tiny feet. Looking at the photos, I feel like I used to when I was on heroin and looking into other people's picture windows, into their well-lit lives. What is it like, this black-and-white, sweet, cuddly world? I thought that by adopting, I was escaping the endless grind of doctors' offices. Here I am right back again.

The doctor is thirty minutes late and by the time she arrives, Tariku is climbing the walls of the reception area. He likes to dart behind counters and hide. He likes to run through open doors. He doesn't listen to me at all. Suzanne says it's mostly my fault; she could get him to listen. She thinks I'm crazy for not giving him time-outs. "No random consequences" is one of the more controversial aspects of the nonviolent parenting we've been studying at the Echo Center. No time-outs, no threats, no bribes, no punishment, no praise. This last one is the hardest. I simply find it impossible and after a while I stop trying. I do at least focus on praising his efforts rather than his results. We are still on board with no time-outs. I think. Honestly, I don't really know anymore. I'm not sure we know anything.

We go into the doctor's office and Scott and I sit across the room on a couch and watch T answer questions across a low table. Tariku stacks blocks to look like hers and when he gets tripped up, he throws them. I sit motionless, telling myself to allow it all. She has to see his challenging behaviors to get a picture of what our life is like. When a block flies my way, I duck.

At the end of a few sessions of this, we have a long, involved conversation with the doctor, who genuinely seems to like Tariku and confirms what the other assessment stated—basically, he's really smart and a total pain.

I ask about attachment disorders.

"Attachment challenges are useful to keep in mind," she says. "I'd be more comfortable saying he has trauma-related behaviors. More specifically, he also has something called sensory processing disorder and it would be useful to him to get into occupational therapy right away. It's a really common situation for children who suffered early childhood trauma. I'm going to write you a prescription. On the prescription, I'm not going to write SPD; I'm going to write PDD, pervasive developmental disorder, not otherwise specified. This is the most innocuous thing I can write, and it's something that can go away, so it won't necessarily follow him around for the rest of his life."

My mind reels. What is sensory processing disorder? What is . . . the other thing she said, whatever it was? I've never even heard of these things. I shudder at diagnosing him at all at this point, worried that it will go into some database and never disappear and someday when he's looking for a job or running for Congress, they'll find it and his whole world will crumble, because I didn't have the foresight to prevent it. But then again, he needs help. Help is expensive. When you need help badly enough, they have you by the balls. We already pay exorbitant amounts of money for medical insurance. Why shouldn't we use it? I decide to accept the prescription, accept the diagnosis, to some extent anyway.

I never know what to think about diagnoses. Doctors have been wrong in the past and they will be wrong again. Our culture is eager to slap a label on a set of symptoms and mistake that for true understanding of an individual child. The medical establishment is even more eager to provide the medication that corresponds to the label. But at this point, if a label gives me access to help for Tariku, I'm willing to accept it, at least for a while.

Sensory processing disorder. Another set of symptoms. Another difficult-to-understand diagnosis. More nights in front of the computer. Another stack of books to plow through. Basically, it means that his nervous system is confused, unable to accept messages from the senses and organize them into appropriate motor and behavioral responses. The Sensory Processing Disorder Foundation website says:

> A person with SPD finds it difficult to process and act upon information received through the senses, which creates challenges in performing countless everyday tasks. Motor clumsiness, behavioral problems, anxiety, depression, school failure, and other impacts may result if the disorder is not treated effectively.

From all the sources we consult, we learn that SPD is best treated through occupational therapy, and we set out in earnest to find a good therapist. It turns out there is a highly recommended OT center that is both covered by our insurance and right down the street. There are yet more assessments, but just as I am feeling hopelessly frustrated with all the testing, wondering when someone is going to stop testing and start helping us already, his therapy starts. The OT center is basically a little gym, with mats covering the floor, colorful exercise balls, and an elaborate climbing structure. The therapist assigned to us is kind and patient. She has Tariku swing on swings and bounce on the balls. She makes little "social stories" with him, which amount to multicolored laminated books about his responses to different stressful situations. She carefully letters them with a Sharpie.

> Hi, my name is Tariku Shriner!
> I love to play and have fun.
> I'm usually happy and love to play with everyone, but . . .
> Sometimes I can get angry or frustrated.
> When I feel like this I might try to bite or hit someone.
> Hitting and biting will hurt others. When people are hurt they feel sad.
> Hitting and biting are NOT okay. Hitting and biting HURT.
> Things I can do when I get angry or frustrated are:
>   1. Taking deep breaths.
>   2. Taking a walk!
>   3. Taking a break!
> If I don't hit or bite people, they will want to share and play with me!
> If I don't hit or bite, I can feel proud!

He loves to read them over and over.

I don't really see a difference in his behavior, but I figure these things take time. The real problem is that there's a conflict in philosophies. When Tariku misbehaves, she puts him in time-out and turns her back to him. I continue to talk to her about it and she continues to disagree with me.

"We simply think that in the long term, it's better for him if we give him time-ins," I say.

She rolls her eyes. "Time-whats?"

I continue, "I don't want to take a child traumatized by separation and turn my back on him. It's withdrawing love as punishment and we don't do it, so I think you and I should try to be consistent. We always sit with him when he's taking a break."

"Well, then, I need you to give me a better suggestion. And please don't say time-in again, because I have no idea what that means. That's just rewarding him with affection for his bad behavior."

She's right that I don't really have a better suggestion. I base all my arguments on the fact that it will benefit our relationship, and Tariku as a human, in the long run if we try to identify the need behind the behavior and give him words for it. Shower the people you love with love. Hug it out. Her attitude toward me goes from eye rolling to deep sighs of frustration in a matter of weeks. I cannot give her a good answer about how to control his behavior in the moment. I tell her that we aren't focused on control but rather empathy.

Though anger flashes behind her eyes when he is being particularly unruly and she feels her hands are tied, basically, she truly seems to like him and we reach a kind of grudging accord. She doesn't give him time-outs, but she does use rewards—mostly in the form of time playing with his favorite light-up airplane toy—as an incentive and she takes the same toy away as a consequence. I don't really see a problem with it, witnessing it in action. But just when we see the first hints of progress, we watch her belly grow and then she's gone, with no projected return date.

Her replacement doesn't carry the same love for Tariku.

When people don't like my son, I understand those cartoons with the steam coming out of characters' ears. My head feels light and my hands go tingly. I want to actually hurt people who don't understand him, who think he's just a bad kid. The lack of impulse control and aggressive behavior in my son are treatable, healable. I know this in my bones. This particular OT does not seem to agree. One afternoon too many, Tariku baffles her, refuses to come off the monkey bars. When she pulls him off, he melts down, honey badger style, and bites her. He doesn't respond to her weighted blankets or her brushing of his skin with a special brush in an attempt to calm him. These things are standard treatments for SPD, but they are inexplicably ineffective for T.

"I think we should end early today," she tells me.

She calls me later and tells me he has graduated. She will send his diploma in the mail. I'm blindsided and confused.

"His *diploma?*"

"His diploma. Congratulations. Thanks a lot. Good-bye."

"Wait, how can you graduate him? From what? I don't understand."

"His fine motor skills are much better. They're in the average range now. You'll see it in my report."

"Wait, we weren't here about his fine motor skills. What about his SPD? What about his aggression? Those aren't better."

"That's because he doesn't have SPD. He didn't respond to the heavy work or the pressure or the brushing or any of the therapies I use to treat it."

"So he therefore doesn't have it? Because you can't treat it? He has a diagnosis from one of the most respected pediatric neurologists in the country. Doesn't that seem like a backward way to undiagnose him?"

"He actually doesn't have a diagnosis of sensory processing disorder on his prescription, if you recall. We were going out of our way to help you with this. The problem is lack of discipline, Mrs. Shriner. Kids need discipline. They need structure and limits."

"Of course they do. We give him structure and limits; we just don't punish him, that's all. Look, we're trying to figure this out, too, okay?"

"I can't help you because you tie my hands."

"Because I don't give him time-outs? You are giving up on him because you don't like my parenting?"

"You don't have to look at it that way. You can just say he graduated."

I'm not sure which is worse when I hang up, my rage or my shame. Maybe we're wrong. Maybe we should just lock him in his room until he calms down, like most people do with their kids. But my intuition about my son is that putting a tighter stranglehold on the situation, battling it out for control, isn't going to help. If we're not addressing the root cause, then it's just going to become a contest about who can scream louder, who wields the most power.

I am willing to entertain the idea that we might be proceeding in too idealistic a way and it's just becoming too exhausting. I, too, want a more immediate solution. I want something that works. Not works as in, he'll be awesome in fifteen years, but works in an immediate sense, so that my entire house isn't set on edge with his constant volatility. I'm willing to concede to Suzanne that using threats and bribes may in fact not make all children into drug dealers and manipulators and bank robbers.

I also know this . . . There will come a day when threats and bribes no longer hold the same weight. I know because it happened with my father and me. When his iron-fisted control over us started to erode, he tightened the fist, and when he realized his grip was still slipping, he got furious. When his own body could no longer comfortably contain his fury, he transferred that fury to our bodies. I remember a day when I wouldn't comply with some request and my father, in a blind rage, interlaced his fingers in my hair and kicked my feet out from under me. Until now, I could never begin to imagine why one would do that to a child. While it is true that I would never go that far, I know now how he felt. I see the metaphor I failed to understand at the time: You need me to stand. If you don't do what I say, I can take the very ground from you.

When the day comes that taking Tariku's TV time away is no longer an effective bargaining chip, if we have built nothing else, where will we be then?

~

Halloween rolls around. Scott and I have thrown a Halloween party every year since we found our house.

"We could dress T as a vampire and just let him go ahead and bite everyone," I say.

"That's one idea. Here's another. Let's cancel," says Scott.

"When you have a sensitive kid," a friend with an autistic son had told me a few weeks earlier, "you can either put your whole life on hold or you can try to find solutions to help him deal."

Emboldened, I go ahead with the party. I have a habit of making plucky, spur-of-the-moment decisions that I regret later. It's one of my best/worst traits.

I decide we're going to dress as a circus family. I think it will be funny to dress T as a baby strongman, with a handlebar mustache and a leopard-print wrestling costume and a fake-muscle shirt. Child-sized fake-muscle shirts only come in "flesh tone," which should be renamed "white tone." I buy it and I spend about four thousand hours hand-sewing brown, stretchy net over it, before I give up and dismantle the whole thing and bring it to the tailor down the street, who nearly falls off her stool laughing. She does a great job with it, though. She even adds her own creative touch: little brown felt nipples.

Auntie Jo agrees to stay glued to him the whole night, so I can be sure that he's safe and isn't going to start pitching our laptops across the room the minute my back is turned. I also close off the upstairs and set up a quiet room for him, with toys and books and DVDs and blankets. That way he has somewhere to go if he gets overwhelmed.

The night of the party, he mostly plays in the backyard with Auntie Jo. A few of our friends' kids come and go. Interacting with the adults makes me uncomfortable. I check on him incessantly, constantly looking over everybody's shoulder to monitor the action. I won't say it's exactly fun, but at least we are not giving up. We're struggling to find our path in the world as a family, not just hiding away. For that, I'm proud of us.

The rest of the holidays tumble by in much the same way. Not exactly fun. Not exactly pleasant, either. But there are moments of real joy sprinkled throughout, even on the days that are colored with envy for the more typical experiences we see people having around us.

I'm finally ready to cook a brisket and I can't call to ask my mother how. There are no presents for T from my parents under our tree this year, as he approaches his third birthday. When he asks about their sudden disappearance from our lives, I tell him that they love him, they just live very far away. He's not old enough to realize that's an absurd explanation. Everywhere we turn, we see grandparents flooding our friends' lives with love.

I remember my mother's crisp latkes, my loud relatives laughing in the candlelit dining room, the shiny blue and silver gift wrap, the windfall of loot that came every Hanukkah. I remember the year my father waited on line at dawn for six hours, because there was a run on Cabbage Patch Kids and he wouldn't let me be the one to go without.

I don't remember a holiday growing up without family: grandparents and aunts and uncles and cousins. The guilt swamps me. I have deprived my child of grandparents.

I hold this sadness, along with the joy of seeing my son's face when we bring the tree in the house. Once when I was about sixteen, I remember sitting in temple, in the throes of an existential crisis about religion (due to copious reading of Camus). My grandmother, dying of cancer and emaciated, held my hand between both of hers, her bones too close to the powdery parchment of her skin, and said to me, "It's okay to hold two conflicting things at the same time, for a while." I miss her, especially this holiday.

We surround ourselves with friends and try to sculpt a holiday that is truly us, combining our different faiths and traditions. I do cook a big, chaotic Christmas Eve dinner of brisket and latkes and I manage to muddle through. Afterward, we listen to carols and drink hot chocolate under the tree. The tree is a masterpiece. You really want to see Christmas done with gusto, go to someone's house who never had one growing up. No one crafts a winter wonderland quite like a Jew.

We all go around and say something we're grateful for.

"I'm grateful for our family," I say. "And for patience when I have it. And faith, which I'm pretty sure is there even when I think it isn't."

Chapter 23

THE next preschool we try is pleasant and small, in a blue house tucked away on a side street in a suburban enclave about twenty-five minutes north of us. The drive is a pain, but will be worth it if it works. It's got some academics. It's not quite as hippie-dippie as the first school we tried. I suspect that some more traditional schoolwork might be a plus for T. He has a voracious appetite for letters, words, numbers. He has already taught himself to write.

At the admission interview, I say, "You have to keep in mind that my kid didn't have parents for a while at a crucial time in his development and this has repercussions. We're working it out. We're healing. We're doing great, actually. And our version of doing great looks different from how it does for kids who have had a typical attachment cycle in the first three years of life. So he's going to need a little extra attention."

As we walk away, Scott says, "Nice one!" and nods appreciatively. It is probably the most articulate I've ever been about our situation, even to myself. It makes me think I'm beginning to get a better grasp on it.

The director calls me later that day. She would be thrilled to welcome us, but he'll need a psychological assessment by her friend/colleague, who will determine if he should attend with a "therapeutic companion," or shadow, which is basically like hiring a private teacher's aide. If he does need a companion, this psychologist will match us with one she deems appropriate and we'll incur all expenses for this, of course.

"We've already had him assessed a couple of times," I say. "Can she just use those?"

"Oh, no, I'm sure she'll want to see him for herself."

The test results are, most definitely, this child needs a companion. She assures us she has someone great for us—a woman with children of her own and a master's degree in early childhood development. The cost is exorbitant. We could literally send him to Harvard for what this is going to cost us.

One or the other of us is also expected to stick around school for the first few months. We decide that it's worth a shot. What if it truly helps? We'll never know unless we try. Maybe with some extra attention and support he'll hit his stride and we won't need to pay for the 24-Karat Shadow for long.

The second time T starts preschool, I don't take pictures. Instead I break down in tears (not a sweet mommy tear—a full snotty cry) in the school bathroom. I hang around the sidelines trying not to let my unease spill over onto him.

We show up early that day, so T can spend some time getting to know the 24-Karat Shadow before the day starts. Her physical presence takes me aback. She is a wan, petite woman with pale strawberry hair and sallow skin. She stands with her shoulders hunched forward slightly and her handshake is tentative and limp. The director hovers nearby, with the memorized unflappable cheeriness of a person who works with kids all day long.

There's no way this bland, limp little thing in front of us is going to be able to handle our little spark plug. He's going to roll right over her. I wish I could tell you that my suspicion gets turned on its head. That she is firm but kind, that she provides a scaffold for him and he uses it to grow straight and tall and confident.

What happens is she gets up in his face right after she takes something away from him that he wants, so he bites her on the cheek. She completely freaks out, leaves him in the middle of the room, and goes to cry in the office.

I say, as gently as I can, "I'm so sorry that happened."

And then I continue, maybe not as gently as I'm trying to sound, "Can I ask, what kinds of challenges do you usually work with?"

I want to ask, "Have you chosen the right profession?"

I mean, people don't hire 24-Karat Shadows unless their kids are presenting significant difficulties, right? She recovers and then makes a big show of being brave and getting back on the horse. The director of the school is encouraging. I don't like this shadow and her air of martyrdom. I don't like the director and the way she coddles her, either.

Foreboding creeps into my shoulders and neck, where it lodges and sits on a nerve, sending shooting pains into my skull. For the rest of the day my headache is so bad that I have to squint through one eye, but we make it. I have a meeting to go to the next day, so Scott attends school with T. On my way home from Beverly Hills, I talk to an old friend back in New York whose son has also been diagnosed with sensory processing disorder. Instead of being aggressive and bonkers like T, her son would retreat into himself and hold his ears, rock, and totally shut down.

"You could do it a lot of ways," she says. "I chose to pull him out of preschool and didn't send him until kindergarten. I just didn't want to subject him to being terrified every day and that's what was happening. Then I chose a school that was highly focused on ritual and structure and flow. He's doing great now, but he's eight. It took a while."

The idea of a terrified child resonates. Even though T has a very different way of showing it, essentially I think that's what's going on. My son is so scared. He loves being around other kids but the stimulation also frightens him. Faced with the fight-or-flight response, T chooses to fight. It's probably the reason he's alive, after all he's been through. I love that fire in him. My goal with school is not to change him. I just hope that eventually he'll feel safe enough that his fighting spirit finds expression in a soccer game rather than an MMA match.

When I get home, Scott and T are already back. I know from Scott's demeanor that it has gone either very well or very poorly, because he seems focused and calm and resolute. This could indicate either triumph or surrender.

T has his airplanes lined up in a neat row across the living room floor. One by one each plane takes off as he makes the sound of a jet engine. He calls this game "magic airport." We slip into the kitchen for a moment and Scott tells me the story in hushed tones.

He begins with, "We're not going back there."

Apparently T bit one of the other kids while his aide wasn't paying attention. The director got angry and yelled at him in front of the whole class, until Scott just picked him up and walked out the door.

"C'mon, little homey," he said. "We're getting out of here."

We have a meeting scheduled with the "team" later in the week and they ask us to keep him at home until then. Another meeting. Another team facing us grimly. Maybe they are a team. They just aren't our team.

At the meeting, we listen to their suggestions. I calmly take notes.

When the director is done talking, Scott says, "We were honest with you about what's going on with him. We spent a lot of money on all these tests he had already done, at your insistence. We hired someone who you told us was capable of handling this situation. When that turned out to not be the case, you shamed my son and yelled at him in front of the class, which was not exactly what you led us to believe was your conflict resolution philosophy. Tariku acted exactly how we told you he would act in the face of such a big transition. The fault isn't with him here."

The director looks shocked.

"I'm sorry. I did the best I could in that moment," she finally responds, after a long pause.

"What does that mean?" asks Scott.

"It means this school isn't the right fit for your family."

We shake hands with them and leave.

"Fuck this," says Scott on our way back to the car. "He's not ready yet. Those people aren't smart enough for him. When Jo goes back to school, I'm hiring you a full-time nanny. A really, really good one."

When I married Scott, I knew he was a terrific guy. I knew he was cute and funny and that he was a shredding bass player. But how could I have known this kick-ass, brave, loyal man was the man I married? I take his hand and feel strangely fine. So this is my son's father. This is who we are.

~

I call Ruth later. She suggests to me that I hold T like a baby and dial the attachment clock back.

I start out easy, with a moment when things are sweet and we're just sitting on the floor of his room together, playing airplanes. We've been at it for hours already, and I can feel his attention start to waver. The transition to another activity is coming, and transitions are always tough.

"Do you remember when you were a little baby and I used to rock you?" I ask.

"How?" he says.

"Do you want to pretend like you're a baby and I'll show you?"

He's game. He laughs. He thinks it's a funny idea. He says, "Goo goo."

I sit cross-legged, my back against his bookcase, and he crawls into my lap. I wrap my arms around him and begin to rock him. This is something we already do, but usually only when he's getting out of the bath, when I swaddle him in a towel. Ruth suggested eye contact, if possible, but that's not happening because he buries his face in my shirt. I rock him and we sit there for a good long time. Longer than he's let me hold him in ages.

Warmth floods my limbs and it's as if my brain is bathed suddenly in a wash of serotonin. We are survivors, the two of us. We're loved. We're safe. We're going to be okay, my son and I. I know this as surely as I knew he was my son the minute I saw his picture. As surely as I have ever known anything.

I wonder if Ruth has tricked me. If this rocking isn't for healing T, but for healing me.

~ Chapter 24

TARIKU inches his oatmeal bowl closer to the edge of the kitchen table, a wicked tilt to his smile. Closer still.

"Do. Not," I tell him.

He is never the first to back down. No retreat, no surrender. Sometimes I think, how can I begrudge him this tendency to fight to the death when it is his spirited personality that helped him to withstand hunger, illness, and trauma? And yet, this selfsame personality drives me to sit, near hopeless, head in hands at the end of every day, wondering why I ever expected motherhood to complete rather than lay waste to me. Wondering how I was so naive to think such a thing as completion possible.

These days, if I put anything in front of him that isn't mac and cheese or chocolate chip cookies, he hurls it at the wall and hollers like his chair is on fire. My chest and arms are still peppered with the scabs of angry bite marks.

My friends whose toddlers contentedly sit on picnic blankets and eat quinoa at jazz concerts in the park are the first to give me advice. Have you tried soothing music? Have you tried a gluten-free diet? Have you called my homeopath?

Of course I have. If I were to be uncensored, I'd react to these sanctimonious, though well-meaning, friends just like my son does

to string beans. I'd look them in the eye, open my mouth, and release a banshee wail that would blow their hats off their heads. I'd
hurl their eco-friendly, fair-trade toys at the windshields of their
Volvos.

Tariku's bowl hits the floor and splatters its contents across the
yellow wall, painted by Scott's father when we first moved in. Once
sunny and perfect, the finish is now a Jackson Pollock work of mystery stains and gouges.

At the moment of the crash, my cell phone quacks. I feel an
unwarranted sense of expectation as I answer it, on my way to get
the paper towels and sponge. Somewhere floating in the periphery
of my thoughts is always the dream of escape. I keep hoping I'll
pick up the phone and find . . . the answer. The answer could be just
about anything other than what's happening in the moment. Perhaps it will be some great piece of news, just the thing to yank me
out of my mundane morning: Scott with a windfall of money, my
agent calling.

But, no. It is Jennifer's ex-husband's new wife, Dylan, on the
other line. Though Dylan and I are friendly and I've always liked her,
it's still unusual for me to receive a call from her. And I've stopped
talking to Jennifer. I love her as much as I ever have, but I got tired of
the rehab waiting rooms, the late-night hysterical phone calls, the
desperate begging for me to come to the hospital after her boyfriend
overdosed, lived, then overdosed again and didn't fare as well the second time. Motherhood has given me the perfect excuse to disappear.

"Jennifer is in the hospital," Dylan begins. She's a therapist and
usually calm, but her tone seems even more measured than usual
today. "She overdosed in her father's bathroom. She's in a coma.
You should come now. We're at the ICU at Mission Community
Hospital. Jillian, there's no brain activity."

I take down the address. I mechanically kneel and clean the
oatmeal, scooping the bland goop into paper towels before spong-
ing down the wall and the floorboards.

"I wouldn't eat this, either." I sigh.

When I'm done, I wash my hands and dry them on a dish towel. Every micromotion of every muscle, every texture that comes into contact with my skin, every sound outside the window is suddenly more defined, set into sharp relief against a big, whirring unnameable thing that seems to be hovering just out of frame. I can't see it, but I know it's there. At the center of me is a smooth, cool ball of nothing, no feeling at all.

I pick up T. He's confused. Why did the battle halt? Did he win? If so, it was an anticlimactic win.

He wiggles, but not for long, resting his head on my neck after a moment. Even though he is now, at three years old, too heavy to tote around for very long, I'm usually grateful for the warmth of him against my chest. The day will soon arrive when I can no longer pick him up at all.

I walk out the back door into the late-winter sun and step barefoot across the dewy grass of the backyard to knock on Scott's studio door.

"Jennifer's in the hospital," I say.

He takes T from my arms.

"I don't know what's going on exactly. I think it's bad. I don't know when I'll be back."

"Okay, just call me when you get there and let me know what's happening."

I know that whatever happens, Scott will scaffold me. If the past few years have taught me nothing else, they have taught me this.

Neither one of us is shocked. We have discussed the possibility that this call might come. And yet, now that it has, I'm convinced there's been some mistake about the brain activity. I'm sure that I'll show up and Jennifer will greet me with a wan, embarrassed smile. I have always believed that there will be a tomorrow in which we'll have a chance to make up. I have always thought that at the end of the world, Jen will be the last person standing, kept company only by the roaches and Cher. She has lived through days darker than most people could dream up in their most baroque nightmares. She is my bright-eyed warrior girl. I know I will arrive to find her awake, alive.

I listen to the new Amy Winehouse album as I drive. I pick it because something about Amy reminds me of Jen—the dramatic eye makeup; the long, dark hair; the rebellious tilt of the chin. They both have that vibrating electricity around them, the sense that things will go either spectacularly well or exactly the opposite. The brief, bright candles of the world.

The buildings lining the freeway seem stretched and strange, the dry, golden hills in the distance glazed with wobbly light. I hit Repeat. Not for the overplayed song about refusing to go to rehab (everyone's favorite drinking song) but rather the vampy "Back to Black."

You go back to her and I go back to . . . earth?
I'm not sure what she says, but I think it's earth.
You go back to her and I go back to earth.

I realize after a few repeats that it's not "earth," it's "us." I go back to us.

In the waiting room for intensive care, I recognize a few people, slouched silently in plastic chairs. My friend Rayna sits with an arm on each armrest, staring at the ground. She wears her perpetual wool cap over her two-tone dyed hair, no makeup, trendily thin, violet eyes glassy with tears. A girl I don't know, an almost-replica of Rayna, is fastened to her side.

I expect there will be people here I haven't met. Jen is incredibly popular. She hates to be alone. We're different that way. This popular business is too much work. I like to have a handful of good girlfriends and get invited to a fun party once in a while. For a long while, Jen gave me both of these things. There was a time we talked every day and made up names for our fake band and got matching tattoos. All of which are really just markers of the same sentiment: you are not alone.

Rayna fills me in. There are two visitor passes, only two people allowed to see Jen at a time. Friends are taking shifts.

"I sat up all night with her," she says.

I sense something vaguely accusatory and smugly proprietary in her reporting of this. Where was I?

Rayna tells me that Jen overdosed on cocaine and heroin in the bathroom of her father's residential hotel and had a massive cardiac arrest. There is, indeed, no brain activity. They have spent the morning trying to reach friends and family. Leon, her ex-husband, has to make the big decisions. Her mother, in Canada, is staying in Canada. Her father is a career junkie himself. He is not expected.

Jen's father met her mother because he was her drug dealer. The couple were beautiful, in a wrecked, down-and-out kind of way. Every photograph of them looks like a set still from *Drugstore Cowboy*. I suspect Jen shot up in his bathroom (rather than out in the open, as he would have done) because she didn't want to let on how much she was holding. Had she been with her father when she went under, he would have administered CPR, as all self-respecting junkies can. A flash of anger infiltrates my still-numb center. My vivacious, brilliant friend is going to die because she didn't want to share her drugs. With her father. I'm not sure if I'm mad at her parents or simply at God. What kind of chance did she have?

Rayna grips both my hands in hers so hard my bones rub together. She looks at me desperately, as if I, a newcomer to the scene, might be carrying some fresh answer for her. Her eyes are a bit demented with sorrow, twisted with magical thinking.

"You never know," she says. "Miracles happen. Miracles happen every day."

Yes, they do. Miracles happen. But unless you are Lazarus, you do not wake from the dead. That is not one of them.

There are alliances and enmities among the people milling about, shell-shocked and at the same time not really surprised at all. The visitor passes slip from hand to hand, sometimes between people who have slept with each other, or at least with each other's boyfriends or girlfriends. These are longtime friends with a flair for drama—people with a history of drugs and sobriety, crime and redemption. The motley crew looks like a holding tank of extras for the biker TV show *Sons of Anarchy*. Almost everyone here has faced each other across hospital waiting rooms before—drugs, car wrecks, motorcycle crashes.

A good friend with shiny chestnut hair to her ass and a chest tattooed with *Love Will Tear Us Apart* in gangster lettering stumbles into my arms and sobs. We wait together, hands clasped. As I sit there, I look down at my arms, the tattoos that have become my skin. One of my arms is fully sleeved with two Japanese koi fish and the other is a purple dragon surrounded by orange flames.

The Japanese folk tale goes: Once upon a time, a school of koi was swimming upstream and came upon a waterfall. Most of the koi turned back, discouraged by the very sight of it, but a small number of them remained and kept swimming. The laughing demons in the sky only increased the height of the falls as the fish fought on. The koi swam upstream against the falls for one hundred years until, with one heroic leap, a single koi reached the top of the falls. As a reward, God transformed the koi into a shining golden dragon, who spent the rest of his days chasing pearls of wisdom across heaven. Since that day, every time a koi fights hard enough to make it to the top of the falls, it becomes a dragon.

Water and fire. Transformation. I have always liked the story.

When a visitor emerges, I take the pass and am buzzed through a locked door. Leon is alone in the room with Jen. He runs his hand through his long, stylishly greasy blond hair. The lines on his face are etched an inch deeper than the last time I saw him.

On the hospital bed lies my friend, my golden dragon, her skin oddly flattened, breathing tube down her throat, monitors stuck to her chest. Her dark bangs are pushed off to the side, as if she is a little girl and her mother has just smoothed her hair out of her eyes. She looks thin. Until now she has always been a zaftig girl—tall and broad shouldered, with wide hips and large breasts. All she's wanted the whole time I've known her is to be skinny like a model. She's lived on string beans and Diet Coke and still she's been a big girl. It's been the bane of her existence, which is sort of crazy, considering her existence. It has been so hard. And still, her biggest concern has always been whether her ass was fat.

I haven't seen her in months. Her frail arms on top of the sheet startle me.

"What happened?" I say to her. "You finally got as thin as you always wanted and you figured you were done?"

Leon smiles. He's composed. He's good in a crisis, as am I. Or at least we hold it together on the outside. Some of our friends show up hysterical. Some, worse, don't show at all, unable to "deal." I spare no judgment for the no-shows. Leaving her alone is unthinkable.

"Her heart is still beating on its own," Leon tells me.

We hold each other. We sit in silence. It may be ten minutes; it may be twenty; I don't know. Eventually he drifts out of the room, drawing the curtains against the harsh midday sun as he goes.

My mother, with her impeccable etiquette, taught me how to be around sickness and death. I know how to navigate hospitals, send condolence cards, show up with food. But I am generally stoic and pragmatic and like to put all my feelings into my hands—cooking, making calls, doing what needs to be done. I only shake and cry later, on the living room couch, alone in the dark, reluctant to let even Scott see me in a moment of such weakness. Or worse, the feelings come out in my gruesome nightmares.

I sit with Jennifer and hold her hand, dry and warm but lifeless. I feel the cold, hard mass in my belly give, just an inch.

"Wait," I say. "This is a mistake. You're the one who makes it."

With our hands joined, the tattoos on her arm seem almost an extension of my own. I wonder why she landed in this bed and I'll walk out of here and return to my everything-I-ever-wanted. It could easily have been me—car accidents, overdoses, dangerous friends, stupid, stupid decisions.

This is the moment when you regret your carelessness. When you vow you will live each moment more fully, will wake up and pay attention, will be present for the love in your life. Of course, it's not set up that way. We vow in times of crisis to be present in every moment but we're lucky if we're present for even one, once in a while.

I first met Scott shortly after Jen's wedding. Jen was a gourmet cook and a sensational entertainer; it was her passion. My cooking expertise went no further than steaming broccoli. I owned about three plates and two forks, all from the 99 Cents Only Store. I have no idea what possessed me when I decided that, for our fourth date, I wanted to cook dinner for Scott in my tiny studio apartment in Hollywood. Jen was excited about the idea and we colluded to make it a grand display, spending hours on the phone planning the simple menu, the music, my outfit—everything. I went to her house the day before and she walked me through how to make feta, herb, and sun-dried tomato–stuffed chicken breasts. She told me exactly when to dress and toss the salad. She wrote a grocery list, ending with brownie mix, vanilla ice cream, and a sprig of mint for dessert. Then she raided her wedding booty and packed a giant box full of a tablecloth, napkins, good plates, glasses, silverware—everything I would need to make my crappy vintage kitchen table into a scene worthy of *Martha Stewart Living*.

I warned Scott that this cooking experiment was a ruse, a one-off, and not to get his hopes up that it would happen again. That turned out to be wrong. Now I'm the one with the table linens and the china, who pores over recipe books early in the morning before anyone else is awake—my moment of stolen pleasure.

For some reason all I keep thinking is how sorry, how very sad I am that she never met Tariku. As if it matters now. As if it would have saved her. It was me he saved, not her.

"I love you, my friend," I say. "You tried so hard. I understand that you couldn't stay."

And then I tell her about Tariku.

"He's like us. He's hurt and on fire and furious. I'm scared for him and I don't know how to help him and I'm worried he's going to turn out as wild and unwise as we did. I wish you had met him. You would love him. He would crack you up . . . Will you help him?"

I don't believe, by the way, that people die and then somehow stick around so they can attend weddings and graduations and nod their ghost heads appreciatively when people mention them in toasts. I don't believe our loved ones hang around dangling their legs from clouds and throwing down protective angel glitter when we pray for it. Or that they wait for their big moment to show up on the infrared cameras of reality TV ghost-hunting charlatans.

And yet, I ask. Because we don't think through what we say in such moments. Because I don't know why some of us survive and some of us don't. Because I don't know where our help comes from at all, and I need some.

I kiss her swollen hand and notice she's been shooting drugs into the punished veins there. I lay my head on her chest and let it rise and fall with her breath. I listen.

Those of us at the hospital spend the rest of the day rotating through the room until I eventually decide to go home to sleep. I arrive after T's bedtime. He's lying on our bed in his Halloween pumpkin pajamas, even though it's already February. His face is slack with sleep and he breathes deeply and easily. I curl myself around him—the edges and softnesses I know more intimately than my own. I put my head to the back of his neck and smell the coconut hair product we use to tame his baby Afro, along with some mixture of grass and french fries and pee that tells me his dad didn't give him a bath.

I weep until I soak the entire back of his jammies and have to gingerly change his top without waking him.

As I lie there, waiting for sleep, I remember a framed picture of Jen, taken at three years old—the same age T is now. She had it displayed on the sideboard of the home she shared with Leon, so I saw it countless times. In it, she has a gap-toothed, wide smile; poorly cut bangs; white Mary Janes. She was precious. I think about the fact that there was a moment, thirty-odd years ago, when Jen was born and she was the answer to someone's prayers. Then I think for some reason of the room in Africa in which my son was born. I think of his young birth mother and wonder, as I have many times, if there was someone there to love her.

I am not there at two A.M. when Jen's heart stops and the machines keep her alive until they can arrange the organ donation. The doctors say it took a damned strong heart to survive a massive cardiac arrest like that and still keep pumping for so long. By the following night it is beating in someone else's chest.

~ Chapter 25

IT has been two weeks since Jennifer died, and I still sob and shake uncontrollably every night. I start lying on the couch until late, so as not to keep Scott awake.

I watch every stupid comedy I can find. I eat and eat, shoving big bags of pistachios and wedges of cheese and spoonfuls of avocado straight from the shell, all of it doused with sea salt, into my mouth. I pull the car over and eat spicy tacos by the side of the road. I buy mangoes marinating in cayenne pepper from cart vendors and eat them while I drive, juice running down my hand and up my sleeve. I leave sticky handprints on the upholstery. One afternoon I cry until I throw up. T is somber and sweet to me that day. When Scott comes home, he says, "Mama cried and barfed."

I thought he hadn't known, but of course he did. He notices every tiny thing.

I'm not sure about the traditional Kübler-Ross five stages of grief. I think my grief actually has five food groups. For the past week I've been in the fifth: chocolate. The sixth is probably Weight Watchers.

I ran away from her. I pretty much stopped taking her calls. I pressed Decline. Decline. I sometimes called back days later and sometimes not at all. Sometimes she lied to me and told me she was sober and looking for a new apartment. Sometimes she told the truth—she felt so desperate. I wasn't sure which type of phone call I disliked more, so I avoided her. And this I know: when she died she felt abandoned by me. This, too, is true: she never abandoned me when I fucked up. Never.

I was a coward. I was half-turned toward the door for years, until I finally took to my heels and ran and left her there. Not long before that, we used to tell people at restaurants and nail salons that we were sisters. "Of course," they'd say. "You look exactly alike."

Was I mostly a good enough friend or was I always lazy and selfish, only good when it was easy and fun? And even if there was nothing more I could have done, would it have been worth it to keep talking to her if only to have a scrap of her voice to remember better now?

Is this who I am? Someone who abandons people? Is this why my child hits me and bites me? Because he can see inside me and he knows I'm a zombie mother, already emotionally dead and gone?

The lights were low at Jennifer's memorial and I was grateful, because there was a purple lump on the side of my face from where T whacked me with a die-cast metal bus. I get scratched and spit at. Yesterday, he pulled a hunk of hair out of my head and then got grossed out and asked for my help getting it out of his mouth.

"Love Daddy this much," he says, with his arms way out to the sides. "Love Mommy this much," he says, chubby hands close together, as if he's trying to juice a kumquat.

"Mommy don't come," he says when we leave the house together as a family, attaching himself to his father's leg.

Nothing I've encountered in my life has hurled me into darkness as fiercely as this rejection by my son. Not Jennifer's death, not stripping, not drugs, not being disowned, not depression, nothing. Even when I'm able to remain grounded and patient and not take it personally all day long (it's a rare day, but it happens), come bedtime I still find myself in tears, thinking that in a million years I never imagined being a mother would feel like this.

I go over and over it in my head. What are the things about our turbulent relationship that might be my fault? What might I be able to control, to change simply by changing me? As if changing were that easy, but I can't help running through the possibilities. What if I worked less? What if I yelled less? What if I was better at the life balance? What if I was a better cook? What if I was more fun? What if I could draw a perfect elephant?

What if I was better? Would that make my child love me?

But even as I castigate myself, I also see a more likely story. With all of the trauma and transition in his short life, it's logical that T would make sure to do the rejecting rather than risk being hurt again.

A boxer friend of mine once told me that in order to be a great boxer you don't just have to like hitting people; you also have to like getting hit. I would say the same thing about writers and rejection. In order to succeed as a writer it helps if you can welcome adversity. In my work, I keep taking punches and standing back up—I keep swinging. So why is it so much harder to stay in the ring of motherhood?

Jennifer's death breaks me down but it also gives me new resolve. I may not have been a good friend to her, but I can at least learn from it. I will get back in the ring with T, I tell myself every night, for as long as it takes. I will never throw in the towel.

Every time he pops me in the nose, I will walk away for a minute to get my bearings and then I will come right back.

~

Every night before bed I eye the stack of novels in my office with longing, but instead I pick up *Toddler Adoption: The Weaver's Craft* or Joe Newman's *Raising Lions* or *Parenting with Love and Logic* or *Too Loud, Too Bright, Too Fast, Too Tight: What to Do if You Are Sensory*

Defensive in an Overstimulating World. I make the same lists over and over again, because in the heat of the moment, I tend to forget everything and yell.

I write:

Identify the need behind the behavior.
Help him to identify his feelings.
Empathize.
Keep your voice quiet and low.
Establish routine.
Be consistent.

I commit these things to memory, figuring that if I study them long and hard enough, they will begin to seem less impossible.

At the same time, I embrace the idea that the answer for T specifically, T the unique human, is not in any one book. In a moment of crisis, parenting theory is about as useful as dance theory. You can't learn to do pirouettes by reading about them. Still, reading is my comfortable place and I know that the words will settle into me somehow, in some configuration, and begin to make sense.

I go in for a private counseling session with Ruth and admit everything. I tell her that I can't stop yelling at T, that I hit him once, a year and a half ago, but never again. I tell her that he can't stand me, that sometimes I can't stand him. I tell her that I subscribe to her methodology in theory, that I want to be empathetic, above all, with my child. But in the moment I just want him to stop acting like such a freaked-out weirdo and do the fucking Music Together correctly, like the other kids. I tell her that I'm embarrassed much of the time. That I'm horrified every time I have to drag him screaming from the store in a fireman's carry.

"Your son has special needs," she says. "Your expectation that he behave like neurotypical children of the same age is doing you both a disservice."

I blanch. "He has what?"

The words land a blow. "Special" meaning, like, a lifetime of being teased? A forever sentence of therapy? Special ed and meds and boarding schools? Even with all the assessments and diagnoses and therapies and Googling, I guess in my heart I always just thought T was going through a phase. I certainly never thought to use the words "special needs."

"Why do you say special needs?" I ask. "Is that what you call his behavior? What if he's just a little asshole?"

She smiles politely but doesn't laugh at my joke. She knows me by now and won't indulge my tendency to use humor to skirt emotions.

"Why don't we look at the book together?" Ruth says.

She asked me to bring his adoption agency Lifebook, which is filled with pictures of his life before he was adopted. It tells his story, as best they knew it. Ruth and I read it together. Near the beginning, there is a picture of Tariku at three months when he was first brought to the orphanage. In the picture he looks unmistakably sick, his eyes confused and gluey and glazed.

She says, "He's not mad at you, you know. He's scared. His behavior is entirely grounded in the assumption that the world is a frightening place in which everyone he loves will abandon him. He's not testing you. He's testing his model. If he can get you to lose your cool, he has proved his hypothesis and can go back to being in control. So you see, every time you let him push you over the edge, you're confirming his assumption that the world is unsafe and reinforcing the trauma. Describe to me what you see in this picture."

"He's so tiny," I say.

My heart aches for the months of his life I missed.

"And?"

"He isn't smiling. When he's not melting down he's always smiling. Always."

"Well, you're right. He's not smiling here. Why do you think that is?"

"When the babies first enter the orphanage they're quarantined for two weeks. So when this picture was taken, that's probably where he was."

"So at three months of age this child loses his mother, her heartbeat, her smell, her body, her milk, and then for two weeks he is essentially alone."

I'm weeping now. I can barely look at the picture. I can imagine him, always smiling until, for the first time in his life, the smile goes away and, judging by the pictures, it's gone a good long time before it begins to creep back.

"He looks terrified."

"Yes, he does."

"His face is too old for a three-month-old."

Ruth reaches over and takes my hand. "Somewhere, this scared little baby is still in there," she says. "And he has needs. A lot of them. And they are special."

~

Scott and I make some changes. I leave my cell in the car when I take him to the park. I force myself to pay attention, to be conscious, to make lots of eye contact, to answer his anger with love. Whenever he socks me, I go back in for more. As Ruth says, I gather him to me.

This crazy metaphysical thing happens. After all this time combing every book and website, going to therapist after therapist, praying and praying for help, help starts to find us.

Christine Moers, a pink-dreadlocked mom who owns an RV park in Texas and has five kids with special needs, has a blog I love called *Welcome to My Brain*, in which she talks about therapeutic parenting. Christine and I become friendly and in one of our exchanges, she mentions a book called *Beyond Consequences, Logic, and*

Control: A Love Based Approach to Helping Children with Severe Behaviors, by Heather Forbes, a psychologist in Florida. Because I find Christine to be about the sanest, smartest, most grounded voice around, I look Heather up and it turns out she is holding a Beyond Consequences seminar in our area the following weekend. Coincidentally, it's located at the offices of our adoption agency.

This is where we first attended the Adoption Options seminar. This is where I looked at a photo album of Ethiopia and told Scott, "That's where our baby is."

The conference room is packed with about two hundred people. Who would come here on a beautiful Saturday if they didn't feel desperate?

"Are there really this many people in the same boat as us?" I ask.

"I know," he says.

I know he's thinking the same thing I am: we've felt so alone.

The crowd is remarkably diverse. There is a couple so sexy and attractive they look like a beer ad. There is a frowsy older woman with stiff yellow hair and a face like an apple doll. There is a roly-poly couple who look like salt and pepper shakers. If you saw this group of people, you would not be able to guess what they had in common.

Heather walks out in front of the room. She is a pretty, no-nonsense-looking blond woman with serious shoes and an infectious smile.

"Trauma," she begins. "Your child's extreme behaviors derive from the neurological effects of early childhood trauma. He isn't just 'being a boy'; he's fighting for his life, as far as his brain is concerned. In the deepest recesses of his soul, he feels unsafe."

For the first half of the day she talks about trauma and its effect on brain development, then she talks nuts and bolts. The basic idea is to change the question from:

How do I get my child to change his behavior?

to

1. What is driving my child's behavior?

and

2. What can I do at this moment to improve my relationship with my child?

There are worksheets and projections. She shares useful tips and inspiring stories.

It's not so different from what I already know, but for some reason, in this conference room with its worn blue carpeting and rickety folding chairs, I start to understand. Not in my head, but in my heart. Maybe because my son has taken a battering ram to it and forced it to open. I finally understand the way that trauma inscribes itself onto the architecture of your gray matter. How it forces a shift in perspective in which the world itself becomes a threat to your very existence.

Lunch is quiet. Scott and I chat for a minute with our social worker, who is also there taking the seminar.

Afterward, Heather takes questions. Scott and I raise our hands and she calls us to the front of the room. Even though we're standing up in front of a roomful of expectant faces, I'm neither nervous nor embarrassed. We are perfectly qualified to be here.

"I have a three-year-old who's intensely aggressive toward me," I say. "To others also, but mostly toward me. All of these 'parenting with empathy' theories are great in the big picture, but how can I stop him from hurting people? Now. I need something that's more immediate."

"The problem with just telling him no all the time is that we don't want to ask him to stuff his emotions. We also don't want him to form a negative self-image," she says. "He needs to get that energy out in some way. Have you ever had him push on you?"

"Um, I don't think so."

Heather stands facing me in her beige slacks and patterned blouse. She puts her hands out in front of her and interlaces her fingers with mine.

"Now push as hard as you can and yell," she says.

"Um." I suddenly feel frozen, foolish. In spite of every goofy exercise I ever did in a college theater class, I can't seem to yell. Aren't I the sane one, the grown-up?

"Here, I'll start," she says. She begins and nearly pushes me over.

"See, that's the thing. You have to push back. He has to know you can support him. You can take it."

We try again and I push back, making the two of us a balanced pyramid of tension. Heather lets out a guttural yell that startles me, but I continue to push.

She stops and nonchalantly says, "That felt good. Okay, you try."

I do. I push and I roar and I feel an instantaneous sense of relief. I think of what she said earlier in the day: separation from the mother at birth alone is enough to cause trauma. Violence, physical and emotional, causes trauma. Trauma builds on trauma. Trauma isn't so much about a particular event; it's about the impact of the event on the specific psyche of an individual. Each human system has its own unique adaptation to trauma.

"Don't be surprised if people are skeptical about trauma," she says. "They'll say, 'Oh, kids are so resilient.' Yes, they are. They don't usually die in the face of trauma; they adapt, they fight back, they take control. To be resilient does not mean that you are unaffected; it only means you are adaptable. Adaptation for survival doesn't always produce traits that are desirable in non-life-threatening situations. People don't want to believe that precious babies get hurt and sometimes stay hurt. They like to believe that babies don't remember, because it assuages the guilt of all their transgressions as well. All the times they feel they fell short as parents."

As Heather talks, I consider my own history—the night terrors, the self-medicating, the years of edge-pushing behavior. Recognition throbs at the base of my skull. Heather isn't talking only about my son here; she's talking about me. I feel suddenly like there's oxygen in the room. I hadn't even noticed that I was suffocating. Something shifts: this understanding is what I've been waiting for. My son has trauma and so do I.

And we are not alone. That is a start.

Chapter 26

THE next day I am at Target with Tariku. As we head to the diaper section, he asks me for the treasured airplane toy I've brought along for him. I reach into my purse and go to hand it to him but I'm careless and drop it. The problem with Tariku's favorite airplanes is that he likes the models instead of the toys, so they're impractically delicate. It hits the linoleum and shatters. His screams are immediate and operatic.

"It's your *fault*," he says. "I *hate* you."

Piece by tiny piece he picks up the airplane and hurls it at me.

"You are *mean*."

He throws himself at me fists first. People stop shopping and stare. We are a rubbernecking attraction in the middle of the sporting goods aisle.

I do not attempt to stop him or take him out of the store. I contain him in the way we've been trained to do, holding him firmly but without "electricity" in my arms. Address the fear instead of doing battle with the behavior, I tell myself. There's no reasoning with him until we can regulate his nervous system.

"This is hard," I say. "Mommy is here. I'm not going anywhere. You're safe."

I say it over and over again. I don't care anymore that people are staring. I hope the idea that he's safe is somewhere nestling into his subconscious. I know it's already soothing me—the idea that I am capable of providing safety. The arms I wrap around my son will be the same arms that give me comfort.

I look at my child and see how terrified he is.

When he calms down a bit, I ask him if he wants to push on me. I show him how it's done, facing each other, hands interlaced, and he tries it, tentatively at first and then with gusto. His face is a twist of concentration and effort. I push back at him, holding him steady.

"*Roar,*" he says, like a tiger. "*Roar.*"

Now people are really gawking, but I couldn't care less, because within sixty seconds, Tariku is, magically, laughing.

~

I'll be honest, when the tantrums come, "Mommy is here. I'm not going anywhere. You're safe" are not the first words that come to mind.

The first words that come to mind are, "Stop throwing shit at me and get in the fucking car already!"

But with practice, I improve. As I get my sea legs with this trauma idea, I start talking to people about it freely. Until now, I've been honest only with our inner circle of friends, family, and therapists. Maybe it wouldn't be a betrayal of our family if I just started telling people the truth in a more general way. I stop worrying so much how people will react to the truth. Since when do I expect to be understood by the majority of the human population? Since when have I made that a condition of speaking my mind? Why did motherhood suddenly make me cower before the masses? Make me want to fit in, to seek approval more than I ever had before in my life? Why, out of all the thousands of hateful things said to me on the Internet by total and complete losers (because no one, I mean, no one other than a loser sits at home anonymously shaming and hating on people), do I only remember the ones that insist I am an unfit mother as a result of the fact that twenty years ago I drank a bunch and ran around in Chanel suits and had sex with some shady characters?

I stop being a parenting purist, mostly out of exhaustion. Sometimes I say, "You can only have a cookie if you finish your dinner." We begin to give him time-outs (yes, yes, we do, though we still stay nearby) and to weave some compassionate but more traditional discipline with our more loosey-goosey progressive ideas. I approach it with curiosity, trying to look at it all as an experiment, a matter of trial and error.

On one thing I do not compromise: telling him he's safe. This much I can do. Take his TV time away or don't; give him a cookie or don't. Just as long as you tell him this over and over.

"Take care of yourself" is the other directive in all the books about parenting trauma.

I'm not sure if they mean manicures or movie nights or what, but I take care of myself in a different way. I start writing the story. I start writing the truth. I post it online. I write articles for parenting magazines.

I stop trying to pretend it's all okay, trying to laugh it off, gloss it over. I say "special needs" like it's something totally okay to say to the woman in line with me at the coffee shop. The first time it crosses my lips, I feel off balance. It's like I'm getting benched, not allowed out on the field with these competitive coffee shop moms who are humble-bragging about their six-year-old playing Chopin.

But over time the idea changes shape in my mind, grows roots in my heart. The truth is almost always a relief. Rather than benching me, it puts me on exactly the right playing field, where I suddenly understand the game.

I say it like it's no big deal now, and I begin to hear an echo. *My kid has special needs, too.*

I find that the echo is coming from people I'd rather spend time with than the Tiger Moms anyway. I'm proud to be among this new group of people. All I wanted was to feel less alone, and now I do. It's not all fixed, but I have something better than fixed: I have hope.

I don't judge the Tiger Moms. I would have been just like them; I was on that same path. What parenting philosophy will get T into the right preschool? What will be the best place to nurture his immense talent in fencing or chess or whatever? Which private school will position him to proceed to a very, very good (if not the best, but okay, probably the best) college of his (okay, my) choosing?

Now I really don't give a shit about fencing. I care that my son will be able to have successful emotional attachments in his life. That he won't remain locked in fear and anxiety forever.

Organically, we start spending more time with the friends who get it. Often they are families with adopted kids. Sometimes they are just families who have faced some challenges that caused them to shift their priorities, as we did.

My friend Claire has written a handful of novels, as well as a book about autism, and she has become a touchstone for me. She has four children, and has mothered both special needs and severe health concerns. She wears it all lightly, with grace and humor. Sure, she cares where her kids go to college, but college is weighted a bit differently when you have watched a couple of your kids almost die.

Her kids are older than T, but they're dear with him and we spend time at her pool. Her teenage daughter is T's favorite person, and they run around in the yard while Claire and I commiserate and eat grapes and compare photo apps on our phones.

T is scared of the water and won't swim, but he likes to sit on the steps and splash, which is annoying but I still grudgingly lower myself into the pool with him. For some reason, when I try to cajole him off the steps, he comes. It is a lazy summer day, the flat midday sun turning the pool deck into a white-hot skillet. The smell of honeysuckle and eucalyptus hangs heavy in the air. A balloon floats over the fence, escaped from a child's birthday party next door.

My son wraps his legs around my waist and his arms around my neck, holding on for dear life, as I wade out into the shallow end, gently bouncing him in the water.

He pats my back, as if comforting me.

"It's okay, Mama," he says. "I've got you. You're safe."

~ Chapter 27

As Tariku turns four, his pediatric neurologist is optimistic. It's hard to say what turns the tide. Maybe his growing grasp of language and the accompanying ability to express himself. Maybe his age. Maybe our increasing facility and patience, or our growing comfort with his challenges and strengths. Words like "regulation" and "dysregulation" come to be second nature to us. Dysregulation refers to an emotional response that is poorly modulated and doesn't fall into the range of developmentally appropriate behaviors. We start to communicate with him about symptoms of dysregulation.

We say, "Your engine is running really hot! Let's see if we can cool it down."

We do deep breathing exercises with him. He learns to "take a breath and take a break." And while he is not always receptive to this once he is too far gone, if we can catch a tantrum while it's ramping up, sometimes we can head it off at the pass.

It helps that emotional dysregulation is physically uncomfortable for T. It feels out of control and frightening, so as he gets a little older and has a hairsbreadth more impulse control, he works even harder than we do to keep it under control. For instance, we have him eating very little wheat and even less sugar and food dye, as many of the books suggest. And we try like hell to avoid the dreaded trifecta of all three together (see: every children's birthday cake ever made). But it's not my habit to tell him absolutely no, unless something is truly hazardous. He doesn't have a dangerous allergy to these foods; they just turn him immediately into a maniac who literally runs in circles until he smacks into something and starts to howl. When Tariku eats a piece of crappy birthday cake, his whole body shakes and his eyes go wiggy and bloodshot. So I bring him other options and I tell him that cake makes him sick; maybe he'd like these cookies I brought. And if he still insists, I let him have some. At which point he invariably feels awful and we have to leave the party.

It doesn't take long for Tariku to have this one dialed. He refuses cake or candy or anything "blue or red or other weird colors." He is so self-aware, in fact, that he leaves his basket of Easter candy in the neighbor's yard.

"You forgot your basket, baby," I tell him.

"It's bad candy," he says. "It makes me sick." He pantomimes puking.

For the entirety of that next spring and summer, things shift tectonically. First it's a day without a violent tantrum, then two. Then we take him to the park, to the museum, to birthday parties without a cloud of foreboding around us. I stop hovering a foot away every time he's near other kids. I move back, and then back some more.

One day, I actually sit on the bench and drink a latte at the park.

I go to the swing set to check in with him. He waves. He makes sure I am watching when he is being a daredevil on the slide—face-first, mouthful of sand, huge smile.

I look around—bored nannies and young families and one grandma wearing a Christmas sweatshirt in June. No one here could guess how hard he is working to keep his hands to himself, to exercise impulse control when someone takes the shovel he wants.

I see him raise his arm for a blow and then put it down again. I doubt anyone else sees the heroism of this moment.

He looks over at me. I give him a giant thumbs-up.

"I am so proud of you, Tariku Moon!" I shout. "You are awesome!"

In a bittersweet twist, I have an overwhelming urge to call my mother and tell her. This happens to me pretty often, and I have found it's like the pain of stubbing your toe. It's so bad you think you might die for a minute, but then you remind yourself that as horrible as it may feel, you are strong, you will live, the throbbing will fade in a minute and all you will see is your son's smile and the blue sky above you both.

~

I'm thinking, with a measure of both apprehension and relief, that we'll homeschool him starting in the fall. I'll seek out regular play-groups in order to work on his social-emotional developmental delay. I'll seek out another OT, with a better attitude, and we'll pay out-of-pocket if need be. For now we while away the final days of summer, eating corn dogs and riding carnival rides, running through the sprinkler, digging for sand crabs at the ocean's edge.

Another wondrous thing—we're welcome again at Suzanne's house, on a trial basis, and it's going swimmingly. T is finally able to play with his adored twins without each day bringing some new disaster.

Suzanne and I hang out on her front porch one day, eating the last figs off the tree, as Violet and T play King and Queen of the Pigs. I tell her my school plans.

"He's doing great! He doesn't need homeschooling," she says. "This is the last thing that kid needs. He'll be way ahead in some things and way behind in others and he doesn't even need preschool for the school part; he needs it for the other kids. Did you check with St. Stephen's? I feel like that's the place for him; I really do. It's structured, cute. It's the most diverse private school in our neighborhood. It has the academics but it's not insane. Please call them. Will you promise?"

And so comes another admission interview. At this one I am both calm and honest, even though this is yet another private school where everyone gets wait-listed. Long gone are the days when I thought a private school rejection was going to be the end of us. We'll be okay.

I don't lead with Tariku's challenges; I lead with his strengths. I do tell the head of early childhood education at this diverse and sweet yet rigorous school that my child will need extra support. That he may have a rocky transition. He's making strides every day and once he has settled into the community here, he'll be a dynamite student, a leader, and a joy. I tell her that he's wildly bright and he's not easy, but no child will bring more humor and enthusiasm to a room.

And do you know what? The head of early childhood education at the school tells us that she is very familiar with everything we're talking about, as she has adopted siblings, one of whom has special needs. Her eyes light up. She listens. She seems excited when we tell her about Tariku.

"If you run into challenges," says Scott, "how committed are you to our child and to us? We're willing to go to any lengths to help this child succeed. We'll do whatever we need to do. But we aren't about to subject him to another place that promises to stick by him and then pulls out at the first sign of trouble."

"We're committed," she says. "I, personally, am committed."

She leaves the room for ten minutes for a conference and when she comes back she is holding admission papers.

"This is unorthodox, but we're going to offer you a place in the preschool class for this fall. If you'd like it, we can take care of it right now."

We sign the papers right there.

~

When September rolls around, I dig through the enormous piles of crap in the garage in an attempt to find the custom lime green lunchboxes with cartoon pictures of my husband's band on them. They sold them at the shows for a while a few years back. I know there's a box of them in here somewhere.

The danger of digging through the garage is that I inevitably wind up getting sucked into a box of journals or notebooks or letters I forgot were there. It's not always a pleasant saunter down memory lane. There are land mines that I don't want to step on when I'm just looking for the bathroom paint color to fix a chip, or some fishing line to hang a mobile.

Honestly, I can't remember what this black opaque plastic file box contains. Most of my archives are painstakingly labeled but this one is anonymous, a potential time bomb, and as a result, irresistible. I flip through a journal from the box and it is, as I feared, one of the reams and reams of notebooks I kept when I was drug addicted and lost in a constant morass of self-pity and bad poetry. I spent many, many hours writing back then. I managed to have plenty of alone time for my writing, mostly because no one wanted to be around me. Too bad the writing itself was terrible. Still, there are always moments in these journals that jump up and grab me. Lucid depictions of a painful life, so different from the one I'm living now.

I find a letter to myself. I remember writing it as if it was yesterday, in Matt's apartment. Not a boyfriend but a friend of a friend, who dealt drugs to bands and pretty girls. I spent a lot of time there. I remember the irregular stair on his front walk, the apple tree obscuring the landing in front of his door. I always paused to rearrange my face before I knocked, trying to iron out the creases of expectation.

The day I wrote the letter, Matt had looked sicker than usual, with a bad case of hepatitis. Yellow eyeballs, hair matted with sweat, teeth gone dark around the edges.

I remember him sitting across the room on the filthy couch, forgetting the lit cigarette in his hand. Every few minutes his sentences trailed off and his head lolled on its hinge. Next to him on a table was a huge fish tank, the water inside turned to thick green sludge. Within the mossy mess I glimpsed an occasional shimmering movement, so I guessed something inside was still alive. I tried not to look at the ashes falling on the carpet and I tried not to look him in the eye too much. I worried that he would see what I thought of him.

In her final days, Jennifer would have been hanging out in rooms like that one.

Eventually he walked to the kitchen for a spoon. I stifled the need that rose to the top of my throat as burning nausea. Listened for the rattle of the silverware.

We'd sit around and I'd tell him stories that had no ending, as I angled for leverage. He gave up more of his dope to keep me around longer. Sometimes I almost didn't mind Matt. It was better being with him than being alone every day and loaded in the middle of the afternoon.

When he nodded out, I'd write on the couch for a while. He'd wake and we'd watch TV or listen to music. We'd order some food and not eat much of it.

I sat there on that orange couch in my glassy heroin slick of profound okay-ness. Fixing felt that way every time, for a while, until it really didn't. I wrote myself a letter that day—the letter I am looking at fifteen years later in my messy garage, searching for the perfect lunchbox with which to send my kid to preschool.

This is what it says:

Dear Jill,

I am on Matt's couch again. Half the time I think I am irretrievably lost and half the time I know that I will not be here forever. This disgusting place with this love of my life. Not

Matt, of course. Gross. Not even heroin. Okay, heroin, yes, heroin. But really it's the relief. The floating glaze of today and today and today. Is it so much to ask for, some relief? Says everyone who has ever made a deal with the devil. Is it so much to ask for?

This is how it feels: My back opens up with waves of light. Radiance flows around my shoulder blades, hooks through the web of my rib cage, and spreads out like wings. Then I rock shut and my need washes over me like rain. How can I leave?

Maybe I'll be a librarian if I ever get out of this. Live swimming in books and words and organization and quiet. I will be an ex-junkie, ex-stripper, vegetarian, yogi librarian with tattoos and a nose ring and some ancient tracks on my arms that you would hardly even notice. It could be good. I could be happy there.

I have a small secret. It's only the size of a dime, yet I can sometimes feel it throbbing in my chest in quiet moments. Maybe it's faith? Maybe it will lead me somewhere new, so that I can grow roots in kinder ground. Maybe it will lead me somewhere that I can get clean. Clean enough to be a mother.

Stay alive. For that, at least.

Maybe you are there already and you are reading this. I like to believe you are. I have always had hope for you.

Love,

Jill

It's a letter from someone else, nodding out on a thrift store couch in some scumbag's apartment because I wanted his drugs and didn't want to be so alone. At the same time it is a letter from me, this same me, one hand always clinging to a buoyant balloon of hope, as ghastly as things seem. What on earth gave me the gall to dream of this life today, when I was nothing but appetite, a pure specimen of selfishness and single-minded desire? A librarian? A mother? The nerve.

I feel Jennifer behind me. I'm not afraid of her ghost; I'm only afraid to turn around and lose her. It's hard getting off drugs. It's so hard. I have no idea how I did it, in the end.

That same fiery creativity that shot Jen to the top of all she did was also her downfall. She was a Roman candle. I'm a free spirit, but I am also a workhorse. I dreamed of being not a rock star or even a writer, but a librarian. I dreamed of being a mother, above all. Practical dreams. Jennifer dreamed of being a prophet, a poet.

She remains a light over my shoulder, a warmth behind me. I miss her and miss her.

I find the lunchbox. I leave the journal behind.

~

On T's first day of preschool, I drop him off, sign the sign-in book, then turn and walk away. I don't say hello to anyone other than the teacher. I hide behind big sunglasses. When I reach the car, I put my head in my hands and I weep. We have been to the meetings and the coffees, have sat in the tiny chairs with what looks like an awfully square bunch of parents to me, and gotten the back-to-school briefing. Many of the parents know each other and were at the school last year.

"I feel like the Addams Family here," I tell Scott on the way home.

"The Addams Family?" he replies. "I feel like the *Manson* Family."

I wonder if we'll never fit in at this uniform-wearing Episcopalian school. Then I remember what I learned from our friends in Ethiopia—I've got Jesus on my side, Morticia Addams or not. Jesus doesn't love people for their blamelessness or their excellent soufflés. That's the cool thing about Jesus. He loves me regardless of if I swear like a sailor, or was a slut, or did buckets of heroin. God, a friend of mine once told me, gives us the gift of unconditional love. Exactly the way we aspire to love our children.

Tariku can't wait to start school, which doesn't mean it's going to work out. It often means the opposite, in fact. He gets so excited to be around other kids—he's the most social person I've ever known—but his excitement sometimes dysregulates him. This can manifest in antisocial behavior and drive kids away. It's not so much biting and hitting anymore as it is grabbing, hugging too hard, talking too loudly, getting in kids' faces. He has made so much progress, but that doesn't mean everything is fixed and better— phew, dust off our hands, thank God that's over. Change is so slow.

He has a rocky start at school, as I could have predicted. There are a few incidents of aggression, including two bites (which land us on probation), and a dazzling escape attempt, where he makes it halfway through the parking lot. My mornings turn into daily meetings in the director's office. T begins refusing to go into the classroom and at the same time refusing to turn back and go home. Every morning he and I wait together in this limbo on the wooden bench in the outdoor hallway, listening to the sounds of children inside the classrooms, until he's ready to go inside. I try just walking away. I try staying. Either way he clings to me and hides. When Scott takes him it seems to work better.

He doesn't tantrum at school, but loses his cool completely every day after he gets home. I practice doing less, and just sitting with him.

I tell him: This is hard. I'm here. You're safe.

My interactions with other parents are stilted. I know some of them are concerned about Tariku's behavior in the classroom because the director has told me as much. I try to be relentlessly friendly at all the school events. We volunteer at the carnival, at the open house, on the diversity committee. I try to make myself valuable to the school, when really I would like to go hide in a hole until it all blows over and T is strong and healed and perfect.

But he is trying so hard. Oh, how he tries. Day after day I watch him pin his shoulders back and screw his courage down and walk into that class. How can I give up when he won't? I go against every nonviolent parenting principle and give him bribes and snacks for every day finished without a major incident—a plastic brachiosaur, some green goo, gluten-free chocolate chip cookies, vegan ice cream, two wooden swords.

I talk to his teacher often, offering suggestions about how to communicate with him about his impulse control. I tell her that it helps to have him do push-ups or jumping jacks. That it helps to stand behind him and press down firmly on his shoulders. I tell her that it's important to tell him if you're going to touch him; if he doesn't see it coming, it startles him and sets his nerves on edge. She is a pleasant, traditional woman, besweatered and apple-cheeked. I suspect my suggestions about push-ups seem silly to her—I can see it in her eyes—but she is kind and listens.

I surmise she's not revealing everything that goes on in class. I tell her as much and she acquiesces, saying she doesn't like to worry parents with every little thing. I encourage her to go ahead and worry me, so we can address any issues as they come up. I have a hard kernel of worry knocking around in my chest, telling me that maybe this is not the right place for him after all. But the other option is to approach the more progressive schools—the ones with all the fairies and knitting and chickens and naked finger-painting. These schools are cool, but way too unstructured for T. Without a firm hand and a ton of routine, Tariku feels unsafe. If he doesn't absolutely know who's in charge, he figures he had better take charge himself. If we send him to a naked chicken school, he'll be running that place within hours, the tiny Don Corleone of the playground. Maybe homeschooling will be the best option after all.

Then slowly, slowly, we start getting reports that he is improving. He has good days; he has great days. He has hard days more often than either of these, but let me emphasize—he has great days. I stop having the daily meetings. People smile at me more on campus.

At the drop-off, he still clings, but for a shorter time. When he walks in, no fewer than five kids jump up and down and shout his name. For the other mothers this is no big deal. For me, it is a small miracle. My kid has friends.

~ Chapter 28

I'M in my office working, basking in the bright and warm parallelogram of sunlight slanting in through the window. I've even gotten to the point where I'm comfortable turning my phone to silent for an hour or so at a time. Ideally, I would get the best writing done if I put my phone in a drawer and didn't look at it for a three-hour stretch, but that seems unrealistic. What if something happened? What if he needed me and I wasn't there?

I turn over the phone at exactly the hour mark—okay, probably the fifty-six-minute mark—and see a digital representation of all my fears, neatly contained on a tiny handheld screen. Two missed calls from the school. Three missed calls from Scott, who has been at the gym.

I sigh, stand, and begin to pack my stuff up as I listen to Scott's message, figuring it'll say more than the school's.

I listen to the second message first.

"Okay, I'm going to pick him up now. Call me when you get this."

And then the first. Scott is pissed.

"Will you please pick up your phone during the day when he's in school? He bit someone again. They've been trying to reach you. Okay, never mind."

I sit back down and nearly lose my smoothie. He bit someone again. We'll surely be kicked out of the school, and then where will we go? I am heartsick.

A memory floats back to me of a trip I once took to the office at my grammar school. I don't know why I never remembered this before. I bit someone, too. A bite—the last weapon of the overpowered, the outnumbered. If you are willing to just sink your teeth in, you can still win. The salty sourness of skin. The surprising metallic taste when you break it.

It's not that I don't understand. It's just that I don't know what the hell we're going to do now. I have been praying and reading and Googling and going to classes and seminars and arranging meditation lessons and martial arts and therapy. This is the third bite in three months. Where do we go from here?

The last time it happened, I marched into the subsequent meeting and said, "This is not going to happen again; he's not a danger to other kids; this incident was an anomaly." I believed it to be true. He had been doing so much better.

Scott comes in the door with Tariku trailing behind. T looks stricken, his face reminding me of when he was eighteen months old, wide-eyed and petrified. One look at him and my righteous "you know better than this" indignation crumbles. He loves that school more than anything. He has been so proud of himself lately.

I wrap my arms around the both of them. A Tariku sandwich, we call it.

"I know we're all upset," I say. "But we're going to work this through together."

His eyes glaze over. He's not hearing anything anymore.

"I want my bottle," he says.

Tariku still uses his bottle to self-soothe. I have heard stories about parents addressing severe attachment challenges in teenagers by hand-feeding them, by rocking them as if they were babies. Because they are, in some ways. Our kids are still babies because they were never babies. That is a ravenous kind of hunger. I pull Tariku into my lap and rock my four-year-old as if he were a newborn, feeding him his bottle. He closes his eyes. I surreptitiously cry into his hair.

We are asked to stay home from school until our scheduled meeting about the incident, which will occur in a couple of weeks, right before the Christmas break. He sits out the Christmas pageant and the Christmas concert and the Christmas party and the Christmas everything. We go to see the decorations at the mall. We pick out a tree and decorate it. Every day, Tariku asks when he can go back and see his friends. It breaks my heart.

I walk through our days with a wooden kind of resignation. He never bites me anymore, but with his newfound language skills have come newly clever and persistent battles. Bath. Breakfast. Bargaining, bargaining, bargaining.

One morning, overcome, I hide my face in a warm pile of laundry and scream, "What the fuck are we gonna do?"

I stand up, feeling sort of foolish, and then I put my head back down.

"I hate my life!" I yell. "I hate it!"

The nerve of me, for this ingratitude. To hate this blessed life, this unimaginably privileged world I live in.

It feels awesome just to admit it for once.

"Fuck you, God," I scream into a staticky pile of warm T-shirts that smell like lavender.

"Fuck you for all the hurt children. Fuck you for all the sick and starving babies. Why would you drop this glorious child into my life only to let me ruin him? I am trying so hard and I am failing and fuck you I have been asking for help long enough fuck you *help me already*."

I sob and sob, until the white T-shirt I'm crying into looks like the Shroud of Turin and I have to throw it back in the hamper. I hear Auntie Jo arrive in the other room, and I figure that's my cue to curl up into the pile of laundry on the bed and do something I haven't done in three years—I go back to sleep.

When I wake up, I'm surprisingly calm and clear. I know exactly what to do. I go straight upstairs and sit down at my computer. One day Tariku's story will be his to tell, but for now, it's my responsibility. A new kind of excitement builds. I may suck at lots about mothering, but this I can do: I can tell a good story.

I write a letter to his school. In this ten-page manifesto, I tell them a story in which Tariku is acknowledged for the exceptionally bright, creative, loving, exuberant, and beautiful soul that he is and not just for his negative behaviors. I tell them a story about all the joy he brings to every room he's in. I tell them about our strategies and tools. I tell them how much progress we've seen. My goal is to enlist them in the cause.

I tell them where Tariku came from. I tell the story of our family and how we came together. I talk about our dreams and our struggles.

I call my friend Claire and my friend Kristen, both writers and moms of kids with special needs, for advice. I grab books off the shelves and pull quotes. I give this fight all that I have, because T loves this school and his friends there; he truly does. I will do almost anything to protect him from yet another disruption in his emotional life.

I write:

> *I am willing to fight hard to make his experience at St. Stephen's a successful one. He has formed such sweet friendships already and has a deep emotional attachment to his teachers and his classmates. I want to honor those attachments. I want him to feel safe in getting to know and love and trust people. He has suffered so much loss, and we try to support consistency in his relationships. If, in fact, St. Stephen's is not the right school for him, I want to know we did everything we could to make it work. I don't think we have yet.*

There was some discussion in our last meeting of Tariku's effect on the classroom dynamic. There is no doubt in my mind that though Tariku has special needs, he belongs in and will reap the most benefit from participating in a class of typically developing peers, preferably one (like St. Stephen's) that offers enough of an academic challenge to satisfy his voracious curiosity. I have been doing some reading and was pleased to discover that there is a great deal of evidence that children perform best in classrooms where a broad range of needs are represented. All the children in the class, not just those with challenges, benefit by learning to accommodate and help a peer who may be struggling.

When I stop in a day and consider the context of his history, remember the frightened, faraway look in his eyes in the very first picture I saw of him, I realize how truly remarkable his progress has been. In this light, I'm absolutely confident that if we can make it over this speed bump, Tariku will be the kind of student you will proudly point to as an example of the value of an education at St. Stephen's.

I am blessed beyond words with my child and all the love and learning he has brought into my life. I am humbled, as always, before the power of healing that I am privileged to witness every day by virtue of being Tariku's mother . . .

I send it, and a week later we go to the meeting and face down the tribunal: an oval-shaped table with ten chairs, all of them filled. It's the same table at which the director first handed us our admission papers.

"Three bites and you're out. That's our policy," says the head of the school, the big kahuna. It's bad news that she's even here. "But we like you. That's the reason we're here now."

I like her, too, actually. She has always struck me as a sort of fun-loving bulldog, a devoted and intelligent woman. She's a

straight shooter, who is a little bit scary but will also oc
wear those bobbly antennae with glitter foam balls on
Coincidentally, the school is holding its International Dress Day, so
during our meeting she is wearing a muumuu from her native Hawaii and a big fake flower in her hair.

"So what are we saying?" I lean in and ask her. "I just want to
be clear. Have you already decided? Is this the meeting where you
break it to us that we're out, or is this the meeting where we're
fielding possible solutions?"

"We're not necessarily asking you to leave. We're not necessarily not," she says. Her honesty sets me at ease. I like people like this;
you never have to wonder what they're thinking. All in all, it's not
a bad group to be facing. The school counselor is a well-known
psychologist who has written great books about mindfulness and
treating the whole child. The head of early childhood education has
always been on our side. The head of the school is unconvinced but
she is frank and fair and I know we have a shot at least.

Tariku's teacher, on the other hand, sits at the head of the table,
flushed with annoyance. She makes no eye contact with us.

I present our case. I have been reading about the volunteer "patient" in any group dynamic. That someone volunteers (not con-
sciously, of course) to be the odd man out, to be the manifestation
of the group's dysfunction. The temptation can be to think that if
you just eject the patient the group will be rid of the problem, but
that isn't the case. The dynamic must be balanced, changed from
within.

I can see that his teacher—overwhelmed by Tariku's needs—
wants him gone. I sense it from the atmosphere of the room—the
sideways glances toward her, the way she becomes redder and more
tight-lipped, breaking a sweat with every suggestion for a solution.

The counselor has recommendations for an early childhood
development therapist and for an occupational therapist, with
whom she works in tandem. This occupational therapist, she as-

sures us, specializes in exactly the kind of sensory challenges Tariku is facing. The counselor's blue eyes are lively if a bit tired and she wears black nail polish, chipping slightly at the edges. The nail polish comforts me maybe more than anything so far. Black is an unusual choice. Chipped stands for imperfect.

Scott and I agree to bring in a full-time aide to the classroom, who will provide the extra support Tariku and his teachers all seem to need. They seem a bit surprised by our willingness. I guess most parents walk in here with their dukes up, resistant to the idea that their child may need help. I think this is the thing that keeps us walking the razor's edge, not getting kicked out. We leave with a new contract that states Tariku may provisionally return to school, to be reassessed in a couple of months.

"This could turn out to be a great thing for all of us," I say.

And I mean it. The teacher will benefit from working with out-of-the-box kids. The school will, I'm convinced, ultimately be gratified for believing in us. And through it all, Scott and I are being introduced to who we truly are, maybe for the first time in our lives. And my son, who has to work so hard to learn the social skills that come easily to most kids, will know himself capable of overcoming daunting obstacles, of fighting for what he wants.

We say good-bye and Merry Christmas. At home, we tell Tariku he can go back to school after the holiday.

"Yes!" he says, doing a fist pump. "Yes!"

~

In the guesthouse of a sweet forties-style ranch in Encino, our new OT puts Tariku through various physical tests: balance beam, puzzles, touch your nose, touch your toes, left side, right side. I am vindicated to learn that the former OT who "graduated" T was wrong. The new OT confirms Tariku's diagnosis of sensory processing disorder and explains it to us with clear charts. She also discovers contributing factors that I would never have guessed. It turns out Tariku can't sit still not just because he has so much energy but because he literally *can't* sit still—he has almost no core strength. It's exhausting for him to hold his own torso up in a chair. When she says this, a light goes on. Of course. He couldn't sit up unassisted until he was ten months old. All his other muscles must have developed to compensate.

One thing I notice about the new therapist is that she often refers to children with special needs as "our children," as a way of distinguishing them from kids who are developing more typically. As in, "It's sometimes hard for our children to handle unexpected touch." Or, "Our children have a difficult time visually organizing new environments."

I find it comforting. It makes me feel less isolated and reminds me that children are raised by communities, not individuals. We may not have asked to be a part of this particular community—but who does? Well, some very exceptional adoptive parents I know do; but most of the rest of us generally don't wake up and say, Wow, I'd really like to go to lots and lots of therapy with my five-year-old until I'm so harried that I need some for myself as well. And yet here we are. We are better, stronger people for it; there is no doubt.

Here are some of the practical things we've put in place by the time school rolls around again:

I find a great therapist of my own. Finally.

We do "kid CrossFit" each morning in the living room—basically Tariku and Scott doing a bunch of calisthenics that focus on core work. T runs laps around the house and does sit-ups and bear crawls while Scott shouts encouragement and times him with a stopwatch. The physical exertion calms Tariku's nervous system and helps to balance some of the unevenly developed muscles, with the added bonus of being adorable.

We have noise-canceling headphones (Peltor Junior Earmuffs, to be specific) for him, which we begin to bring to loud and over-stimulating environments. This changes our whole life. Suddenly, when we're in the grocery store his eyes don't glaze over. He stops ignoring and running away from us, or collapsing into a hair-trigger tantrum every ten minutes.

We give him jobs. This is probably the greatest help of all. We give him a task to focus on. When we're at the grocery store, Scott says, "Okay, go get broccoli and an avocado and three beautiful apples."

We give him heavy things to carry: books, backpacks, bags of groceries. It puts pressure on his joints in a way that relaxes and regulates him.

We get a trampoline.

We keep him running, keep him active, keep him breathing. We make a balance beam out of a two-by-four.

We breathe. Breathe. We play games like moving a cotton ball by blowing through a straw.

We interview candidate after candidate until we find a school aide who seems almost too good to be true. Gia (that's Miss Gia to you) is a gentle, hip woman with a careful way of speaking and an unmistakable confidence and solidity. She has both a master's degree and four children of her own. She came to this work when her youngest daughter began to present multiple special needs and she found she had a facility for addressing the challenges. Her daughter's therapist, after the treatment was done, took Gia under her wing and trained her. When the school year starts up again, Gia is at T's side.

It is tricky in all the usual ways at first, but I feel oddly unruffled. If it doesn't work this time, we'll know we've tried everything. We'll know we need a more dedicated special needs environment of some sort and that will be okay, too.

And then.

In a week, he starts to turn it around. In two weeks, his teacher greets me not just with eye contact but with an enthusiastic hug and a wide smile. In three weeks, *three weeks*, he is a different child entirely.

Miss Gia would correct me. He is the same child, she'd say. The goal, she would say, is never to make Tariku not be Tariku. Tariku is amazing just how he is. She means it. She loves my child. The goal is to help him control his impulses so he can function. And that is exactly what starts to happen.

Gia teaches not just Tariku but me. I learn from her that security and routine are key for him. He needs to know what's coming and that someone has his back. We write out elaborate calendars and set timers for every transition.

When I was trying to get pregnant, I feared I was undeserving and beyond help. It was so easy to believe those things about myself. Now I look at my son and see that we are all children of God. None of us is undeserving and beyond help.

I had read every book and taken every class and practically spent our last dollar. I was beating my head against a wall unable to figure out how the healing was going to happen. Now I know you just keep hammering away at it. And then one day things shift a fraction of a degree and the entire world changes.

~

Three months later, Scott and I pack up the car with crafting supplies, an Ethiopian feast, decorations and paper goods, and the all-important PowerPoint presentation. You do realize they're five, right? Scott asked me when I was hunched over the slides late into the night. It's our family's turn to do "International Day" at St. Stephen's. I was unreasonably stressed about organizing the whole thing, because Ethiopia carries significance for T beyond what other kids feel for, say, Greece or China or Ireland. He has a real sense of pride and excitement about it. I want to do something super fun and engaging for the kids. I want them to get to know my son.

I sit at the front of the room with Tariku next to me.

"Ethiopia is a very special country for our family because Tariku was born there and that's where we adopted him."

Six hands shoot up.

What's adoption?

Whoa. I was not expecting that one. I came with injera bread and pictures of antelope. Naively, I did not come prepared to explain what adoption is to a bunch of five-year-olds. None of these kids' parents have explained to them what adoption is? From her perch in the corner, Miss Gia gives me a look of silent support.

Here goes.

"Families are formed in lots of different ways," I say. "Our family was formed through adoption. Tariku didn't grow in my belly. He grew in his birth mom's belly and then we adopted him. So he has two moms, his birth mom and his forever mom—that's me!"

Six more hands shoot up. Shit.

What happened to his real mom?

Are you gonna show us pictures of his real mom?

I get the on-the-spot, I-don't-have-the-answer brain freeze, like I've been caught in a lie or have been asked too hard a question on an oral exam. After a long breath, I realize I actually do know the answer.

I explain that I am Tariku's mom. That he also has a birth mom. That we are both real moms. Then I tell them these are private questions and it is up to T if and when he wants to talk about it. T looks confused. He didn't expect all that, either. It never occurred to him that most of his friends had no idea what adoption is. I manage to shift the conversation back to Ethiopia.

All of this is upstaged by the fact that they're allowed to eat Ethiopian food with their fingers, which quickly makes it everyone's favorite food.

Actually seeing him in the classroom, I'm floored by the progress T has made over the past few months. He is still energetic and enthusiastic and dancing every five minutes, of course. He's still T. But he can sit still and keep his hands to himself. He's polite and raises his hand.

On our way out the door, I run into the head of the school, walking toward us down the hallway.

"It's our little success story!" she says.

Us. A success story.

We have a few more meetings with the team and if the mood in the room were any more jubilant, we'd all be slamming shots—including the teacher (especially the teacher).

I go from talking to the head of the preschool every day to not getting an e-mail back from her for a few days at a time sometimes.

"She forgot about us." I say to Scott. "There are more important things on her plate. We're falling off the map!"

At the meeting before spring break, they offer us a reenrollment contract to the school.

Chapter 29

SUZANNE often brings her three kids over to play in the early afternoon. A couple of my other mom friends sometimes show up, and at least one of the aunties pops by after work nearly every day. Our house always has someone or other sitting at the dining room table, climbing the camphor tree out front, jumping on the trampoline in the yard. Scott composes in the studio out back, and it is to the deep tones of his bass that I make chili and corn bread, Southwestern beef stew, bubbling three-cheese lasagna, comfort food with easily enough for ten. The little boy I thought would condemn us to isolation is suddenly the locus of the most vibrant, comfortable social life I've ever had.

Tariku has a sibling relationship with Suzanne's twins. They play for hours on end, hatch plots, bicker. For the first time in my life as a mother, I relax on the sidelines, tuck my feet up under me, and gossip with my friends. Rarely do I have to sprint and wedge myself into the middle of a conflict anymore. It can, at times, feel . . . (I'm hesitant to write this, lest a lightning bolt come out of the sky and strike me down for my hubris) easy.

I could say that the change has come because Scott and I now lovingly enforce a system of clear and consistent consequences and rewards, or, more specifically, consequences and toy airplanes. Or that we have finally found the right team of teachers and therapists, plus a godsend of a tireless French nanny with industrial-strength boundaries (not to mention an excellent coq au vin recipe and an encyclopedic knowledge of all things related to the band Kiss). Or maybe it's because Tariku's growing language skills have made him less frustrated with communicating. Or the fact that his nervous system is calming down, as he feels safer and comes to trust that we are on his team, that we are not going anywhere.

It's definitely not because I found the answer, although it might have something to do with the fact that I have stopped expecting one. I loosen my grip on my parenting, on the house, on life in general. I try out different things, constantly in flux. Some days I have patience and some days I still snap and yell. Some days it works and some days it doesn't; some are good and some are bad.

But some are good. Some are good.

Tariku jumps and jumps on the trampoline. It soothes him. Sometimes, when he gets off, he is so regulated that I almost think I imagined the whole thing. He's not making strange faces and holding his head at an improbable angle or having loud verbal outbursts. His body seems to have a more stable axis, rather than the way he sometimes moves, which is a kind of herky-jerky dance. He doesn't fall for no reason at all. He doesn't get his face one inch from everyone around him and make growly dinosaur faces and talk too loudly.

But the most notable thing that has changed, so slowly that I didn't even notice the tipping point, is that T has stopped rejecting me. Emotionally, it is as if a light has been turned on, all at once. I know that it was once dark, but it seems so long ago now.

He puts his arms around my waist and stands there beside me. He holds my hand and kisses it. He whispers in my ear, "I love you to the moon and back two thousand hundred times."

One afternoon in April, Suzanne and the kids come over, as they often do, but this time we have a mission. We plan to drive to higher ground around five P.M. to see the solar eclipse. We have eclipse viewers, snacks, and jackets packed in their backpacks, waiting by the door.

My mother texts me. We are texting now. We speak on the phone now and then. It's not the same as it once was, with our daily chat sessions, but maybe that's not a bad thing. Maybe there is room now for some change that needed to happen for a long time. I'm honestly not sure what the future holds for my parents and me. The wounds are deep on both sides. But if I have learned anything in my first few years of parenting, it is that healing is a baffling and slow thing, but it exists. Whether or not we know it, we are reaching for it all the time.

For now, my mother and I are each tentatively holding out an olive branch.

Are you watching? she texts.

Not yet. Troops not mobilizing. Trampoline v. Eclipse . . .

The kids couldn't care less about the sun and the moon crossing paths, once they get in the backyard and there is wrestling and trampoline jumping and baseball to be had. They ignore us when we ask, and when we ask louder they whinily protest. It's not my policy to give in to whining and wheedling, but Suzanne and I are the only ones who cared about this eclipse in the first place and we decide instead to surrender to a languid early evening, juicing lemons off the tree.

Tariku gently pushes Violet in the swing. We have come to trust them together, to turn our backs, even. The jasmine is in bloom and the air is thick with the fragrance. We pull our sweaters more tightly around us as the evening turns chilly, tell the kids to stop putting dirt in their hair, pick up a stray Wiffle ball or two and throw them in the toy bin.

Somewhere behind us in the solar system, somewhere we can't see, the sun is eclipsed by the moon and we miss it. But it is a gorgeous twilight, with cool grass to lie down on and light that is amber and altered. The shadows melt into the driveway. There is lemonade and a friend to sit with and the kids are happy and safe.

Missed it. Ah well. Good luck with your luncheon, Ma. Love you.

I have learned to release my expectations. Sometimes, you have to be content to face east instead of west, miss the eclipse, feel the strangeness at your back, and know that there will be other marvels. You have no idea. The world is full of them.

~ Epilogue

I once screamed, "Fuck you, God," to an unfeeling sky (or an unfeeling pile of laundry, as the case may be). Now I find myself driving around spontaneously thanking God for our challenges, for the way I have grown to know the fierce and brave heart of my son, for the fact that I have come to value more fully the strength of my marriage (oh yeah and sorry about that fuck-you thing). Through the trials of the past few years, I have come to understand myself to be selfish, vain, petulant, and unequal to the task of mothering, to be sure, but also resilient and determined and resourceful—who knew?—and possessed of a rock-solid belief in my family.

Scott and I have always talked about a second adoption, never considering that Tariku would stay an only child. As life around the house becomes less chaotic and scary, we decide it's time to grow our family again. Ethiopian adoptions have become increasingly complicated and fraught in the years since we adopted T, so we decide to pursue an adoption through the L.A. County foster care system, where we know there's great need for families. We had a good relationship with the agency we used, so I set up a call to get things in motion. I'm surprised to find that I'm on a conference call with both our social worker and the head of the adoption agency.

"Hi! This is a surprise—nice to talk to you. We're excited to get started," I say.

There is an awkward silence. Followed by all of us talking over each other. Followed by uncomfortable laughter.

"Go ahead."

"No, I'm sorry, go ahead."

"Since you adopted Tariku, you published a book," says the head of the agency. "We've had the opportunity to read it and we feel that you were not completely honest with us. You're not who you said you were. We're not interested in facilitating another adoption for you."

The creative license we took on our initial adoption application has come back to bite us in the ass. I know, I know. I'm the only one who didn't see it coming.

There is some back and forth. I apologize and ask for their understanding.

"Can we have another chance?" I ask.

"I'm afraid not, no. Not with us. You can go somewhere else, start over from the beginning, and tell them the truth."

After I hang up, I lie on the floor for a long time looking at the ceiling fan, embarrassed, blindsided, devastated. I breathe. Breathe.

Every mother has her past, I figure. Every woman has a big idea of what will make her acceptable as a mother, what will put the USDA stamp of approval on her and make her feel worthy of this human experience. And every mother has her whole self, which rarely aligns neatly with either pole.

This house is full of love and warmth and music. And we try like hell; really we do.

Make a mistake and start again? If nothing else, this I know how to do. I look up the number of another agency, pick up the phone, and call.

"Hello," I say. "We're interested in adopting a child."

The truth? Here it is.

Some Notes on Trauma

I wish I could offer you a fail-safe strategy, a magic pill, a miracle cure. There are plenty of people out there willing to say they
have it. I am not one of them.

Some people look at me skeptically when I discuss the impact
of early childhood trauma and the profound effects of PTSD. We
have a hard time considering a slippery, invisible emotional problem, with very few black-and-white answers. It's hard to bear witness to the suffering of our fellow humans, especially children, and
not know how to address it. But denying the existence of the
wounds won't make them go away.

So many things have helped our family along the way and I'm
not even always sure what they were exactly. I believe it was our
effort itself as much as anything. It was the strategies, yes, but ultimately it was love and faith. Trauma victims are deeply afraid in
places the conscious mind can't access. You have to go at it with
love—conscious, persistent, and fearless love. Some of these recommended resources contain contradictory information, but all have
in common the fact that they focus on relationships rather than
diagnoses and overmedication. It's common in the special needs

community to say that love is not enough. I get the point—we need education, tools, willingness, patience. All that said, I maintain that it *is* enough. That, in fact, it is all we have.

~

Here are a handful of our favorite resources:

Aronson, Jane. *Carried in Our Hearts: The Gift of Adoption.* New York: Jeremy P. Tarcher, 2013.

Best, Denise L. *Therapeutic Parenting Manual for Traumatized Children.* Iowa City: Adoption and Attachment Treatment Center of Iowa, 2009.

Bosnak, Robert. *Embodiment: Creative Imagination in Medicine, Art, and Travel.* New York: Routledge, 2007.

Cline, Foster, and Jim Fay. *Parenting with Love and Logic: Teaching Children Responsibility.* Colorado Springs: NavPress, 2006.

Forbes, Heather T., and B. Bryan Post. *Beyond Consequences, Logic, and Control: A Love Based Approach to Helping Children with Severe Behaviors,* vol. 1, 2nd ed. Boulder, CO: Beyond Consequences Institute, 2010.

Forbes, Heather T., and B. Bryan Post. *Beyond Consequences, Logic, and Control: A Love Based Approach to Helping Children with Severe Behaviors,* vol. 2, 2nd ed. Boulder, CO: Beyond Consequences Institute, 2009.

Gray, Deborah D. *Attaching in Adoption: Practical Tools for Today's Parents,* 2nd ed. Philadelphia: Jessica Kingsley, 2012.

Heller, Sharon. *Too Loud, Too Bright, Too Fast, Too Tight: What to Do if You Are Sensory Defensive in an Overstimulating World.* New York: Harper Perennial, 2003.

Hopkins-Best, Mary. *Toddler Adoption: The Weaver's Craft,* rev. ed. Philadelphia: Jessica Kingsley, 2012.

Koegel, Lynn Kern, and Claire LaZebnik. *Overcoming Autism:*

Finding the Answers, Strategies, and Hope That Can Transform a Child's Life. New York: Penguin, 2005.

Moers, Christine, and Billy Kaplan. *Chaos to Healing: Therapeutic Parenting 101*. DVD.

Newman, Joe. *Raising Lions: The Art of Compassionate Discipline*. CreateSpace, 2010.

Purvis, Karyn B., David R. Cross, and Wendy Lyons Sunshine. *The Connected Child: Bring Hope and Healing to Your Adoptive Family*. New York: McGraw Hill, 2007.

Siegel, Daniel J., and Tina Payne Bryson. *No-Drama Discipline: The Whole-Brain Way to Calm the Chaos and Nurture Your Child's Developing Mind*. New York: Bantam, 2014.

Stutz, Phil, and Barry Michels. *The Tools: Transform Your Problems into Courage, Confidence, and Creativity*. New York: Spiegel and Grau, 2012.

Wright, Marguerite A. *I'm Chocolate, You're Vanilla: Raising Healthy Black and Biracial Children in a Race-Conscious World*. San Francisco: Jossey-Bass, 2000.

Kristen Howerton at *Rage Against the Minivan*: www.rageagainst-theminivan.com

Christine Moers at *Welcome to My Brain*: www.welcometomybrain.net

Christine Moers, Parent Coach: christineparentcoaching.com

Parenting in SPACE: www.housecallscounseling.com/parenting-in-space/

Dr. Tina Payne Bryson: tinabryson.com

In Los Angeles:

Los Angeles Child Guidance Clinic: www.lacgc.org/index.htm

Echo Parenting and Education: www.echoparenting.org

Dr. Uyen Nguyen at the Developmental Therapy Alliance

Dr. Mona Delahooke: www.monadelahooke.com

Dr. Mitesh Parekh: miteshparekh.com
Ann D'Angelo: bemindfulbreathe.com
The Children's Ranch: www.thechildrensranch.org
Cheerful Helpers Child and Family Study Center: www.cheerful
    helpers.org

If I had to pick one thing (okay, two things):

3M Peltor Junior Earmuff: www.amazon.com/3M-Peltor-Junior-
    Earmuff-Blve/dp/B0015UX2EK
JumpSport 10x17 Rectangular Trampoline with Safety Enclosure:
    www.jumpsport.com

Acknowledgments

THIS book is, in part, my eulogy for Jennifer Alicia Grant. You are always remembered, my beautiful friend.

Deepest gratitude to my agent, dear friend, and coconspirator, Alexandra Machinist; my editor, Becky Cole; and everyone at Plume/Penguin.

Scott and I treasure all the love and support from our Ethiopian travel group, our extended family. Amaseganalou!

Big love to the whole Weezer community.

Thank you, Meg Bowles, Catherine Burns, and everyone at The Moth for helping me figure out what a story is, and how to tell it.

There are no words to thank Suzanne Luke for her contributions to my life and work. She is not only a cherished friend but also practically the ghostwriter of my entire oeuvre. Thanks also to all of our amazing neighbors on Mount Royal Drive.

Deepest gratitude to Kelly, Sarah, Bailey, Gia, Heather, Tina, Janelle, Doreen, Zanita, and our whole school team, for being the kind of teachers and administrators who change lives.

J-Wolf, my Charlotte; Claire Bidwell Smith, my touchstone—you know.

I wrote the majority of this book in the Suite 8 coworking space, with Joshua Wolf Shenk, Annabelle Gurwitch, Carina Chocano, Keshni Kashyap, Benj Hewitt, Heather Havrilesky, Erica Rothschild, Janelle Brown, Danielle Parsons, Tim Kirkman, and all the other Suite 8–ers at my side. I am so grateful for this wellspring of invaluable camaraderie and inspiration.

I am also eternally indebted to the community of writers and friends who believed in me and buoyed me up throughout this quixotic endeavor: Rachel Weintraub, Joe Gratziano, the Scovell/Summers/LaZebnik clan (sorry, you're never getting rid of us), Meredith Maran, Christine Moers, Matthew Specktor, Kurt Gutjahr, Anne Dailey, Gina Frangello, Jamie Rose, Samantha Dunn, Amanda Fletcher, Tammy Stoner, Rob Roberge, Leonard Chang, Jim Krusoe, Craig Clevenger, Meg Howrey, Bernadette Murphy, Patrick O'Neil, Julie Fogliano, Brian Joseph, Chad Harbach, Marti Mattox, Paul Quin, Vincey Blaskovitch, Andre Lambert, Aislinn Cassels-Hyde, Christophe Liglet, D. J. Mendel, Robert Cucuzza, and Garrett Finney, Meghan Daum, and Ben Decter.

Super thanks to Kristen Howerton, my secret weapon.

Other invaluable sources of support have included Echo Parenting and Education, Ruth Beaglehole, Uyen Nguyen, Dr. Mona Delahooke, Dr. Tina Bryson, Dr. Mitesh Parekh, and Dr. Alessia Gottleib.

Huge gratitude to Dr. Judith White, because if Momma ain't sane, ain't nobody sane.

I am thankful for the grace and humor of the Shriners, the Dreskins, Sherri Carpenter, and all the rest of my relations, who are unfortunate enough to have been saddled with a memoirist in the family.

And to my husband, bashert, and partner in crime, Scott Shriner: I'd say that none of this would have been possible without you, but that's so obvious. I love you crazy.